James Castrission (Cas), 30, is an author, writer, photographer and renowned Australian explorer. Most recently, on 26 January 2012, alongside his best mate Justin Jones (Jonesy), he made history by completing the longest unsupported polar expedition of all time: the first return journey from the coast of Antarctica to the South Pole without assistance. In 2008, the duo became the first kayakers to cross the Tasman Sea. James has led mountaineering expeditions to some of the most challenging peaks around the world, run numerous ultra-marathons and sailed to remote destinations across the globe. He is now one of Australia's most sought-after corporate speakers. *Extreme South*, the story of Cas and Jonesy's epic Crossing the Ice expedition, is his second book. James lives with his wife, Mia, in Sydney.

JAMES CASTRISSION

EXTREME SOUTH

hachette
AUSTRALIA

The diet, nutritional information and training regimes described in this book should not be adopted without consulting a qualified medical practitioner. Neither the authors nor the publisher can be held responsible for any loss or claim arising out of the use, or misuse, of the suggestions made or the failure to take medical advice.

hachette
AUSTRALIA

Published in Australia and New Zealand in 2012
by Hachette Australia
(an imprint of Hachette Australia Pty Limited)
Level 17, 207 Kent Street, Sydney NSW 2000
www.hachette.com.au

10 9 8 7 6 5 4 3 2 1

National Library of Australia
Cataloguing-in-Publication data

Castrission, James, 1982–
   Extreme south / James Castrission.

   978 0 7336 2798 9 (pbk.)

   Castrission, James, 1982–
   Jones, Justin.
   Adventure and adventurers – Antarctica – Biography.
   Explorers – Antarctica – Biography.
   Antarctica – Description and travel.
   Antarctica – Discovery and exploration – Australian.

919.8904092

Cover design by Blue Cork/Luke Causby
Text, map and picture section design by Christabella Designs
Typeset in Bembo by Graeme Jones
Printed in Australia by Griffin Press, Adelaide, an Accredited ISO AS/NZS 4001:2004 Environmental Management Systems printer

FSC
www.fsc.org
MIX
Paper from
responsible sources
FSC® C009448

The paper this book is printed on is certified against the Forest Stewardship Council® Standards. Griffin Press holds FSC chain of custody certification SGS-COC-005088. FSC promotes environmentally responsible, socially beneficial and economically viable management of the world's forests.

To the Norwegian polar explorer
Aleksander Gamme, for showing me what adventure
is all about

Get the free mobile app at
http://gettag.mobi

Video journal
www.casandjonesy.com.au/extremesouth

A picture is worth a thousand words ...

If you own a smartphone you can scan the QR tags throughout this book to connect to our favourite short videos. These look like mini black and white Tetris puzzles, as shown above. These codes make life easier and save you having to type long URLs or short text codes. Here's how to get up and running:

1. Download the free tag app at http://gettag.mobi
2. Open the application on your phone
3. Hold your phone camera 10 centimetres away from the QR tag placed on the page
4. It will automatically recognise the code and play the video.

Simple! The videos are well worth a look and really enhance the reading experience.

If you don't have a smartphone you can still access the videos by visiting our website: **www.casandjonesy.com.au/extremesouth**

J.C.

A note from the author

I am, first and foremost, an adventurer and my research stands proudly on the shoulders of the great works of many explorers, writers and historians who have gone before me. It was their stories of danger, of daring, of remarkable stamina that inspired me to head extreme south. The inclusion of information about previous forays in Antarctica is about humanising these mythic ice-men (a task made more difficult by the emotional reservedness of both that time in history and the nature of these men). In doing so, my intention is not to tarnish their memory, it is quite the opposite – I want to bring these great men to life and share their inspiring feats. Turning around at the South Pole and marching back to the coast has given me a unique understanding into the challenges explorers of yesteryear faced, which I have shared honestly throughout.

In this book I have chosen to express all distances in kilometres. Distances used in past literature on Antarctica have traditionally been expressed in statute (standard) miles, geographic (or nautical) miles or, more recently, kilometres. There is little consistency between different accounts. For instance, Mawson's diaries used statute miles while Scott wrote in geographic miles. Some purists may squirm, but most readers in Australia have a clearer understanding of kilometres – so kilometres it is!

1 kilometre = 0.54 nautical miles = 0.62 statute miles

1 degree of latitude = approximately 111 kilometres

For similar reasons, I have used Celsius not Fahrenheit for temperature readings.

I hope *Extreme South* gives you a fresh insight into the lives and motivations of explorers past and present, and that you enjoy reading our story as much as I have enjoyed writing it.

James Castrission

June 2012

Sydney

CONTENTS

Our expedition started at Hercules Inlet (altitude 130 metres) on the edge of the Ronne Ice Shelf in the Chilean-managed segment of Antarctica. The straight line distance to the South Pole from Hercules Inlet is 1130 kilometres. Although this was not the shortest route to the Pole, we decided it was the safest option to take, avoiding major crevassed areas as much as possible.

The South Pole lies at an altitude of approximately 2830 metres (600 metres taller than Australia's highest mountain, Mount Kosciuszko). This means our journey to the South Pole was almost entirely uphill. Although the majority of the route was a barely perceptible incline, there were two major rises: climbing out of Hercules Inlet, while we had our fully weighted sleds (600 vertical metres); and the climb from approximately 86° 30' to the Polar Plateau at 88° (1200 vertical metres).

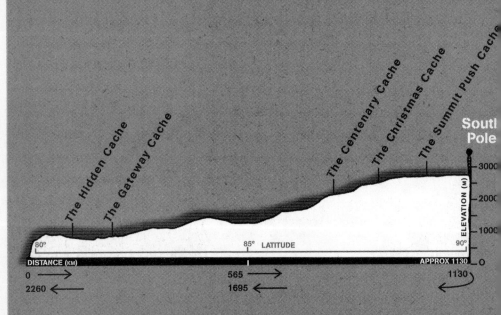

The coast
Hercules Inlet

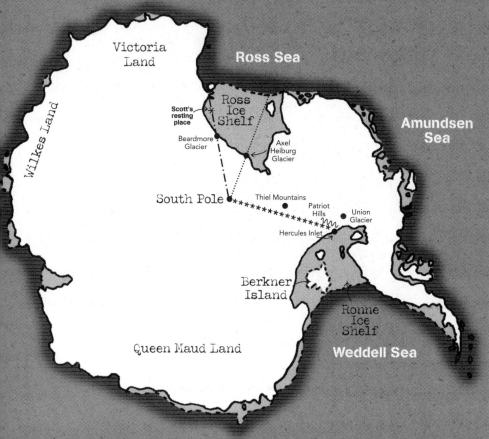

ANTARCTICA

AUSTRALIA

Southern Ocean

Victoria Land

Ross Sea

Wilkes Land

Amundsen Sea

Scott's resting place

Ross Ice Shelf

Beardmore Glacier

Axel Heiburg Glacier

South Pole

Thiel Mountains

Patriot Hills

Union Glacier

Hercules Inlet

Berkner Island

Ronne Ice Shelf

Queen Maud Land

Weddell Sea

AS & JONESY'S ROUTE ★★★★★★★★★★

SCOTT'S ROUTE —·—·—·—·—

AMUNDSEN'S ROUTE ·················

Southern Ocean

CHILE AND ARGENTINA

KILOMETRES

500   1000

'One hour of life, crowded to the full with glorious action, and filled with noble risks, is worth whole years of those mean observances of paltry decorum, in which men steal through existence, like sluggish waters through a marsh, without either honour or observation.'

SIR WALTER SCOTT

The relentless plodding had become familiar. I was no longer being as careful as I should have. When I'd seen the first crack in the ice a few hours earlier I cautiously poked it with my ski pole and gingerly shuffled across the delicate snow bridge. It was solid, and it held. I knew what lay beneath, and didn't want either of us following the fate of explorers past who had been swallowed up by this white continent. But when the cracks became more frequent, I stopped being as prudent. We plodded on, one foot in front of the other, dragging our sleds behind us.

All I could hear was my heart pounding as I sucked in the frigid polar air. Suddenly my leg punctured through the snow and I plunged downward. I might have screamed, but as quickly as it started the falling sensation stopped. I looked down. The trace-line back to my sled had saved my life, leaving me dangling above a gaping chasm. The hole in the fragile snow bridge allowed a shaft of light to dance off the contorted wall of the crevasse for a short distance before disappearing into a deathly blackness. In the fall my ski pole had snapped. I took a deep breath to calm the rising panic and shouted for Jonesy.

PART I

THE EARLY DAYS

'We shall not cease from exploration, and the end of all our exploring will be to arrive where we started and know the place for the first time.'

T. S. ELIOT

Chapter One

DREAMS OF ICE

I thought I was content. It was 2010, two years since I had crossed the Tasman in a leaky kayak with my mate Justin Jones – Jonesy. We'd spent sixty-two days on the wild ocean and had become the first people to successfully kayak from Australia to New Zealand. I had gone from wearing a suit and crunching numbers all day as an accountant, to a sunburnt rogue in a kayak. Surely that was enough? That adventure had answered questions about myself that had plagued me for years, and when we pulled it off I was finally happy.

Back on dry land, I was living a lifestyle that had eluded me for years – I fell in love and proposed to the most wonderful girl, Mia, established a successful business and was getting out climbing regularly and hard (well, that's a relative term, but I was pretty stoked with my progress). Many of the motivations that had driven me to cross the Tasman had been put to rest. I did not have the same anger, nor was I dealing with the same self-esteem issues that plagued my youth. I had nothing more to prove to the world or to myself. I no longer felt like a prisoner of institutionalisation, and the anger and frustration that had helped spur me on weren't driving me anymore. In fact, if you'd asked me five years earlier where I'd like to be with my life, I couldn't have dreamt of being in a happier place than I was in 2010. I was a different person since we crossed the ditch. But even though so much had been resolved in my life, the magnetic pull of adventure and the thrill I got from pushing myself to see what I could achieve hadn't been extinguished – within a few weeks of crossing the ditch Antarctica had begun to call.

At first it was just a whisper, tickling and playing with me. Thoughts and questions popped into my head that had me daydreaming for hours: what is that place like – the coldest, windiest, driest place at the bottom of the earth? What does breathing air at -50° Celsius feel like? I wanted to experience the blizzards, ski over sastrugi and hear the dry snow crunch beneath my boots. Then other thoughts came into play too. The Tasman journey had taken four years to prepare for, and Jonesy and I learnt more about ourselves in those sixty-two days at sea than the previous twenty-five years had taught us. Looking back on everything that happened – the sharks that tore at our hull, the thirty-foot waves that crashed over our cabin, the extreme food and sleep deprivation – I couldn't help but wonder whether we'd fluked the crossing. Had we just got lucky?

Perhaps the most valuable lesson the Tasman taught us was how to tackle an objective that we had no idea about, and I wanted to test those skills again. Sure, I could have done that in lots of different ways, but I wanted to commit myself to another world-class objective, to push myself even further in a completely foreign environment and experience that knee-trembling rush of fear and adrenaline that comes with being out of my comfort zone. The very thought of putting together an expedition down to Antarctica made excitement flow through my blood, generating the same energy as when I first began to dream of the Tasman.

With that in mind, in April 2008, a couple of months after returning from the Tasman, I was heading up to the Blue Mountains for a weekend of climbing when I made the call. I was a bit surprised by how nervous I felt. As with the Tasman, I knew I couldn't do this expedition without Jonesy.

'How'd you like to catch up for dinner?' I asked.

'You're not really my kind of guy,' Jonesy said and chuckled. 'Anyway, this sounds ominous – I'm sensing déjà vu.'

Jonesy could see right through me.

We arranged to have dinner a few days later at the same pizzeria where I had asked Jonesy, back in 2004, to paddle to New Zealand with me. There was the same big barrel-chested man with the same moustache making the same pizzas. Returning from an adventure, I always seemed to be more aware of people who stayed with the same job year in, year out. I admired their commitment. Occasionally I wish I could be like that, and wasn't as restless as I am (and so does my poor mother). At times I think a stable life would be so much easier.

I could tell Jonesy had been partying hard. There were bags under his eyes and his skin had a grey tinge to it.

'Don't ask,' he said before I had time to question him. 'Had a couple of massive nights.'

That made me laugh – we'd only been back a few months, and had so easily reverted to our same old habits.

We spent a few minutes chatting about what we'd done the previous weekend, but before long Jonesy said, 'Tell me what you're thinking, Cas.'

I decided to launch straight in. 'Antarctica, mate,' I excitedly belted out. 'How 'bout it? I've got this idea to do something truly amazing down there.'

His face lit up and, without hesitation, he smiled. 'I'm in – let's do it!'

Signalling to the waitress to bring us a pen, we looked down at the paper tablecloth and started scribbling. We felt alive as the ideas hit the table.

Our starting block was that we wanted to undertake a big adventure down south, but there were so many options of what we could do down there. For Jonesy and me, the attraction has always been in attempting a journey or voyage that has not been done before. Why? Because we get to write our own blueprint and try to solve problems that have stumped previous explorers. When it's a worthy objective, we both find it incredibly inspiring and rewarding to make all the pieces of the jigsaw fit together. But the only way you can ever know if your planning and preparation are good enough is by following through. American explorer Robert Peary says:

> the process of reaching the Pole may be identified with a game of chess, where all the moves leading to a favorable outcome have been thoroughly thought of in advance, long before the beginning of the game.

Sure, things can happen once you're there, but that is what makes it all the more challenging, trying to foresee problems and come up with solutions long before you have to.

Many people think that all of the big adventure 'firsts' have been successfully completed around the world, but I argue that improved technology, lighter gear and a deeper understanding of human physiology is allowing us to push boundaries that wouldn't have been dreamt of twenty years ago. In 1984, explorer Roger Mear set out with Robert Swan and Gareth Wood in their In the Footsteps of Scott expedition to make an unsupported one-way journey to the South Pole. At the time, Mear said:

A possibility excited me, why not dispense with all the clutter and go alone and unsupported, in one push with a minimum of food – no depots, no air support, no dogs, ponies or mechanised vehicles – just two men hauling sledges on the longest white walk in history? Of course, it could never be a two-way journey on foot as Scott's journey had been, for no-one could drag the weight of five months' food, but the thought of being out there, in such awesome isolation, with just a pair of skis, a sledge and a tent made the artificiality of a one-way journey acceptable.

Jonesy and I wanted to push it further – why not a two-way journey on foot? Since Robert Swan's In the Footsteps of Scott expedition, one-way trips to the South Pole have become the norm. But to us, the notion of marching to the South Pole and not provisioning for the return seemed incomplete. How can a trip be called 'In the footsteps of' when only covering half the distance of the original pioneers? In so many ways Swan's expedition had beautifully romantic ideals. They had sailed out of London, wintered down in Antarctica and set off for the Pole with no communications gear, but had not provisioned for the return. This bugged me. How would it be received if climbers were flown off the summit of Mount Everest? Most mountaineers would be disgusted, as the climb back down is part of the journey. And how is that any different from getting a ride back from the Pole? Why had this become accepted? At the turn of the last century, the North Pole had been conquered a few years earlier than the South Pole. Similarly, the first and only unsupported return journey to the North Pole had been completed in 1995 by Richard Weber and Mikhail Malakhov. The same had not yet been done in Antarctica.

By the time we left the pizzeria that night, we were grinning like idiots.

———

In the adventure world, the purist way to attempt any adventure is to do it 'naked', with no provisions or water and by hunting or gathering all your own food. Each element you add to that detracts from the overall purity of the adventure, but it also helps to manage the risks.

Adventure is all about defining a level of risk that you're willing to accept and going from there. Jonesy and I did this before embarking on the Tasman expedition, and were required to do the same for this journey in Antarctica. Understanding our risk profile allowed us to make decisions about the nature of the journey – where to start from, what means of transport we would use, and what style (unsupported versus supported) of expedition it would be.

With all our past adventures, it had always been important to both of us for the journey to be as self-reliant and self-sufficient as possible. Nothing had changed in that regard, so we were keen for this Antarctic journey to be an unsupported one. This meant we had to carry all our food, fuel, medical supplies and equipment for the entire trip, and could in no way rely on outside support. The other option would have been for a support party to drop food and fuel caches that we'd pick up en route to the Pole, but this didn't hold much traction with our adventuring beliefs.

Another decision we needed to make was whether to harness the wind through the use of kites – after all, Antarctica is the windiest place on earth. In recent times, kiting technology has improved drastically and has allowed people to travel up to 600 kilometres in a twenty-four hour period when the wind is right. It was something that could help us succeed, but would our journey be truly unassisted? On the Tasman we did not use sails, and after talking it through we felt the same way about this expedition. We wanted to do it under our own steam, with no wind assistance.

Then there was the question of where to start our journey. The logical place for a sled-hauling expedition is from right on the edge of Antarctica, with one toe dipped in the water. Back in the eighties and nineties, expeditions started from a place called Berkner Island, as it was believed this was the true edge of Antarctica. But it's not. The island is not accessible by sea and year round it is surrounded by the Ronne Ice Shelf, with its northern point approximately 20 kilometres from the ocean. This arbitrary start point (which would've cost an additional A$200,000 to get to) did not attract us any more than what had now become customary. The convention these days is to start from the coast, basically where the beach would be if there was no ice around. It is affected by tidal influence, but you're never going to see the ocean, as it is covered in approximately 130 metres of ice. This location is a place called Hercules Inlet. It was where others had begun the journey and so it seemed logical for us to leave from there too.

Slowly our questions were being answered, and we named the expedition: Crossing the Ice. Now that we knew what we wanted to do, we had to work out how we were going to pull off a journey that had eluded so many before us. The first attempt of an unsupported return journey in Antarctica was by a team of three – Eric Philips, Jon Muir and Peter Hillary (son of Sir Edmund, the first person to climb Mount Everest) – in 1998. They set off from Ross Island but following one air resupply, their attempt ended at the Pole after eighty-four days. They not only failed to make the return journey, but their one-way trip to the Pole was the slowest in history. After reading all about their attempt, the importance of strong, positive team dynamics was really driven home to us.

In 2006–07, Kiwi duo and good mates Kevin Biggar and Jamie Fitzgerald attempted the return journey from Hercules Inlet. They were fit, strong and were planning on using the prevailing winds to kite back from the Pole. Unfortunately, both lost an enormous amount of weight on the outward journey and Jamie tore both his hamstrings. Their bid ended after reaching the Pole in fifty-two days. We learnt from their attempt the importance of being efficient cross-country skiers and keeping sled weight to a minimum.

Also in 2006–07, British explorer John Wilton-Davies attempted the return journey solo, but his attempt ended short of reaching the South Pole due to a whole array of reasons ranging from failed sponsor obligations, his gear not being ready in time, poor route finding and a lack of experience in the cold. He wrote on his expedition blog:

> Some of these problems could have been avoided in better planning. Primarily my experience in the crevasses cost me a lot of time. If I had more experience of the conditions I should expect I would have avoided most of those problems ... To be realistic I failed because I went too slowly earlier on, and because I lost my confidence in the crevasses. After that episode I was certainly less driven to succeed.

In 2008–09, UK paratrooper Mark Langridge set out feeling hopeful, but the weight of his sled and the intimidating prospect of the return leg saw him drop most of his weight at the beginning of the journey, leaving him only able to commit to a one-way trek to the Pole. More recently, in 2010–11, Chris Foot, an English ex-SAS soldier, attempted the return journey, but due to a late start from Hercules Inlet, he didn't have enough time at the back end of the short Antarctic summer for the return.

In a way, all these failed attempts added to the allure. The teams that had tried previously weren't scrawny badminton players, rather they each had solid adventuring credentials. To be more successful than those who had tried before us, we'd need to haul all our supplies (which we estimated would weigh somewhere around the 150 kilogram mark) over 2200 kilometres. This distance was 500 kilometres further than had ever been achieved without support, and would probably take us about three months. Now we were talking!

For us, this adventure really stood out as being right on the limit of physiological and technological endurance. It sat on the boundary of what was possible. In fact, with so many strong teams having tried and failed, was it just a little out of reach, and was failure inevitable? We didn't know – but it was worth a shot. We were going to try to be the first unsupported team to travel to the South Pole and back, on foot, without kites or any assistance other than skis. This uncertainty is what made it an adventure. Jonesy and I had a lot of work to do, but we were determined to embrace that fine Aussie phrase yelled out by spectators at sporting events across the country: 'Have a go, ya mug!'

The rich history of that vast seventh continent lay like a dare just to Australia's south. Known for its harshness, its beauty, its unforgiving and uncompromising rawness, it had beaten so many before us. It was the ultimate challenge – to follow in the footsteps of Scott and Amundsen and take on the world's last great frontier.

Chapter Two

IN THE FOOTSTEPS OF ...

'Just before the turn of the last century, mankind knew more about the surface of the moon than it did about the seventh continent at the bottom of the world, the frozen lost land called Antarctica. In the famed Heroic Age of Antarctic exploration that followed, the icy veils that had so long covered the face and form of this mysterious place were courageously lifted, one by one, to reveal that frozen face in all its terrible splendour and though many men died in the process four men in particular became legends.'

PETER FITZSIMONS, *MAWSON AND THE ICE MEN OF THE HEROIC AGE*

As a kid, stories from the Heroic Age of Antarctic Exploration awakened my imagination more than any novel ever did. Don't get me wrong, I did enjoy *The Adventures of Tintin*; I followed Frodo Baggins through *Lord of the Rings* and was intrigued by the *Adventures of Robinson Crusoe*, but nothing entranced me more than the epic tales of Amundsen, Scott, Shackleton and Mawson, to name just a few. I daydreamed for hours about their adventures in the south, wondered about the conditions they faced, the decisions they made, and dwelt on the lives that were lost. The stories of the first men who tried to reach the South Pole had captivated me. Their heroic struggles and tales of mateship, their pain from frostbite, crevasse falls and cold injuries, and the tragic deaths that plagued their expeditions had me asking questions that books alone couldn't answer for me.

Interestingly, the only book prize I ever won at school – The John Coleman Memorial Prize for Meritorious Effort – saw me receive a copy of *Extreme South: Struggles and triumph of the first Australian team to the Pole* by Ian Brown. It is a book I treasure, and a title that eventually found its way back into my life.

Now, I'm no general history buff but, when it comes to things Antarctic, I know some. The stories of that time captured my attention like nothing before or since. They helped spark my addiction to adventure. Stories like how in 1773, a few years after Captain Cook sailed into Botany Bay, the great mariner was overtaken by the urge to discover what lay below this great southern land. Over the next few years, while in command of the HMS *Resolution*, Cook pushed his men and his ship through the Roaring Forties and Furious Fifties, further south than man had ever dared go. As the air temperature plunged, the nose of his ship began nudging icebergs around a latitude of 70 degrees south. With only sails to provide forward momentum, navigating among these icebergs was fraught with difficulty and danger. The decks, rigging and sails needed to be constantly freed from ice to avoid the risk of the ship becoming too top-heavy and capsizing. During these forays into the Southern Ocean, Cook discovered that Antarctica was not connected to any other continent, but due to the pack ice he was unable to explore far enough south to view the seventh continent.

Over the next one hundred years, few journeys of discovery were made to that part of the world. There was no reason for them. What drove ships at the time were commercial incentives and the money that came with transporting spices, fabric and food. Men didn't strive to explore further south until the realisation dawned that there were vast quantities of fat and fur available from the well-insulated animals such as seals, elephant seals, penguins and whales. Their pelts and blubber were highly desirable for fur and to light lanterns in Europe and North America through the 1800s. Money is a big motivator and all of a sudden men of adventure had the backing to push themselves further and travel to the unknown south to hunt these beautiful creatures – unfortunately, as it turned out, to near extinction.

Closing in on the end of the 1800s, the Sixth International Geographical Congress at the Royal Geographical Society's Headquarters in London passed a resolution that 'exploration of the Antarctic Regions is the greatest piece of geographical exploration still to be undertaken'. Antarctica was officially back on the agenda and with the recent invention of steam- and coal-powered engines, vessels had more manoeuvrability through the ice. Impetus and ability combined, and the next twenty-six years would become one of the most active periods of exploration and adventure the Southern Ocean had ever seen.

In 1897–98, the Geographical Society of Brussels sponsored a scientific expedition to explore the long finger of the Antarctic Peninsula and spend the winter in Antarctica. Up until then, vessels had darted into these southern latitudes but had scurried north when the end of summer approached. The Belgian ship, the *Belgica*, was heavily fitted out and provisions considered as best they could be so that the men on board could survive being trapped in the floating sea ice through the twenty-four hour darkness of winter. But no-one could prepare a man for the strangeness of the experience. All on board suffered in their floating prison, the ship's surgeon Frederick A. Cook wrote:

> The dense throbbing blackness of the polar night became ever more menacing, so too did a certain blackness show up in the morale of the men, matched only by a slowly enveloping blackness of mind.

Many of the men suffered horribly with madness and depression. In early June, one young man died of heart problems, exacerbated by the lack of food, warmth and light. I read and I wondered – could I have withstood that?

One of the men on board the *Belgica* was a strapping young Norwegian first mate by the name of Roald Amundsen. In his youth, Amundsen's mother had pressured him to become a doctor and he had not wanted to go against her will. I understood the pressure of this type of expectation and had struggled with it myself. Reading of Amundsen, I learnt that when his mother passed away, when he was twenty-one, he quit university and headed to sea. Inspired by Fridtjof Nansen's crossing of Greenland in 1888, Amundsen held a hidden desire to pursue a life of intense exploration. Once free to follow his desire, Roald Amundsen wasn't to be stopped. He returned from Antarctica and immediately set to work putting an expedition together to be the first vessel to navigate the Northwest Passage. During this groundbreaking expedition, which charted the first sea route through the Arctic

Ocean along the north coast of the Americas, Amundsen learnt many valuable polar survival skills from the indigenous Netsilik people that would prove invaluable in later years.

After successfully navigating through the Northwest Passage (a voyage that had eluded sailors for hundreds of years), Amundsen returned to Norway and set the wheels in motion to undertake an expedition to become the first man to reach the North Pole. A familiar issue would dog him as it did me and Jonesy all those years later – problems raising the vast sum of funds needed. In 1909, while Amundsen was organising his trip, two parties claimed to have reached the North Pole – Frederick Cook, the surgeon from the *Belgica*, and an American explorer, Robert Peary. Their claims were not without controversy, and many questioned the truth of their achievements, but Amundsen did not. He owed a large part of his survival on the *Belgica* to Cook, and had no reason to doubt the news. He decided to change his objective and re-route to Antarctica to conquer the South Pole instead. No point being third when you can be the first! Much to the disgust of many British, he did not make these plans known and even kept his decision from his own crew, his sponsors and most of all from Robert F. Scott, who had already revealed his plans to set out to become the first man to reach the South Pole. In early June 1910, Amundsen left Norway and only when underway did he inform his men that they were heading south. A few weeks later he sent a short telegram to Scott informing him of his change of plans.

I had read a lot about Robert Falcon Scott. A military man, he was born in 1868, and rose through the naval ranks from young cadet to captain. He was from a relatively well-to-do family, however, later in life, his father made some poor investment decisions and found himself close to bankruptcy. At the age of thirty, Scott found his two younger sisters and mother were totally financially dependent on him. This pressure must have been immense. How could he focus on adventure when his family needed his financial support? Then, in 1899, Scott had a chance encounter with the president of the Royal Geographical Society, Sir Clements Markham, who a few days later invited Scott to lead an expedition down to Antarctica. The opportunity was too attractive to turn down:

> The authorities and public are apathetic and slow to be moved but he must be dull indeed who does not appreciate that there will be great glory for this man and for the country of this man who first of human beings stands on the axis of this world.

Scott willingly took command of the Discovery expedition of 1901–1904. The participants were predominantly comprised of British Navy personnel and men from the merchant navy who had never been on skis and had no idea how to use them. Many of the expedition's scientific and discovery objectives would be hampered by their inexperience in polar environments and confusion on how to manage a dog team and horses. Still, Scott along with Ernest Shackleton, who was described by a fellow crewmate as being 'the most popular of the officers among the crew, being a good mixer', and Edward Wilson set out for the South Pole. Their journey was described as 'a combination of success and failure'. On one hand they pushed further south than any other expedition to date but, on the other, they still fell roughly 800 kilometres short of the South Pole. They suffered from snow blindness, frostbite and, ultimately, scurvy and, on the return journey Shackleton broke down. Wilson's diary entry for 14 January 1903 reads:

Shackleton has been anything but up to the mark, and today he is decidedly worse, very short winded and coughing constantly, with more serious symptoms that need not be detailed here but which are of no small consequence one hundred and sixty miles from the ship.

Although they maintained a public façade of mutual respect, Shackleton's attitude to Scott was one of 'smouldering scorn and dislike'. Shackleton set to work trying to launch his own expedition to the South Pole. Forget the goal of stamping the Union Jack at the South Pole for God, Queen, country and good ol' British sportsmanship; these two military men were focused on outdoing each other. On hearing of Shackleton's intentions, Scott sent him a letter immediately:

I see by the *Times* of Feb 12 that you are organising an expedition to go on our old tracks; and this is the first I have heard of it. The situation is awkward for me as I have already announced my intentions to try again in the old place. You see therefore that your announcement cuts right across my plans and to an extent … I needn't tell you that I don't wish to hurt you and your plans but in one way I feel I have a sort of right to my own field of work …

Yours very sincerely,

R. F. Scott

P.S. I feel sure with a little discussion we can work in accord rather than in opposition.

As the tension between the two explorers escalated, Scott wrote again:

It must be clear to you now that you have placed yourself directly in the line of my life's work ... two expeditions cannot go to the same spot either together or within the compass of several years ...

Yours ever,

R. F. Scott

This was close to the bone. In 2006, Jonesy and I wrote a similar letter to Andrew McAuley when we found out about his intentions to also kayak across the Tasman Sea. It was a shock to all involved to realise we were aiming for the same goal. I sympathised with where Scott was coming from. He justifiably felt there simply weren't the funds, public interest or expedition members around to support two big endeavours south.

Claims to a 'first' adventure or climb have plagued explorers for generations. Does an individual have the right to claim sovereignty of an objective? Of course they don't. But it doesn't make the notion any less fraught or emotionally charged for those invested in a goal. In rock climbing, climbers who prepare a new line often tag the bottom of the climb with a red flag which marks a 'closed project' – it's symbolically like a dog peeing on a lamp-post. A red flag says to other climbers: 'This is my line, back off'. Sure enough, there have been plenty of disputes over the years and it leads to many debates on such topics as to how long you can lay claim to that climb.

There are no hard and fast rules about exclusive rights to an adventure. But there is pride. As the French polar explorer Jean-Baptiste Charcot said:

There can be no doubt that the best way to the Pole is by way of the Great Ice Barrier, but this we regard as belonging to the English explorers, and I do not propose to trespass on other people's grounds.

The squabble between Scott and Shackleton did not impede on the latter gaining traction and heading to Antarctica in 1907 on the Nimrod expedition. Using the knowledge attained from the Discovery expedition, Shackleton pushed the 'furthest south' benchmark to *only* 180 kilometres from the Pole. He established a route up the treacherous Beardmore Glacier that connected the Ross Ice Shelf to the Polar Plateau – the gateway to the South Pole. Turning back from the Pole a mere 180 kilometres short was a decision that surely saved his life.

When Shackleton returned to Britain, the only comment he made to his wife, Emily, about not reaching the Pole was: 'I thought, dear, that you would rather have a live ass than a dead lion.'

———

It was now or never for Scott. Public interest was at an all-time high. A route to the South Pole had been established, so Scott got to work raising the £40,000 needed to launch an expedition (that's equivalent to about A$4.5 million today). When he announced his plans to recruit a team of men, no fewer than 8000 from around the world applied.

While Shackleton was living down in Antarctica, Scott had been busy progressing his naval career when a beautiful young bohemian sculptor entered his life. Swept away by love, Scott quickly proposed to Kathleen Bruce and the couple married a few short months later. But marriage was not going to stop Scott from pursuing his dream.

In July 1908, while Scott was tossing around the logistics of the expedition, Kathleen wrote to him:

Write and tell me that you shall go to the Pole. Oh dear
me what's the use of having energy and enterprise if a
little thing like that can't be done. It's got to be done,
so hurry up and don't leave a stone unturned - and
love me more and more, because I need it.

When I'd first read about Scott, Kathleen's part in his life had barely
registered with me. I was a young bloke and love stories weren't
my thing. But re-reading many of the stories closer to travelling
to Antarctica, I couldn't help but see some similarities to my own
circumstances. It's hard enough to organise an expedition, raise
funds and get your body and your head right, but it would be even
harder if you had to battle with your girlfriend, your wife or your
family as well. I was lucky that Mia fully supported my expedition
just as Kathleen had supported Scott.

On 13 September 1909, Scott made his plans public: 'The main
object of the expedition is to reach the South Pole and secure for
the British Empire the honour of that achievement.' The very next
day a son, Peter, was born to Kathleen and Scott.

There was a lot going on in Scott's world and many critics argue
that he was woefully unprepared for his journey. I disagree. He had
learnt many valuable lessons on the Discovery expedition of 1901–04
and had always carefully considered alternative methods of transport.
On his most recent foray south during the Terra Nova expedition,
Scott planned on using a variety of modes of transport, including white
horses from Siberia (they had to be white because apparently they
performed better on the snow!), motor sledges, dogs and manhauling.
He even examined the use of sledges with small roller wheels. Scott
had spent years developing his skills and exploring ways to achieve the
best results in the frozen, unpredictable southern continent. He was
determined to become the first man to reach the South Pole.

In June 1910, Scott's ship, the *Terra Nova*, farewelled England to a cheering crowd. Scott remained behind to keep fundraising for an additional six weeks before leaving with Kathleen to join the ship in South Africa en route to Melbourne for final preparations before heading south. It was here he found out Amundsen was also aiming to reach the South Pole.

The *Terra Nova* left Melbourne and darted across the Tasman to Dunedin, on New Zealand's south island, before heading full steam ahead to the south. Most of the men on board were sick, and they were battered by Southern Ocean storms including one that ripped ten tons of coal overboard. By early January 1911, the *Terra Nova* had docked in Cape Evans, and the men began construction on the hut in which they planned to spend the twenty-four hour darkness of polar winter, before their attempt at the Pole in the coming summer.

By late January the depot laying was underway. Captain Scott led a team of twelve men, eight ponies and twenty-six dogs out onto the ice to lay caches for the return journey. They made poor progress, averaging less than 19 kilometres a day, and in mid-February Scott made the call to establish their furthest cache away from their winter quarters 74 kilometres short of where they initially intended to do so. One of the men under Scott's command, Lawrence 'Titus' Oates, strongly believed that this was foolish, as it would be too far for the Pole party to get back to. But Scott was worried that pushing further south would cost them the lives of a few of their ponies. 'I have had enough of this cruelty to animals and I am not going to defy my feelings for the sake of a few days march,' he wrote. Oates was immensely frustrated and with remarkable foresight said, 'I'm afraid you'll come to regret not taking my advice.'

'Regret it or not, I have taken my decision as a Christian gentleman,' Scott replied. He would not be swayed and so the men established One Ton Depot 74 kilometres short of where Oates wanted to bury the 2000 pounds of food and fuel. After enduring the harsh winter in their hut, the Brits began their assault on the Pole on 1 November 1911. Following a gruelling seventy-seven days, the British team finally reached their destination. Scott and four companions – Oates, Henry Bowers, Edward Wilson and Edgar 'Taff' Evans – were dragging their sledge across the coarse snow crystals of the Polar Plateau when they saw something fluttering in the wind. Tied to a sled runner, they found the Norwegian flag and a tent left behind by Amundsen. The Norwegians had arrived over a month earlier and were at that very moment only a week away from arriving back at their ship the *Fram*. The Norwegians had nailed it. They'd travelled quickly and efficiently, and incredibly Amundsen arrived back at the ship weighing more than when he left. By this stage Scott and his men were starving and devastated – the impact on morale shouldn't be underestimated.

Tragically, one by one, the men in Scott's Pole party began to collapse and perish in their tracks. First to die was the largest and strongest – Taff Evans. It is suspected that a blow to his head in a crevasse fall a few days earlier was the primary cause of his death. The explorers faced extremely difficult conditions on the return journey, mainly due to the exceptionally adverse weather, poor food supply, injuries sustained from falls, and the effects of scurvy and frostbite, all of which slowed their progress. The next to go was Oates, at the foot of the Beardmore Glacier. He walked from the tent into a blizzard, with his famous last words, 'I am just going outside and may be some time.' His death is seen as an act of self-sacrifice when, aware his ill health was compromising his three companions' chances of survival, he chose certain death rather than hold them back.

Unfortunately, his self-sacrifice wasn't enough to save his three other desperate companions. On meagre rations, Scott, Bowers and

Wilson trudged on towards the biggest depot established on the southern journey – One Ton Depot. Cruelly, Antarctica unleashed its fury when the men were a mere 18 kilometres short of the depot – if only Scott had listened to Oates the summer before, things could have turned out very differently. A blizzard forced them to set up tent. Knowing that he was nearing the end, with frostbitten fingers he scrawled in his diary a note to his beloved Kathleen:

> The worst aspect of this situation is the thought I shall never see you again ... How much better has it been than lounging in too great comfort at home - but, oh, what a price to pay - to forfeit the sight of your dear, dear face.

With the storm raging for days, they consumed all of their food and fuel and with no energy left, became entombed in their iced-up sleeping-bags and heavily frosted tent. Scott's last diary entry haunts me. I struggled to understand why he didn't keep fighting. Surely curling up in your tent is admitting defeat?

> Had we lived, I should have had a tale to tell of the hardihood, endurance and courage of my companions which would have stirred the heart of every Englishman. These rough notes and our dead bodies must tell the tale.

While Scott's men were attempting to claw their way back to the *Terra Nova*, Douglas Mawson, an Australian geologist who had accompanied Shackleton on the Nimrod expedition, had launched his own Australasian Antarctic expedition. Mawson – a strong manhauler, talented scientist and well-liked crew member – had turned down a position in Scott's Pole party as he showed no interest in a 'boy's own adventure' attempt on the South Pole. Mawson was a man of science and wanted to explore the geographic coastline of Antarctica below Australia. His dedication to science was quite unique among explorers, as Sir Edmund Hillary once said:

Nobody climbs mountains for scientific reasons. Science is used to raise money for the expeditions, but you really climb for the hell of it.

Mawson set an ambitious scientific agenda and took charge of the Far Eastern expedition, with two other companions. When the team was 499 kilometres from their hut, one of these men, Belgrave Ninnis, crashed through the bridge of a large crevasse with a sledge and dog team and was completely swallowed. This left Mawson and Xavier Mertz with seriously depleted provisions. They quickly began their return, progressively using their dogs to supplement their food supply. What they didn't know was that the dog liver they had been eating was very rich in vitamin A and toxic. After twenty-five days on the return journey, and the combined effects of hard physical exertion and starvation, this toxicity led to Mertz becoming ever weaker and, just before his death, suffering from oppressive madness. Mawson, himself seriously debilitated, discarded everything that was not essential for survival, except his geological specimens and records of the journey. Using a pocket saw, he cut his sledge in half and dragged it unaided the last 160 kilometres, taking another thirty days to reach Main Base. During this epic struggle for survival his body was failing but he kept on going:

The thickened skin of the soles had separated in each
case as a complete layer, and abundant watery fluid
had escaped into the socks. The new skin underneath
was very much abraded and raw.

Clumps of hair fell from his head and infections burst all over his body. The same fate that stole the life of Ninnis, Mertz and the dogs was perilously close. Yet he kept inching forward, at times having to crawl. Two things drove Mawson on: the motivation to get back to his fiancée, Paquita, and the outer-world theological experience that Mawson describes as 'Providence'. Crevasse falls were frequent and his daily mileage slipped.

Finally, when all the other men back at Commonwealth Bay had given up hope, Mawson stumbled into camp two and a half weeks late. At first glance, the men at the station thought they were seeing a ghost, before realising it was a human – but who? Mawson had returned! Heartbreakingly, the relief ship, *Aurora*, which was destined to carry Mawson and his men back to Australia, had left that morning. Attempts by the skipper to find Mawson and his team were hampered by gales and the impossibility of getting the ship close enough to shore. Making one of the most difficult decisions of his life, Captain Davis made the call to leave a rescue party behind and sail north for the winter, before the ship froze into the pack ice. Mawson and the rescue party endured their second winter in darkness before finally returning to Adelaide in December 1913 where he was met with a hero's welcome and his beloved Paquita.

After Shackleton's Nimrod expedition, he returned to Britain a national hero and was knighted for his efforts. He took kindly to his new status and filled his diary with public appearances, lectures and social engagements. He also tried his luck with a couple of high-risk business ventures and money-making schemes that all seemed to peter out. After the Pole had been reached by Scott and Amundsen in 1911–12, he believed there to be only one final great journey left in Antarctica – the crossing of the continent. It was a highly ambitious, dangerous journey that was a logistical nightmare. It meant using two ships – one on either side of the continent – with the men of the ship *Aurora* laying depots across the Ross Ice Shelf up to the Beardmore Glacier for Shackleton's team who would start from the other side of the continent, then pick up these vital provisions after having passed the Pole.

Unfortunately, the journey ended before it even began and the attempted crossing never eventuated. Shackleton's vessel, the *Endurance*, became locked in ice in the Weddell Sea and the crew had to prepare to survive the long dark stormy winter aboard the ship. Then, to their horror, the ship began to be crushed. It sank leaving the men stranded with what provisions they could throw overboard before it disappeared into the depths. Their odds of survival were slim to none.

No-one was coming to rescue them – if they wanted to live they would have to fight for it. Shackleton left most of his men and went for help. He sailed north in a small, open boat, the *James Caird*, through some of the most treacherous and freezing waters in the world to a known whaling settlement on South Georgia Island, over 1500 kilometres away. This perilous journey was near-suicide but somehow, after fourteen days at sea, the weary explorers stumbled into the settlement. The rest of Shackleton's team were eventually rescued, after having survived off seal meat for 105 days. Shackleton didn't ever get to attempt the crossing of Antarctica but the rescue of all of his men has gone down as one of the greatest survival stories of all time. It was the final chapter in the Heroic Age of Antarctic Exploration.

I knew all these stories. I had read about the hardships and the conditions faced in Antarctica, I knew the worst-case scenarios, and I knew that not much had changed in one hundred years. Though there are now satellite phones, GPS tracking devices and EPIRBs, there is no technology or rescue available when you are trapped in your tent by a wild Antarctic storm, or dangling down inside the yawn of a hidden, bottomless crevasse. Like Scott and Mawson, I had a love waiting for me. Like Amundsen, I had shaken off expectation and embraced adventure. But did I have the spirit, the determination and the mental toughness to achieve what no-one had before? Mawson once described the characteristics that made Shackleton such a great explorer as being his 'never failing fund of optimism, great determination, unknowing of fear, ambition and a fine physique'. Did we have any of these traits?

All these great men had travelled to the South Pole, but no-one had yet claimed the prize for the unsupported return journey. Amundsen had returned, but he had used the assistance of dogs and pre-laid depots established the summer before. Back then there was little to no emphasis on the style of the journey. Polar explorers were judged on being the first to reach the Pole and making it back alive. If they were available at the time, aircraft would have been used.

I had already shown I could put in the hard yards of preparation needed to tackle the unknown. And now, with Jonesy, I was going to push myself once more. And this time we'd both be taken to the limit. We were heading to 90 degrees south, a place that had always held a starry-eyed fascination for me – it was the factory of adventure and home to some of the most inhospitable beauty on the planet. This time we were going to push ourselves further than we'd ever gone before.

Chapter Three

FIT, FAT AND FLEXIBLE

Fighting the urge to throw snowballs at each other or lie down to make snow angels, we strapped cross-country skis to our feet down at the Aussie Alps in the winter of 2010. Having grown up in the suburbs of Sydney, neither Jonesy or I had ever skied before, so we thought now was a good time to learn.

Cross-country skis are about half the width of regular downhill skis, and have scales (or skins) on the bottom that grip the snow as you step forward but still allow you to glide efficiently between steps. By this stage we knew we wanted to attempt to travel to the South Pole and back, but we were still working out the finer details, like how to ski. It took a few minutes to figure out how to clip the bindings to our boots, then, like someone learning to ice-skate in a slapstick movie, neither of us could stay on our feet – let alone ski! After more than a few minutes of laughter, propping each other up we finally gathered enough confidence to try to move forward.

Slam! Back on our bums again.

The jokes and laughter began to subside as we started to get incredibly frustrated and concerned by how bad we actually were. It was beyond funny; it was embarrassing.

Cross-country skiers are fringe dwellers. They're the sinewy bearded types wearing scruffy 'Where's Wally' thermals, their ears popping out of their woollen beanies. They have never been (and are never likely to be) as cool as snowboarders, with their pants down near their knees, or as competent as downhill racers in their colourful lycra. The only people less cool on the slopes than cross-country skiers are hopeless wanna-be cross-country skiers. That was us.

Video journal – First time skiing
www.casandjonesy.com.au/extremesouth

Trying to keep in mind a lesson I'd learnt boxing at university – it doesn't matter how many times you get knocked down, so long as you get back up – we kept at it. Pretty soon we felt comfortable standing up on the skis. Then we started to waddle like ducks (on dead-flat ground) in the kiddies' learn-to-ski area at Perisher. Progress on the first day was slow, but by the time the sun was setting, our bodies were aching and it was time to head back to our accommodation in Jindabyne for the evening. In the car we talked about what we'd get up to the next day.

'How about we ski up Mount Kosciuszko?' I asked.

'Are you crazy?' Jonesy replied.

I thought it was a really good idea. Besides, if we couldn't ski up Kosci, how were we ever going to ski to the South Pole? And Jonesy couldn't argue with that kind of logic.

So, the following morning we woke early, took the Kosciuszko Express chairlift to the top of Thredbo and began waddling over towards Australia's highest mountain, which really isn't all that high at all. Our progress was slow with frequent falls, but by lunchtime, we began to scale its final slopes and before long we were on top! The feeling of elation was quickly dashed when we looked at the terrain we were meant to ski down – oh boy, what a lesson to learn: skiing up is *much* easier than skiing down steep terrain. The snow was icy, which meant we couldn't just take off our skis and walk, so after a quick 'godspeed' and 'good luck' we pointed our skis downhill for a kamikaze-like descent. Fortunately, we couldn't stay on our feet long enough to build up proper speed. Perfect!

That was the first weekend of many that saw us driving down to the Aussie ski fields and slowly, but surely, learning to ski. Early on, we were fortunate enough to meet our Ski Yoda – Bruce Easton from Wilderness Sports in Jindabyne – and we quickly became his young naïve padawans. Bruce began to teach us how to travel over snow with the correct technique – snow ploughs, sidesteps, tip turns, kick turns and herringbones all became part of our vocabulary, and some even became part of our ski repertoire. By the end of winter we were regularly making day-long excursions into the back country and even managed a two-day jaunt with our camping gear up to Blue Lake.

Jonesy and I come from a bushwalking background, and just like sea kayaking had opened us up to 'walking on water', cross-country skiing had now given us access to the beautiful back country of the Snowy Mountains. Once we could stand up long enough, we loved it! Skiing in the back country through contorted snow gums, their boughs dusted with ice and glistening in the late afternoon spring light, quickly became one of my favourite things to do in one of my favourite places in the world. The way the snow sits on leaves and the light bounces off streaked trunks in crazy prisms of colour depending on the time of day is breathtakingly beautiful.

After a while, we were spending more time upright than on our bums, but learning to ski was only a tiny part of the physical preparation required for our Antarctic expedition – we also had to get fit, fat and flexible.

Reinhold Messner, the world's greatest mountaineer, once described sledging as 'the work of horses, not humans'. We'd read countless Antarctic stories where the weight of explorers' sleds initially shocked them, then proceeded to almost tear them in half. As mentioned earlier, two mates of ours from across the Tasman – Kevin Biggar and Jamie Fitzgerald – attempted the return journey back in 2006, and were one of the fittest teams ever to head down to Antarctica. They trained hard and were in prime physical condition when they attempted their trip. Their advice to us was: 'Fellas, the best way to train for pulling heavy things in cold places is to pull heavy things in cold places.'

That's all well and good, but unfortunately in Australia it's not always easy to find cold places to pull heavy things. Even so, we put together a training regime as best we could. Structured training for expeditions is a relatively new concept. Up until the last ten or fifteen years, adventurers had tried to fit in a few jogs, the occasional tyre drag and that was about it. We understood how critical it was to get ourselves physically ready for the journey and we'd learnt from the Tasman preparation that a structured training regime was the best way to do this.

Enter Action Man. Tipping the scales at over 120 kilograms and towering at a height of 200 centimetres, we found probably the most qualified person on earth to design our program. Perth-based adventurer Tom Smitheringale started his career in the army before moving to the personal-training arena. Recently he's been pushing boundaries of adventure under the branding of One Man Epic. For most of us, a title like this might be considered a little presumptuous, but for Tom it couldn't be more accurate. In 2010, Tom almost became the third man in history to ski solo and unsupported to the North Pole. After skating across thin ice (literally), suffering frostbite and dodging polar bears he dramatically fell through the ice and required rescue. From the lessons that Tom learnt in the Arctic, he designed a brutal six-month program that was aimed at increasing both our strength and endurance. Training up to thirty hours a week, the phases and cycles involved a range of activities and exercises – pack marches, swimming, gym sessions – but at the core of all our training were the dreaded tyre-pulling sessions. This involved strapping two truck tyres together and dragging them along the streets and beaches of Sydney for up to eight hours a session. It's hard to think of a more painful, heartbreaking and soul-crushing experience. Cyclists would pass us and sling comments our way like:

'You know it's easier to put them up the other way.'

'You've lost the rest of your car.'

'Mate – there's something behind you.'

Yeah, ha ha, very funny.

And at times, people would innocently ask what the hell we were doing. To be honest, some days I wasn't sure! But having spent so much time out on the streets strapped to these instruments of torture we came up with some replies.

'Car broke down.'

'Just taking my tyre for a walk.'

'Real men don't need the frame.'

Pretty early on in our training it became apparent that if there was one thing Jonesy was designed to do in life, it was to drag heavy things in cold places. He was a machine, strong as an ox right from the start. Starting his sporting life as a rugby front rower and always being a 'big-boned' lad, he had the driving strength to just keep plodding away, regardless of the gradient, the surface, or how many tyres he was dragging. A year earlier, we were both competing in a one hundred kilometre 'ultra-marathon' in the Blue Mountains. Twelve kilometres in Jonesy broke his ankle and hobbled through the next 88 kilometres – refusing to give up. When he sets his mind to something, nothing gets in his way.

Me, on the other hand, well, I'd been doing a lot of rock climbing and was pretty lean when we commenced the program. Right from the start I found it hard to keep up with Jonesy on these sessions, and I hated it. It wasn't a matter of having to feel superior to him or better than him, it was just the way it's always been, and now it was tough always lagging behind – it played with my head. I was worried that maybe I had lost my edge because I couldn't match his efforts. With all the adventures we'd shared together over the previous fifteen years – kayaking, bushwalking, climbing, trail running – I'd always been fitter than Jonesy, which allowed me to lead from the front. We'd come to accept this natural order of things, and had learnt to manage each other and how hard to push accordingly. Tyre-pulling changed all that. And it wasn't a pretty transition.

CAS DIARY ENTRY – 9 MAY 2011

'If this is the way we're going to interact we're not even going to get halfway to the South Pole you a**hole.'

Gloves off, we then went at it. We were forty minutes into pulling tyres in Centennial Park (we'd done a two-hour pack march earlier in the day) and I cracked it. I'm really struggling with being weaker than Jonesy in this tyre-pulling stuff. I hate not being able to keep up, being the weaker one.

I guess what irked me the most on Saturday was the way Jonesy was 'managing me' ... or not, as the case may be. No encouragement, no support ... just leaving me behind and I hated it. Sure, I've left him behind before when paddling/hiking but I like to think a lot of the time I waited for him and tried to pick up his spirits when he was down. After the initial yelling we calmed down and had a bit of a chat about it. He feels uncomfortable being the stronger one and doesn't know how to handle it. He knows that if he encourages me too much and is patronising that's just as bad as not giving any support.

As confronting as it was, it was crucial that we'd identified this as a massive source of tension before heading south. Many adventurers train, organise gear modifications and sponsorship individually, and it's only when they get on the expedition with their teammates that they discover issues like the one we were having, and by then it is often too late. Poor group dynamics have caused many expeditions to fail, and we knew from talking to other explorers that one of the driving factors of this can often be team members moving at different speeds. By realising that this was a source of conflict we were able to address it early on. It was pretty simple really: Jonesy needed to learn how to lead, and I needed to learn not to be so stroppy about following.

By this stage of our planning we had realised that in order to make this project happen and give ourselves the best chance of success we had to live and breathe the project above everything else. We moved into Jonesy's apartment to create a centralised expedition headquarters. Jonesy's lounge room became our office – framed paintings that had hung on the walls were replaced with maps of Antarctica – and foam rollers, weights, Swiss balls and Thera-Bands crowded the floor. The kitchen was stacked high with protein powders and supplements, and the bathroom was used for ice baths after big sessions.

This would have been fine and well for two smelly blokes, but my fiancée, Mia, also moved in and became an integral part of the team. Right from the start she was incredible. She encouraged us when we needed a push and gave me the space I needed to make this happen without letting me ignore important relationships. A big issue I'd confronted when preparing for the Tasman was the way I'd concentrated solely on that and had alienated myself from all the people close to me. I pushed family and good mates away. If I wasn't paddling or talking about the Tasman I wasn't interested. One of my big goals with this expedition was to make sure I didn't do the same thing again, especially with Mia.

From the inception of the Antarctic idea, she was privy to all aspects of the expedition and she began to live the journey with us. The fact that Mia is a dietician helped enormously. She was able to design one of the most scientifically advanced polar diets to date. Each gram we carried had been carefully accounted for in numerous spreadsheets to ensure we consumed the ultimate combination of macro and micro nutrients. And even while we were training she worked out what we should be eating to put on the weight we needed to fatten up for the long, cold journey ahead.

For over a year our tyre-pulling playground became a loop in Centennial Park where we designed a four kilometre course around the outside of the park. We had to be careful to avoid the horses as they went berko whenever they saw us pulling; maybe they were worried we were trying to do them out of a job. Initially it took me almost two hours to get through the course and by the end I looked as sick as a pack-a-day smoker who'd just run a marathon. Within six months we'd built it up to four laps, each taking just under ninety minutes, with a 150-minute pack march thrown in at the end of the day.

As our fitness was shaping up, we were also getting fat. Yep, fat and proud of it.

One of the most valuable lessons we learnt from the Tasman paddle was the impact different muscle and fat stores had on performance. Both prior and post Tasman we had DEXA (dual-energy X-ray absorptiometry) scans done. These are carried out on a machine that looks somewhat similar to an MRI unit, which scans up and down your body compiling information on the muscle, fat and bone density of each limb.

The results were fascinating: over the course of that expedition, Jonesy had lost approximately 12 kilograms, of which six kilograms was muscle and six kilograms was fat. I'd lost approximately 6.5 kilograms, but 90 per cent of that weight loss was muscle and only 10 per cent was fat. My percentage of body fat actually went up through the expedition as I lost proportionally more muscle than fat. These results showed that I should either have had a higher fat percentage going into the expedition (Jonesy kept telling me I should have been supersizing each and every meal – maybe he was right!) or my diet should have had a higher percentage of protein. This would have prevented my body from cannibalising muscle stores when it got hungry.

Many expeditioners over the years have argued on both sides of the fence as to the benefits of pre-expedition bulking up. From our experience, we're definitely of the opinion that it's beneficial to bulk up both fat and muscle stores. Back in the seventies, in Kathmandu on the way to Mount Everest, the famous British mountaineer Don Whillans was given grief about his excess weight compared to his lean teammates. His reply: 'In three months' time I'll look like them and they'll probably be dead.' Science has progressed since that time, but the principles remain the same. Because of the intense cold in Antarctica and the extreme physical exertion we'd be putting ourselves through, we were going to be burning more calories than we could consume (there was only so much food we could carry in our sleds) and therefore we'd be losing weight from day one. As a result, from early 2011 we started devouring whatever food we could get our hands on. Even with thirty hours training a week, I saw my weight skyrocket from about 80 kilograms to just over a hundred! Eating steaks for breakfast, burgers as snacks and double serves of ice cream for dinner was great fun, until the clothes I was wearing got tighter and tighter. And then the inevitable day came when they no longer fitted at all! Fortunately, Jonesy was still the bigger one, and I was able to slip comfortably into some of his old clothes.

While improving our fitness levels and increasing our weight, we also had to maintain our flexibility to reduce the risk of injury while training. I felt pity for the sinewy participants who took their positions in the Pilates and yoga classes we attended. No-one should ever be subjected to the rear view of Jonesy and me when we're weighing over a hundred kilograms (with close to 30 kilograms of that being pure fat) and trying to stretch while busting out of our Lycra.

So we'd begun in earnest to pull heavy things in very warm places. Probably the worst (and stupidest) session we subjected ourselves to was when we decided to set our tyre-pulling baseline on a steaming hot January day in Sydney. Oh, and that also involved finding the steepest, longest and most brutal hill we could: Vista Street in Sydney's leafy northern suburb of St Ives.

Video journal – Vista Street tyre-pulling
www.casandjonesy.com.au/extremesouth

It was important to establish fitness benchmarks so that we could measure the effectiveness of our training. With two tyres each, we started to haul them up the 400-metre, 30-degree hill that had heat waves bubbling off its surface. Within ten metres I began to feel it was a really bad idea, but with Jonesy focused and already pulling away from me, I knew we were committed. Seconds felt like hours as the sweat poured off me. Under the immense strain of the weight, I drunkenly stumbled slowly upwards. With my belly button being wrenched into my spine, my progress slowed even more. Jonesy kept consistent – left, right, left, right. My calves were flaming. The incline was so steep I tried to clamber on all fours like a husky before collapsing. I was only halfway up. Again and again I jerked in the harness, making minuscule progress. Jonesy's feet consistently plodded forward like a metronome. Finally he made it to the top, dropped to one knee and puked in the gutter. I still had another fifty metres to go. With Jonesy by my side encouraging me I made it to the top and we both collapsed in the middle of the road, unable to move. How the hell were we going to haul 160 kilograms for three months down in Antarctica? We had a long way to go.

Chapter Four

YOU SWEAT, YOU DIE

Luck

'I may say that this is the greatest factor – the
way in which the expedition is equipped – the
way in which every difficulty is foreseen, and
precautions taken for meeting or avoiding it.
Victory awaits him who has everything in order –
luck, people call it. Defeat is certain for him who
has neglected to take the necessary precautions
in time; this is called bad luck.'

ROALD AMUNDSEN,
THE SOUTH POLE

Okay, okay it's true – I often get massive man crushes. One such
crush is on the legendary polar explorer Roald Amundsen. Ever
since Jonesy and I attempted our first big expedition, Amundsen's
meticulous and scrupulous attitude towards planning, risk

management and preparation has heavily influenced how we formulated our own plans. Jonesy and I really enjoy setting ourselves seemingly impossible objectives that we know very little about, then breaking that objective down into its components and identifying strategies to combat the risks that we will face at each stage.

Jonesy has always been a bit of a maths nerd and he drummed into me the numbers supporting detailed risk management work and the importance of redundancies. In a nutshell, this is it: let's assume that there are only ten situations that, if they were to occur, could cause the expedition to fail. These situations could include a tent fire, falling in a crevasse, food contamination, etc. If these events each have a 5 per cent chance of occurring (a reasonable level of risk) then the expedition actually has a 40.1 per cent chance of one of these events occurring. So, the expedition has a 40.1 per cent chance of failing.

If we are able to add a level of redundancy (a backup) to each of the ten situations, such as having a second tent, etc., then we reduce the chance of the expedition failing to 2.5 per cent. The chance of one of the events occurring is still great (40.1 per cent) but the chance of one of the events occurring and then the backup also failing is quite small (2.5 per cent). If a second level of redundancy was added this probability of failure drops even more significantly.

Many of the risks that lay ahead in our Antarctic expedition – frostbite, hypothermia, cold injuries – are very difficult to imagine and train for when you grew up kayaking in Sydney. Even if we could wave Harry Potter's wand, transfigure into frozen peas and jump into the freezer at home for a day, that still wouldn't be cold enough. Not even close. The average domestic freezer sits at a balmy -12° Celsius. We needed to train and experience temperatures down to -40° Celsius – and that's not taking the wind chill into account. At these temperatures the condensation from breathing freezes as a cloud in front of your face and the hairs in your nostrils become crusty. The only way for us to experience temperatures similar to what we were going to encounter in Antarctica (without actually going there) was to head up to the Arctic Circle. So, in February 2011, we did.

Iqaluit is a small Canadian coastal town positioned 2000 kilometres north of Ottawa on the southern end of Baffin Island. The surf is rarely up because for eight months of the year the ocean is frozen in Frobisher Bay. We planned to spend three weeks there with Matty McNair and her kids, Eric and Sarah. Between them, these polar gurus have skied to the North Pole four times and the South Pole eight times and Matty is internationally acknowledged as one of the world's premier polar guides. The first ten days we were planning on learning everything we could from the McNairs about the art of polar travel then, equipped with this newly gained knowledge, we were going to head out for our own mini-expedition.

Stepping off the plane into the frigid Arctic air at Iqaluit, we felt like Han Solo and Chewbacca in that scene from *Star Wars* when they're in the bar on Tatooine – it was like we'd entered another world, and my body felt exactly the same way! Within a few minutes I had an allergic reaction to the cold. Much to the delight of overzealous aunties, I've always had chubby cheeks that have attracted much pinching. For some reason, the cold made them balloon out and my head became round like a soccer ball. On the Tasman I was 'allergic' to the ocean, in that I suffered from horrendous sea-sickness, now I was showing signs of being allergic to the cold. Are you serious?

Video journal – Allergic to the cold?
www.casandjonesy.com.au/extremesouth

Waiting in the taxi line we were both hit by ice-cream headaches just from breathing the cold air. Once the taxi was loaded, we gave the driver the house number (Iqaluit is so small that there aren't street names, just numbers) and we got the sense pretty quickly that if we'd just given him a name he would have told us their life story.

When you are dealing with these freezing temperatures everything becomes an effort at first. Taking your dog for a walk brings on a different meaning in Iqaluit. In Sydney it might mean throwing on a singlet and strolling around the block with your poodle, up there it means strapping a team of dogs (that howl and scratch like wolves) to a *qomatiqs* (Inuit-style sled) and rocketing off over a frozen ocean. Everything freezes there. Before the ten days of training started we walked up to the supermarket to buy some snacks. Jonesy picked up a soda for the walk home. Within a minute of stepping out of the supermarket, crystals of ice started floating in the can and by the time we arrived back at Matty's house the last quarter was frozen solid. It was *that* cold.

Dashing out of the taxi, we were welcomed into Matty's house by the sweet smell of brownies and coffee, but she didn't let us slack around too long. She dived straight into the course introduction. You could tell right from the start that she'd spent a decent chunk of her life in these remote areas. Matty appeared to be in her late forties, with an authoritative voice and a small, fit body topped by a mass of wild frizzy grey hair. She explained that polar travel wasn't about suffering and returning home with stumps for fingers, but rather, if done properly, could be fun and enjoyable. What? That seemed to go against every account we'd read about Antarctica and the Arctic. We liked the sound of this!

The first few days were spent going through clothing and sleeping systems, the theory of polar navigation, cold injuries and cold weather survival. One of the biggest lessons we took away was that no gear on earth is designed for polar travel. There just simply isn't enough demand for the highly specialised gear required for these expeditions. If you think about it, why would companies bother to manufacture it? While over 5000 people have climbed Mount Everest, less than a hundred humans have skied unsupported to the South Pole. As a result, we were going to need to adapt, modify and tweak every item of gear that came off the shelf. It was time for us to learn how to sew. We discussed clothing layers, boot and binding combinations, burn rates of different stoves and fuels, tent options – the depth of Matty's knowledge was incredible.

We were fascinated to learn that 'moisture management' is one of the fundamental challenges of polar travel. At first I didn't have a clue what Matty was talking about. If it's -40° Celsius surely sweating is the least of your concerns? Apparently not. When you're pulling a heavy sled and working hard, if you have too many layers on you'll start to overheat. It's fine when you're moving, but as soon as you stop that sweat turns to ice almost instantly. That's bad and must be avoided at all costs. Matty had a saying that became one of our mantras: *you sweat, you die.* The same issue needed to be addressed when we were sleeping. If we sweated into our sleeping-bag, that sweat would turn to ice. Interestingly, on our first five-day mini-expedition we weighed our sleeping-bags prior to leaving and when we returned. The weight increased from 3.9 kilograms to 6.5 kilograms purely from our night sweat freezing in our bags. By the end of this excursion, chunks of ice had formed in our down sleeping-bags and if that had been on a fifty-day expedition our bags would have been full of ice and would end up weighing over 25 kilograms each. We were sleeping too warm. Fail. There were many other painful lessons we would have to learn. Frostbite on toe – fail. Windburn on face – fail. These were mistakes we could not afford to make in Antarctica.

After a few days of theory, drinking too much coffee and eating way too many brownies, it was time to head out onto the bay and get cold. I'm not going to lie, I was seriously intimidated. Any skin that was exposed to the elements would get frostbite in less than a minute. It makes heading up the road to buy milk a challenge in these parts of the world! Jonesy and I set up a buddy system to continually check and recheck each other's faces. If he got damage on his face due to exposed skin it was my fault, and vice versa.

As we skied over the frozen beach onto the 'ocean' the surface became all crumpled and distorted by the motion of the tides crushing the ice. Skiing over this rough ice was pretty unnerving as it was constantly moving, creaking and groaning. Fortunately, it was a few metres thick so there was little chance of us breaking through, even though we were carrying a few extra kilos. These conditions lasted for a few hundred metres until it smoothed out. Being out there, we were immediately able to pick up brilliant pieces of advice like how to keep your goggles from fogging up, how to de-fog them if they do fog up, what to do if you happen to break through the ice into the subzero water, the idea of using a spoon to shovel trail mix into your gob instead of trying to use your clunky mitts, and the fact that waterproof zips freeze up in the cold so we needed to use non-waterproof ones. In order to prevent ourselves from sweating as we skied in -40° Celsius temperatures we were basically wearing the same clothing that we would've on a cold winter's day in the Blue Mountains – a thermal, mid-layer fleece and a shell jacket over the top. When we stopped at breaks, we'd frantically throw on a big puffy jacket to trap as much heat as possible.

It was all invaluable, but the biggest lesson I learnt up there was that there are different kinds of cold. In Iqaluit, we did most of our training on a frozen ocean, and as a result there was a lot of 'humidity' in the air. In Antarctica, it's much drier, in fact, it's classified as a desert. The moisture in the air up north wreaks havoc with your moisture management. In a very short period, everything becomes covered in fluffy layers of frost – your face, your sleeping-bag and the inside of your tent to name a few. Sure, it makes for great photos, but it gets really annoying really fast. Just from breathing through the night, the inside layer of the tent gets plastered in this frost and if there is any wind about these ice crystals shower down on you.

Video journal – Arctic training at Baffin Island
www.casandjonesy.com.au/extremesouth

The experience up north made for great training, and we knew if we could establish systems to deal with the moisture up there then Antarctica would be comparatively easy. A few months later, once we reached Antarctica, Jonesy and I asked a Norwegian for some strategies to minimise frost inside the tent. His nonchalant response was, 'Stop breathing – it's the only way.'

On many of the adventures that Jonesy and I have shared he has always been ridiculously unselfish (apart from when food is low and then he eyes it off like a ravenous, rabid dog). He's always the last to get into the tent and the first to offer assistance to a struggling group member. The flip side of this personality trait is that when it comes to managing his own body, he often puts others first and is somewhat blasé at tending to himself. Bushwalking or paddling in Australia, you can afford to do this, but a massive lesson that Jonesy learnt on Baffin Island is that you cannot put aside your own needs and comfort in such an extreme climate. It's like how in the air-safety briefings before a flight takes off they tell you to put your own oxygen mask on, before tending to others – the same rules apply in polar travel.

I guess one of the big takeaway lessons is that Jonesy's really gotta look after himself more. Coming back to Sydney he had a frostbitten toe, frostnipped fingertips and a windburnt face. That's just not good enough in Antarctica. He's so mentally strong ... he just doesn't listen to his body – he switches off. This can be an awesome and desirable trait on expeditions, but it can also be a huge concern. He's always been so giving when we're out there. In Antarctica, he needs to be more selfish and take care of himself more.

Over the following couple of weeks in Iqaluit, our forays into the polar wilderness became longer as we learnt to manage ourselves in this foreign environment. During each excursion we made notes on what worked, what didn't and what to modify. We'd come back to town, make the modifications then head out again to test them.

It was the perfect training ground for Antarctica and when the time came to leave we had a final briefing with the McNairs. We discussed our objective with them and together we pulled apart our strengths, our weaknesses and how they thought we'd fare. On the pro side of things they said we were 'strong and had a good dynamic with one another'. Our biggest weakness was that we were 'sloppy'. We knew instantly where they were coming from, we were slow to set up camp and break camp, took too long at breaks etc. We knew this was stuff we could work on back home in the Aussie Alps. The other 'warning' we received was that with our limited polar experience we should be happy with attempting a one-way unsupported ski expedition as there had been many teams – both more qualified and stronger than us – that had attempted the return journey, and all had come up short. What made us think we were any different?

Chapter Five

POW!

We'd been working on a design concept, and if it worked it could alter the way heavy loads were transported across snow and ice. It seemed insane that after a hundred years of polar travel, humans were still dragging sleds that weren't very different from what Amundsen and Scott used in 1911. Think about the advances that have been made in cars since the Ford Model T or computers over the last twenty years. And yet, the only real difference that could be seen in sleds were the materials used to make them lighter and stronger. This is where the idea of the POW (Pulk On Wheels) came in.

For Jonesy and me, adventure isn't only about pushing yourself physically in extreme environments. There are so many more layers to it than that. One aspect of crossing the Tasman that we loved was designing a kayak that we could live in for two months. The designing, engineering, building and testing were all incredibly important and just as critical as building up our fitness levels. Our approach and philosophy was to not just accept what had been done in the past, but to see if we could challenge current methods of polar travel and come up with a more efficient way of transporting heavy loads.

Adventure isn't about 'conquering' nature, breaking records, doing things faster or younger – these bring a competitive element to the outdoors, which detracts from the purity of it all. Goals like these are more fitting for a competition or race. I see adventure as a philosophy for living. It's an attitude towards challenging yourself in all facets of life where risk needs to be managed, and committing to a just-out-of-reach objective. This often sees you living outside your comfort zone, a place where you learn who you truly are and what makes you tick. The simplicity and purity of waking up each day and working towards a clear objective in an unfamiliar and hostile environment, cuts through parts of your personality that may keep you alive in the city, like ego, deception and manipulation.

There wasn't all that much we could do to improve on our equipment, but there was one thing that could possibly make a difference. The wheel. No, it's not new, and has in fact been around for almost as long as man has been walking on two legs. The idea to use wheels instead of sleds has also been examined in the past. Back when the race was on to become the first man to reach the South Pole, many modes of transport were examined by the British and Norwegians – manhauling sleds, Manchurian ponies, huskies, motorised sledges – and all were used to carry heavy loads into the interior of Antarctica with mixed results. Captain Scott even examined using wheels on sleds but decided against it. In 2008, two Aussie adventurers, Chris Bray and Clark Carter, designed a cart system with big truck inner-tube tyres to become the first people to walk across Victoria Island in Northern Canada. They were able to pull these carts (which they called PACs – Paddleable Amphibious Carts) loaded with over 200 kilograms of provisions over jagged rocks, thick mud, tundra – you name it, these carts handled it. After testing a number of prototypes, they identified the key to success was designing massive wheels, which seemed to do a better job of handling a variety of different terrains. Taking on board the lessons learnt from their Aussie innovation, as well as looking at carts that other Aussie adventurers had used to cross deserts on foot, we thought we could adapt these designs for polar travel.

Over a few beers (always a good idea), we had some preliminary chats with a good climbing mate of ours who is an engineer, Dave 'Gravy' Johnston. Apart from having a brilliant mechanical mind, Gravy exudes a calmness about him like a Zen monk – he's a good man to have on your team. We couldn't figure out why the concept hadn't been examined further in Antarctica. The surface is predominantly hard ice and firm underfoot. Why couldn't we drag sleds on wheels rather than the traditional sled slides? We brainstormed for a while and identified some small obstacles, but just couldn't find a reason why they wouldn't work. We had to give it a go.

Gravy designed the wheels, hubs and axles and we had a boat builder up on the Central Coast of New South Wales make them for us. A massive design consideration right from the start was to have a redundancy in place so that if the wheels didn't work, we still had a sled built into the design and could keep moving without them. Hence the name: POW (Pulk On Wheels). Pulling tyres along the beach was one thing, but the POW was something else – they looked ridiculous! Picture two 1.4 metre high carbon kevlar wheels (which look like massive Trivial Pursuit pieces) on either side of a 1.8 metre sled. By June, we were doing our first tests in Sydney on fire trails and on the beach. The results were inspiring. We were able to move loads of up to 250 kilograms much more efficiently and faster than two truck tyres on the ground (which we'd figured out had a similar drag to 150 kilograms on snow). The next test – the most important one – was to take them down to the Aussie Alps and see how they performed on snow.

This test was a big one and we were nervous. If the system worked in the Aussie snow fields, then we'd be taking the POW to Antarctica. I had flashbacks of the day our kayak *Lot 41* touched the water for the first time. It hadn't gone so well. She would not sit upright, but instead tilted at 30 degrees from one side to the other. We hoped this would go better, and loaded the POW with only 100 kilograms of weight for the first trial, hoping to add more weight if all went well.

Rolling to the snow the POW moved the load beautifully, but as soon as the wheels touched the snow she snagged up a little. Jonesy heaved forward with more grunt, and ... and ... nothing. She wouldn't budge. What was going on? This wasn't supposed to happen! After pulling for a few minutes like a dog leashed to a lamp-post, Jonesy fell to the ground punching the snow with his fist. The disappointment was all consuming. We'd both been quietly confident that we were onto a winner and that the POW was going to work a charm. One of the reasons the unsupported return journey had failed in the past was that teams had travelled too slowly at the start when their loads were heaviest. We were hoping that the POW would help us overcome this challenge. The first issue was that the wheels were sinking into the snow and creating a ditch that they would sink into and then couldn't roll over. Adding to the problem was a huge amount of snow sticking to the wheel rim which added to the weight and hindered mobility.

When *Lot 41* flopped on her side, we knew the basic design was right and that we needed to do some tweaking, either adding ballast or widening the kayak to improve its initial stability. It was a matter of sticking with the project. Sometimes, however, that isn't an option and there is a fundamental design problem no amount of tweaking will fix. Unfortunately, with the POW, in order to pursue the concept we needed to go right back to the drawing board, and this was something we didn't have time for.

Video journal – The POW
www.casandjonesy.com.au/extremesouth

Our morale took a massive hit. We packed up the wheels, and didn't talk much on the five-hour drive back to Sydney with the POW bouncing around in the trailer. Apart from all the time and resources spent in getting the POW off the ground, emotionally we'd invested so much more. We needed to change our focus and approach. Our success was no longer dependent on an innovation, now we had to do exactly what others before us had done – but better.

Chapter Six

POLAR PRICE TAG

Antarctica has never been a cheap place to get to. Captain Scott estimated the total cost of the Terra Nova expedition to be around £40,000 (about A$4.5 million in today's terms). If I told you that you'd need to front up A$150,000 for the four-hour return air journey just to get to your starting point you'd probably laugh in my face. Trust me, that's not flying first class in a private jet with a personal chef and numerous air hostesses, but more on that later. And flights make up only a portion of the total budget. Add to that the cost of equipment, provisions, training and we weren't going to be left with much change from half a million dollars. And that's if it all went without a hitch. The most important thing is to plan for the worst-case outcome but hope for the best. So Jonesy and I needed to raise enough funds to cover the cost of both a successful and unsuccessful trip and it was pretty serious cash for what's been described to us as a 'very expensive camping holiday in the cold'.

You have to get the balance right. There is no point focusing all your attention on raising money if you don't also pay attention to the physical side of things. Organising a big expedition is like training for the Olympics while simultaneously fundraising for and project-managing the building of your own stadium. There are so many facets that need to come together just to reach the starting line. But we'd learnt that you also have to look ahead. In the years leading up to our Crossing the Ditch expedition, planning and training had consumed us entirely. We had the attitude that every minute spent pre-expedition needed to be focused on how to stay alive out there, not what we'd do for money and work after we finished. When we arrived at Ngamotu beach in New Zealand we were broke and shoeless – we hadn't even packed a bag of clothes for our arrival as that was 'non-critical' to the objective. We both knew we didn't want to go back to our former lives – Jonesy as an exercise physiologist and me as an accountant – but neither of us knew what we did want to do in the real world. Out on the Tasman we talked up some ideas, like how it'd be cool to write a book and produce a documentary, but we knew neither was going to sell like the Harry Potter series – we'd still need to do *something* to earn a living.

On our return to Australia, we were inundated with requests from all over the world from people wanting to hear more about our story. Maybe the book and documentary were a good idea after all? We decided to put a speaking tour together for the general public and started sharing our story with a few corporate audiences. Many of the lessons we'd learnt from the voyage were transferable to people's everyday lives and businesses. We thought we could stretch these talks out for a year before interest in us started to wane – that would allow us to run our own business, put off going back to our grown-up jobs for a bit longer and have a completely new adventure exploring a whole new skill set.

The biggest issue Jonesy and I faced in getting a speaking tour off the ground was a phobia many of us experience – standing up and speaking in front of an audience. As kids at school both of us often had panic attacks when we had to stand up in front of a class and read out our homework. It was something we had to address, and if we could cross the Tasman surely we could overcome this fear? And surprisingly we did. Overcoming the hardships and adversity of those sixty-two days on the Tasman had ignited a confidence in both of us that allowed us to get up in front of audiences and tell our story. It helped that it was a story that we knew better than anyone and one that we really enjoyed telling. We were able to weave into our presentations subtle business and motivational themes like goal setting, teamwork and risk management. Right from the start we understood that we were two young blokes and were never going to go down the path of shoving these messages down the throats of our audiences. All we could do was tell our own story and let the audience take what they wanted from it. To our shock, year on year, the number of bookings we were taking kept on growing as organisations started booking us not just to hear about our adventure but as corporate presenters. At the time of writing this book, we've presented to a little over 150,000 people. And the best thing was we were making a good enough living out of it to keep paying the bills. But it was never going to be enough to fund a big Antarctic expedition.

Crossing the ditch had taught us many valuable lessons in how to find funding. The number one lesson was that sponsorship isn't a charity donation. It's a value proposition, and we have to be able to provide a tangible return to each prospective sponsor. Before we sent out each proposal we'd ask ourselves, what's in it for them? We'd only proceed with the pitch if we felt that we'd accept the offer if it was sent to us. It was also important to keep in mind that each potential sponsor had different measures of quantifying a return on investment. We'd learnt that cold calling corporations or sending a sponsorship proposal to the sponsorships@XYZ.com generic email address was going to get us nowhere.

In searching for sponsorship for the Tasman, we employed an approach that Jonesy had tested while on Uni Games a few years earlier. It involved approaching girls in a pub and simply asking, 'Will you kiss me?' Surprisingly, four out of thirty replied 'yes'. Okay, maybe a little weird, but effective. If we could garner similar results by cold calling sponsors then surely we'd be well on our way to raising the funds needed. How wrong we were! We approached 130 companies and close to a hundred didn't even get back to us despite numerous follow-ups. Twenty-nine politely declined and we managed to secure just one face-to-face meeting. It didn't go so well. When faced with the simple statement by a potential airline sponsor: 'We love your passion and detailed planning, but we're not quite sure how sponsoring you guys will result in more bums on seats,' Jonesy and I looked blankly at one another before dopily replying: 'Neither are we'. And that was that.

Fortunately, now that we'd presented to a vast array of different companies, we had a starting point to avoid the cold calling. It's interesting to note that a round of lectures kick-started Scott's fundraising back in 1908. Our Tasman keynote had broken the ice (so to speak) and established our credentials, giving us a connection with the very people who make these decisions. With most sponsors, the two most quantifiable returns on their investment are increasing brand awareness and staff engagement. Looking at the latter, our keynote presentation is a retrospective reflection on an adventure. This is all well and good, however with our Antarctic expedition, we were passionate to work with our sponsors in ensuring their staff lived the entire journey with us in real time – the planning, the preparation and then the journey itself.

As with the Tasman, before we approached a prospective sponsor we developed an extensive risk-management document, which was a blueprint of how we were going to attempt the journey and manage the risks we were to face. It was initially designed for us, but it proved to be a really useful document in convincing stakeholders that it was possible for two young Aussies with basically no skiing experience to succeed in the longest unsupported manhauling expedition of all time.

Once the risk-management document answered all the big questions, the next phase was to design a sexy sponsorship proposal, which became the starting point for many meetings that followed. These meetings were less about selling the idea to people and more about discussing a partnership that was mutually beneficial. We also made clear in those early meetings that a partnership is exactly that, both parties need to work together. A partnership wasn't just about a company fronting up with the cash and then expecting everything to be done. Jonesy and my focus had to be driven by safety, successfully completing the expedition and providing the infrastructure to ensure each sponsor could leverage their investment. It required resources and work on both sides of the fence to extrapolate maximum return.

Following the global financial crisis we knew that many companies had slashed their marketing and advertising budgets and that securing funds was going to be like finding water in the desert. A number of other expeditioners around the world had postponed their plans due to budget issues. This meant the sponsorship landscape was tough, however by the end of 2010 a number of sponsors had come on board, our gear sponsorships were taken care of and we were well on our way to securing a decent whack of funding. After presenting at the annual conference for REDgroup (Borders book stores) they had also shown interest in coming on as a partner. After numerous meetings, tele-conferences and emails, we'd finally reached an agreement that would position them as the major sponsor of the expedition. Drafts of the contract bounced back and forth and then, just as we reached the 'time to sign the contract part' all contact stopped. What was going on? Where were they? After countless emails and voicemails went unanswered we were getting seriously worried that we'd said something wrong or somehow blown it. But nobody was talking to us and we had no clue. Then finally, after nearly two weeks of silence, I received a phone call. It was from the head of marketing, who explained that since we'd last spoken she'd had to lay off all her staff and that as a publicly listed company she wasn't able to tell me any more, except that the company was going to make an announcement to the media the following day. It didn't bode well.

The front page of the newspaper the following morning read 'Borders bookstores placed under voluntary administration'. Jonesy and I were gobsmacked. How could a company's marketing department be planning an extensive two-year marketing campaign when they were staring down the barrel of bankruptcy? This hit delivered a massive hole to our budget and timeline. We'd aimed to have our funding sorted six months prior to the expedition so we could focus on training, gear modifications and taking the staff of our sponsors on the preparation journey with us through regular updates. We had received that call just before we left for Iqaluit so the timing couldn't have been worse. The funds we thought we had coming weren't, and we couldn't do anything about it at that moment because we were heading to the Arctic. We knew that when we returned we needed to get back on the hunt.

One potential source of funding for expeditions is the media. Many expeditions going right back to the Heroic Age of Antarctic Exploration had covered their costs by selling rights to their stories. Scott's exclusive story had been sold to *Central News* for £2500. At least the doomed men's bereaved families were informed of the tragic outcome before the news outlet, so they didn't receive the devastating information via the press (something that is not always assured these days). After successfully reaching the South

Pole and returning to Tasmania, Amundsen dropped the *Fram*'s anchor 'in splendid isolation' and once onshore refused to answer any questions from the gaggle of waiting press, as he had an exclusive deal with the London *Daily Chronicle* worth £2000. Shackleton had sold exclusive newspaper rights to the *Daily Mail* for the Nimrod expedition in 1907 and to the *Daily Chronicle* for the Endurance expedition. And from then on many explorers did deals with media outlets to access cash. But this wasn't the good ol' eighties where there'd been stories of Alan Bond or Kerry Packer funding entire expeditions or projects like the America's Cup. The media play a hard game, and we knew that if we were to sign over exclusivity rights to the expedition, it would bind us tightly. On the positive side, it was another source of funding, and if we could secure it we would be guaranteed a level of exposure, even though it would limit the media generated across other networks. This was a difficult decision because if we signed with the wrong network and they didn't deliver adequate exposure, we were hindering the return our other sponsors would be able to generate. Intense negotiations with all major Australian networks followed. The deciding factor to go with Channel Seven was the cross-network commitment they were willing to make, their commitment to film a pre-story in New Zealand, sending a crew down to Antarctica to film our arrival, and offering more flexibility in allowing us to share content online. It was a great result, but even with this deal signed, we still needed to find additional funds.

We presented to an agency, Naked Communications, who thought our Crossing the Ice expedition and our philosophy towards adventure matched perfectly with one of their client's campaigns – the Sony Bloggie. The campaign was designed around the line 'shoot, connect and share', with a portion of funds raised from sales being donated to the Sony Foundation's You Can campaign. We loved it. On our prior expeditions we had tried to raise funds and awareness for different causes we believed in. Our fundraising on the Tasman crossing was abruptly brought to a halt when Andrew McAuley was tragically lost at sea. The Sydney Children's Hospital sent us a letter saying that 'they were in the business of saving lives', and that they could no longer be associated with our expedition. Jonesy and I were so disappointed, as over the course of the expedition we had over 1.6 million unique visitors to our expedition website and I believe we could've raised a lot of money for the hospital.

We researched You Can and liked what we saw. You Can is focused on building specialised cancer-treatment facilities for young people across Australia. This immediately struck a chord with Jonesy and I, as a surprising number of our mates from school had been through arduous cancer journeys over the previous few years. Cancer is the leading cause of disease-related death among Australia's teenagers, and one in one hundred Australians is diagnosed with cancer before the age of thirty. Add to this the fact that in the last twenty-five years there has been virtually no improvement in survival outcomes for fifteen- to thirty-year-olds and we could see that there was an obvious and urgent need for action. We were on board!

The next great bit of news was hearing that Sony Bloggie wanted to come on board as the expedition's major sponsor. We were stoked. We could now focus our energies on getting our equipment and gear modified and our bodies moulded into sled-pulling machines.

Chapter Seven

ON THE HOME FRONT

With a good team of sponsors behind us by July 2011, we then had to lock in the finer logistical details. For that we needed help. Prior to departing on the Tasman attempt, we had engaged Captain Pat Brothers as our Operations Manager to keep things together while we were out on the ocean. Pat was brilliant, but we needed a slightly different structure for our Antarctic expedition. This time, the risk-management side of things would need to be more closely managed by us on the ground and from the base in Antarctica, but we still needed a point of contact back home to keep all stakeholders – sponsors, media, family, mission-critical team members (doctors, Gravy, electrical engineer, etc.) – engaged and managed.

We tossed around a few options, but through happenstance met a close friend of a friend, Rebecca Riel, who had been in the army and was great with people. Bec was in between jobs and had the skills we needed to back us up. She was a physically and mentally strong woman, supremely organised and more than able to cope with the demanding role of an operations manager, and also with me and Jonesy. Tick, tick, tick. She agreed to come on board in

August as our expedition logistics manager and, right from the start, she impressed us. Bec moved into the third room in our expedition headquarters and became an integral member of our team. She was going to be our point of contact with the outside world when we were down in Antarctica. We'd be doing daily skeds with her and all RFIs (requests for information) would come through her. Back in Sydney, she would also play the important role of keeping our sponsors, friends and family informed and aware of how we were travelling. I needed to know someone was looking after everything so I wouldn't obsess or worry too much.

I had learnt my lessons from the Tasman crossing, and I was trying hard not to lose myself completely in preparations for Antarctica. Employing a good logistics manager was one way of protecting myself and my relationships. But it was still something I had to watch. There is a fine line between focus and obsession and I was hoping I was on the right side of it. But I was worried I just wasn't spending any quality time with Mia.

Mia and I met just after I returned to Australia following the Crossing the Ditch expedition in 2008. Initially it was quite an unlikely match: a scruffy adventurer and an ex-professional ballerina – who'd have thought! Love took a little while to develop and in a typical bloke's way I remember very early on when Mia bought us tickets to see *Billy Elliot* together four weeks later, it made me nervous. This was a long-term relationship! But after a few dates it became very clear that Mia and I had similar attitudes towards life, and before I knew it I was madly in love with her. I asked Mia to marry me at 5.26 am on 5 December 2010 at the summit of Mount Kilimanjaro and I will never forget the moment. The sun had just started to rise when we reached the summit flags and I was as nervous as all hell, but I couldn't stop and think or I might have freaked out. I remember clumsily pulling off my puffy gloves, reaching into my jacket pocket, finding the ring and dropping down on my left knee. Mia looked shocked but I didn't hesitate.

'Mia, will you marry me?'

Her reaction wasn't what I'd imagined. There was no reply, just a few nervous giggles and grunts that didn't resemble anything like a yes ... or a no, for that matter. It was going to be a long, awkward walk down the mountain if I didn't get a positive reaction.

Not quite knowing how to respond, I prodded: 'So ... should I take that as a yes or a no?'

'YES,' she *finally* shouted.

Still on one knee, I slipped the ring on her finger. The diamond sparkled brilliantly in the early morning light. We hugged each other, symbolically making a pact that this was the dawn of our new life together.

Standing with Mia on Kilimanjaro's summit meant more to me than any other mountain I'd climbed before. From that moment I could see she got it. She got me. I could see in her an understanding of what it meant to climb mountains – in essence, what it meant to be me – and best of all she seemed to like it. The climb had allowed the person I wanted to spend the rest of my life with to finally understand what it is to be an adventurer.

A few weeks later we were back into the hustle of Sydney life. At a friend's wedding, one of Mia's friends asked what the attraction of walking up a big hill was. Mia replied with a dash of George Mallory-esque passion: 'For the sheer joy of it! Why don't you join us next weekend in the Blue Mountains?'

I couldn't believe my luck that I had found a woman who completely supported my love for adventure and had even agreed that she would organise our wedding while I was in Antarctica. We'd decided we would get married about a month after Jonesy and I were scheduled to get back at the end of February 2012. It was a huge leap of faith for both of us. But I couldn't allow thoughts of failure or worse, to enter my mind. Yes, you have to consider worst-case scenarios and there is always a chance that you will die on any extreme adventure. But you can also die walking to the shops to buy milk, so I wasn't going to dwell on the negative. Did you know that there is more chance of dying playing table tennis than there is rock climbing (0.86/100,000 versus 0.31/100,000)? And I know I keep saying it, but preparation and risk management is the key to it all.

Gathering information and wisdom from people like Matty, Sarah and Eric McNair, Eric Philips, Kevin Biggar, Jamie Fitzgerald, James Cracknell, Ben Fogle, Tom Smitheringale and Dr Glenn Singleman to name a few, meant we were learning from the best. Dr Glenn had been our expedition doctor on the Tasman and we knew he would play a critical role in diagnosing issues and prescribing treatments when down south. A base-jumper and mountaineer himself, Dr Glenn knew better than anyone the challenges faced on expeditions. Eric Philips is Australia's leading polar guide, with fifteen years' invaluable polar experience and wisdom. He mentored and advised us throughout the project on an array of different topics from mental attitude to intricate gear modifications. With Bec looking after logistics, Mia looking after our food, and all the other experts offering wisdom and knowledge we truly had a world class team behind us.

I just had to make sure I didn't lose sight of what was important to me while preparing for Antarctica. Mia, my friends and family knew how single-minded I could get, but I still had to ensure I didn't take anything or anyone for granted. If there was one person I didn't think I had to worry about it was Jonesy. He was like a brother to me and I thought we had no secrets. We were together so often, it was how it had to be. But not everything was as it seemed, and I would find that out soon enough.

Chapter Eight

CHECKLIST

I'm a gear junkie – it's one aspect of expeditions that I get way too excited about. Most of the expedition gear and equipment Jonesy and I needed for Antarctica came from overseas. After our trip to Iqaluit, we knew what we needed but also realised that there would be quite a lead-time in getting it all. Sleds from Norway, wolverine fur ruffs from Alaska, reindeer mitts from Canada – you can't just pop down to the local camping disposal store for that kind of stuff. These highly specialised items take time to source and even more time to clear customs.

And then, once we received the items, that's when the work really began. Matty taught us that no garment bought off the shelf is designed to handle the rigours of polar travel, everything needs to be tweaked, adapted and modified. Our shell jackets had no fewer than fifteen individual modifications each. And the tent needed extra special attention. Normally, setting up a tent in a campground will take upwards of ten minutes by the time you unfold all the tent poles, thread them through the sleeves and erect it. Ten minutes is far too long in Antarctic conditions. When your fingers are frozen and the wind is blowing at 100 kilometres per hour it's a recipe for a disaster, or death. We had to cut that time down, so we rigged up a system to erect the tent in less than a minute, and over the course of a three-month expedition, this saved us approximately 13.5 hours. This same attitude to refine, modify and enhance was taken to each piece of equipment. Every minute we saved in efficiency meant we could spend more time skiing or resting. We knew this was important, but it would become more crucial than we could ever imagine.

Many modifications were designed to make life manageable with a big set of mitts on. To get a feel of how frustrating even the simplest task might be, I challenge you to whack on a pair of oven mitts and try to do all your household chores one Saturday morning – washing, cleaning, dressing, feeding the dog – without taking them off. It's incredibly frustrating and difficult to say the least. Every small knob, zipper or button needed to be made bigger; systems even needed to be put in place so that we could eat our rations on the trail efficiently. Try shoving your oven mitt into a ziplock bag to get a handful of nuts or scroggin and you'll see what I mean.

All this modifying meant lots of sewing and unfortunately Jonesy and I were as bad at sewing as we were at skiing when we first started – useless. To overcome this problem, we threw out a call for help on our Facebook page. The response was overwhelming and we were inundated by friends, family and a whole bunch of people we'd never met offering to come over on a weekend to assist. Awesome! Three months out from departure we had nearly thirty people rock up each weekend to my parents' garage in the northern suburbs of Sydney to help out. The atmosphere was inspiring. Everyone rolled up their sleeves and dived into whatever needed doing, we were all out of our comfort zone but it didn't matter.

Gravy, our engineer from the POW attempt, took a lead role in driving many of the modifications and examining each item for obvious points of failure. We then had to ensure that every critical item either had a back-up or a way we could fix it on the ice. Developing the tools and spares for the expedition was a constant battle between keeping weight to a minimum and ensuring there was enough redundancy in the spares so that the expedition could continue on when there were failures. It's difficult to predict how often individual items are going to break – what were the chances of us snapping a ski pole? How many spares do we need? Could we substitute the spares (which are generally heavier) with a method of fixing a broken pole, a splint maybe? Okay, we could take a splint, but what gear do we have that could act as a splint – a tent peg? In the cold, what tools did we have to cut a peg to the right length and bend it into shape? The discussions went on and on for every item of gear. Weighing up what you can carry with what you can't afford to be without and what you can is one of the fundamental challenges of any unsupported expedition, whether it's through the desert, on water or on ice. You have to make it the whole way without any assistance at all. Once we'd decided on the tools and spares, we'd go through every 'mission-critical' item of gear and 'hypothetically' break it and make sure we had a way of fixing it.

Once the first big wave of modifications was completed, we headed across to the Tasman Glacier (thankfully not paddling this time) in New Zealand's mighty Southern Alps for a final shakedown to test our gear one last time before we headed to Antarctica. Our departure date for South America was set for 3 October. From there we'd fly across the Drake Passage and aimed to leave Hercules Inlet on 16 October. If all went to plan, we would get back to our starting point within eighty days.

The launching pad to fly up onto the Tasman Glacier is a quaint village in Aoraki-Mount Cook National Park, a place I'd called home for four summers in my youth. Each summer I'd spent weeks there mountaineering, and returning played heavily on my emotions. Many of the mountains that we stared up at had a story or a memory attached for me. Some of my memories were incredibly positive, like reaching the summit of Mount Cook, others not so much. Remembering watching the lifeless bodies of four Slovenian climbers being carried from the helipad in the centre of the village and looking up at some of the routes where I'd taken falls or been caught in storms stirred powerful feelings and rekindled some dark thoughts that had mostly been laid to rest.

If family camping holidays were the genesis of my adventuring life then Mount Cook represented my reckless teenage years and the place when the adventure bug really took hold. When I first hitched a ride there I was nineteen years old and confused about my place in this world. I was seriously lacking self-confidence and felt like a misfit. Spending time in the mountains played a crucial role in my self-discovery. The drug of my youth wasn't pot or pills, it was climbing. Apart from having an absolute blast, it helped me develop a self-assurance that I just couldn't find in city life. Those summers mountaineering in New Zealand showed me what adventure was all about.

Walking into the Chamois Bar made me reflect on many of the climbers I'd shared a Speight's with after tough excursions into the hills. Some had gone off to climb Everest, others had taken a step back from mountaineering and pursued other adventures in their lives. The constant was the bonds I'd formed with those climbers, a strength of friendship that is hard to forge sipping lattes in a café or taking the dog for a walk in Centennial Park.

Jonesy and I loaded our fully laden sleds onto the single-engine Porter PC6, jumped on board and took off. It was a strange sensation looking down at the chaotic moraine from a bird's-eye view. When I'd been there ten years earlier I was living on five bucks a day, and couldn't afford to fly up into the mountains. Instead, we'd load our packs up heavily and walk up the glacier. The mountains on either side of the glacier flickered past like station walls when you're on a train. Before we knew it we were stepping out onto the upper Tasman Ranges in perfect weather. It is a wild, beautiful place with craggy mountains dusted white by heavy snow, and deep valleys with winding rivers dotted through the region. The first thing I noticed was how soft the snow was – Jonesy and I were sinking up to our knees. Apparently it had just dumped the week before, which was spectacular to look at but was going to make pulling our sleds difficult.

'Oh well, at least Antarctica won't be like this,' Jonesy said reassuringly (if only we knew!).

As the Porter roared off, we filled a number of food bags with snow (we wanted to replicate the weight of carrying 100 days worth of food), buckled into our harnesses and set off. The primary objective of being up there wasn't to physically destroy our bodies but to work on improving the 'sloppiness' Matty had referred to up in Iqaluit. We did drills where we set up and took down the tent, timing our efficiency and working hard to get the seconds down. Everything we had on the Tasman Glacier was what we were intending to take to Antarctica. We tested everything, from sock combinations to uploading videos to our website, and paid special attention to many of our modifications to see if they needed more tweaking. This was a live simulation so we did skeds every twenty-four hours over the satellite phone just like we would be doing in Antarctica.

We knew that from the moment we touched down in Antarctica it had to be game on. We were expecting the first few weeks to be the most brutal and we couldn't afford to play around and figure things out down there. Each of our exercises on the Tasman Glacier had a necessary urgency about them. When one of us dropped a glove or suffered sunburn on our face we felt as though we had failed. There was no room in Antarctica for complacency or anything short of being switched on 100 per cent of the time.

After just over a week up there we'd almost filled a sixty-four page exercise book with notes on further modifications and tweaks we wanted to make. We arrived back in Sydney with a huge to-do list and just one month left until we flew to South America.

Just when it looked like we were right on track, I couldn't believe it when my body started giving me grief. I'd had surgery on my left knee twelve years earlier, and with the additional 20 kilograms of weight I was carrying, combined with the intense training and heavy lifting we were doing, it started giving me problems. At first I didn't think it was anything serious and just started icing it after big sessions and trying to reduce the range of movement in exercises like squats and leg presses. But on a tyre-pulling hill session one morning, I was really worried when grinding and clicking noises started to come from it.

It didn't sound good. I gave my younger sister, Lil, who is a physiotherapist, a call to ask her what I should do.

'*Rest*,' she practically barked down the phone, 'I'll do an examination on it, don't aggravate it any more.'

Lil's advice made me really edgy. Jonesy was still stronger than me and resting was the last thing I wanted to be doing. But I did what I was told. After her initial examination, she booked me straight in to get an MRI done and then recommended I see Dr Ken Crichton. At my appointment with him, the results weren't good.

My knee showed significant bone bruising, with a damaged surface on the base of the fibula. It looked like if I kept up the intensity of my training there was a significant risk of a chunk of

cartilage and the fibula breaking off. The doc recommended I take
four weeks off training and seriously reconsider heading down to
Antarctica. It was only four weeks until we left! I decided I needed
a second opinion and met with Dr Glenn. He gave me a similar
prognosis: 'If you go to Antarctica, you can bet that your knee is
going to crap out at some stage. You seriously need to consider the
price you're willing to pay for the choices you make.'

Adventure had always been about coming back alive and not
doing any long-term damage to my body. As I get older, I want
to get stronger and fitter, not be crippled by a bad knee. The
physical disability was bad enough but the whole 'what if' scenario
also started to weigh heavily on my mind. One of the critical
psychological components of any expedition is having confidence
in your body and your fitness – I would have plenty of other things
to worry about without stressing that my knee might blow out. The
one ray of light that I held onto tightly was that the knee movement
during sled-hauling is quite restricted, it's a shuffle movement.
The knee rarely bends more than 30 degrees and it was only in the
bigger range of motions that the pain in my knee was occurring.

With only a few weeks to go until we departed Australia, we
kept to our plans and continued to modify gear, and check and
double-check our provisions, weights, spares, tools, etc. We also
spent a fair bit of time speaking to the media, which was initially
focused on getting the word out about the expedition, then on
driving donations for You Can. These last weeks were intense but
nothing like the month before our Crossing the Ditch expedition.
That had been manic, with massively long days; we'd only really
finished getting the kayak ready the evening before we left for our
starting point.

We were organised and pragmatic with our time, which meant
things weren't as crazy this time around. However, we were still

under the pump and every hour was now focused on getting ready for Antarctica. I was again troubled with how little time I was spending alone with Mia. She'd become a key member in the whole campaign and was giving so much to the project. Every weekend she helped with the modifications and during the week she spent countless hours tweaking our nutrition plan and sourcing its contents. But I am not sure many fiancées would have been happy to spend hours making lists of foods and weighing and analysing the energy components. Mia did it all without complaining.

For the expedition, it wasn't appropriate for us to take food in its original packaging, and each day's food needed to be packed into ration packs to save on weight (the weight saved by doing this was 12 kilograms) and to ensure food was ready to go (to save on time). Also, certain items like Mars Bars and cheese would freeze the moment we touched down in Antarctica and needed to be cut into bite-sized chunks so that we could suck on them while on the trail and not have the impossible task of trying to segment frozen food.

Unfortunately, this work couldn't be done in Australia as Chilean Customs wouldn't let the food through the border. Everything needed to be in its original packaging and then repacked over in South America, a process that we thought would take two weeks. Gravy, Mia and Bec were coming with Jonesy and me to Chile to help with final preparations. Before I knew it, a month had flown by and we were packing our gear and provisions into sixteen massive North Face duffels.

On 3 October 2011, there was a teary farewell with close family and friends. Neither Jonesy or I felt the same emotion we had back in 2007 when we left Forster for New Zealand. Back then, hugging Mum was absolutely gut wrenching, and Dad had actually left the night before because he couldn't handle the intensity of saying goodbye. After Andrew McAuley's tragic disappearance a mere six months before, there was quite a sombre cloud sitting over the dock. Everyone's faces had a 'Are we ever going to see you again?' kinda look.

I guess this time around, the expedition proper was still a few weeks away and the close team was travelling with us. I had a feeling of relief more than anything, we were finally on our way to Punta Arenas! The journey had begun.

Chapter Nine

BELOW THE BELT

We checked our duffels into LAN Chile flight LA0800 without too much drama, passed through Australian Customs and before long were up over the Tasman Sea on our way towards the Pacific. Looking down at the ocean, I contemplated the journey that had led us here. I wondered if I still had what it took to get across that ocean? Self-doubt is a funny thing, it eats away at you until it's time to do the job and then all is forgotten. Franklin Roosevelt hit it on the knocker in his Inaugural Address by saying, 'The only thing we have to fear is fear itself.' This is so true. Before any major climb, paddle and now on this trip, it was the anticipation of the unknown that scared me the most. Once I'm out there doing it, it's not so scary (most of the time). From then on I just have to focus on one small step after another.

Chilean Customs have a reputation for being almost as strict as New Zealand (on our trip to the Tasman Glacier, Jonesy had accidentally left a banana in his laptop bag and this heinous crime resulted in a A$400 fine and he had to sit through a thirty-minute video on border protection). We had the majority of our food for the expedition with us and were nervous about getting everything through. Fortunately, the officers seemed a little overwhelmed by the number of bags we had and after a half-hearted poke in one or two of them just let us through.

Our launchpad for Antarctica was Punta Arenas, a small, sleepy, wind-scoured town on the tailbone of South America. It's the gateway to the strait of Magellan and Patagonia, and back in the day sailors used to stop in before proceeding around Cape Horn. In 1914, Shackleton also stayed here while planning the rescue of his men from Elephant Island. You probably wouldn't make the effort to fly 3090 kilometres to the south from Santiago to see it. We found the most interesting attractions were the healthiest looking homeless dogs on the planet, and the cemetery, which seems to make every tourist brochure on the place. As fate had it, Bec booked us into a hostel that was opposite the cemetery so we had uninterrupted views of the ornate mausoleums and decrepit plots. Luckily, I'm not a superstitious kind of guy.

When the five of us arrived in Punta Arenas, we were greeted by my brother Clary and his girlfriend, Kit. They'd been travelling around South America for a couple of months and had kindly offered to take a break from travelling to help in getting our food packed.

We converted each of our rooms into a provision-packing production line and got to work weighing, repackaging, and chopping up any food that was larger than bite-sized. We were Mia's troops and she scrupulously watched over our shoulders to ensure we weren't over or under by more than a couple of grams. The seriousness of what Jonesy and I were about to subject ourselves to down in Antarctica was something out of Mia's control. The one thing that she could have a massive impact on was what we were eating and she wanted to ensure that when we hit the ground she couldn't have done any more for our preparation. The biggest 'engaged couple' tiff we had during the food packing was whether to pack the coffee rations in daily tiny bags or whether we could get away with a few weeks in one bag. Mia argued that the composition in the bigger bags between powdered milk, sugar and coffee would not be consistent between days – I argued that we were talking about such a small percentage of our daily calorie intake it didn't matter. Mia won that battle. She took her job very seriously and I understood later that she felt an enormous amount of responsibility for our welfare, and worried that if she didn't get our food right, there was a chance we could die. I loved her for her determination and feistiness, so I couldn't complain that she got her way. Unbeknown to Jonesy and I at the time, Mia had glued notes on our snack bags from family, friends and school children back home.

Food packing in Punta Arenas
www.casandjonesy.com.au/extremesouth

While the food packing was progressing well, Gravy was double-checking and rechecking our spares, tools and bindings 'one last time'. He felt the same responsibility towards equipment as Mia did towards our food. I didn't want either of them to carry that burden of guilt if something went wrong. Ultimately, what Jonesy and I had to tell them was that they'd done an incredible job but it was our responsibility if the food wasn't right or we had problems with the gear. With any adventure, you cannot outsource responsibility for the success or failure of the endeavour. Actually, the same goes for life. We are all responsible for our own actions and it is ultimately up to us to weigh up risk and preparation and choose to step forward or hold back.

The atmosphere in South America was pretty relaxed. No-one appeared overly nervous and we had given ourselves plenty of time to do what was needed. I was feeling calm and ready for what was to come. Jonesy and I had worked through the tension caused by our different speeds of travel and I had (mostly) come to terms with the fact he was just plain stronger than me. We were only days away from leaving when Jonesy handed me his phone to upload an image of us packing our food to Facebook. As I opened the application, I couldn't miss the incriminating text message trail between Bec and Jonesy. My throat tightened, and I felt like I'd been hit in the guts.

CAS DIARY ENTRY – 6 OCTOBER 2011

Jonesy has been sleeping with Bec behind my back since before New Zealand. For months he's been deceiving me. When we did a pro/con analysis of whether Bec should come on board as our logistics manager we were looking for someone not emotionally invested – impartial. Yes, we wanted to be mates with them but more importantly it was a professional relationship ...

For fifteen years, Jonesy and I had been best mates. We'd shared everything with each other, or so I thought. Mia and I had been living in the same apartment as Bec and Jonesy and we didn't have a clue. That worried me a lot. What else didn't I know about my best friend and expedition partner?

The truth is, Jonesy is much more to me than an expedition partner, business partner or friend; he's become more like a brother. We've shared all our big adventures together and our deepest, darkest secrets. One of the strengths of our relationship is that we know each other better than anyone else on the planet knows us. I guess that's why finding out about this whole mess the way I did hurt so much.

What we were about to undertake meant we had to trust each other implicitly and that trust had been compromised. Bec was our logistics manager so she had to be emotionally detached from us in case something went wrong. A logistics manager might need to make decisions or draw conclusions that could mean life or death. She was our link to the outside world and the person who, if necessary, would have to initiate a rescue, organise an airdrop, a medical evacuation, the list goes on. That evening I sat down in a smoke-filled bar and confronted Jonesy about it. At first, he was really evasive about the whole thing. That blew me away. Maybe he was trying to call my bluff. When he realised I wasn't joking, his excuse was that he is a 'weak individual'. He tried to explain that his intention wasn't to hurt me, but my trust in Jonesy was shattered. If it was a drunken one-off I would've found it easy to get over but this was a consistent and regular act of secrecy which I saw as a betrayal of our friendship. The thought that they were sneaking into each other's rooms at night and were both actively deceiving Mia and me made me feel physically ill.

How was I going to trust Jonesy with my life in Antarctica? If we'd been back home and we weren't about to embark on the biggest adventure of our lives, time and distance would've helped mend the friendship. Unfortunately, we didn't have that luxury. I found myself in a position where we were going to need to lean on each other, to trust each other just to survive and yet he hadn't trusted me enough to tell me what was going on with someone we both needed professionally. His action had potentially jeopardised our trip. What if Bec and he had fought and she'd walked out on him and her job just before we left? We'd have been stuffed. There were so many reasons why their relationship was a bad idea, but I am not judging that. I would never stand in the way of someone else's relationship, especially Jonesy's. What I couldn't deal with was the deception. You can't compartmentalise your life when you are a team like we were, relying on each other and looking to push ourselves to the limit.

On prior expeditions, one of the factors that had enabled us to push as hard as we did was the motivation of not wanting to let our best mate down. This may sound soft and mushy, but the strength of it shouldn't be underestimated. I feel this factor alone can be more powerful than the individual skill sets of expeditioners making up a team. Time and time again there have been instances in history where professional adventurers have teamed up for a common, ambitious objective and failed. Not because of a lack of skill, the weather or poor equipment choice but because their team dynamics failed. The 1998–99 Icetrek expedition with Peter Hillary, Jon Muir and Eric Philips that I mentioned earlier is one such bitter story. Throughout their journey they were dogged by differences of opinion, ethics, speed of travel – just to name a few. On their return, the media, books and documentaries about their journey became the court that the mud-slinging balls bounced back and forth over. Comments from the men included, 'There has been one person with a level of decorum and another one who has been like a spoilt brat.' Not surprisingly, many sponsors distanced themselves from the controversy and post-expedition lectures were cancelled.

Hillary, Muir and Philips weren't the first expedition team members to part on bitter terms, and they won't be the last. Tension, and lack of trust and respect, can have a much bigger impact on the success of an expedition than just making life in the tent each night uncomfortable. It can result in failure. Unfortunately, trust is a quality that is earned over years and cannot be mended by a simple apology. The challenge Jonesy and I faced was that we didn't have years to mend things, we would be sharing a tent for three months in a very short time and we needed to work it through.

While Mia, Bec and Gravy were with us in Punta, the tension lingered. The three of us needed to find a way to keep things on track and make it work so we were all comfortable. One strategy we decided on was for Jonesy to do the skeds with Bec each night as I was still too angry.

With the blue-ice runway at Hercules Inlet covered in fresh snow and post-winter blizzards keeping more snow coming faster than the team on the ground could clear it, we were grounded in Punta Arenas. Our scheduled departure date of 16 October came and went. Things between Jonesy and me were still tense and the delay didn't help. Then, on 18 October, our team had to fly back home to Australia. They were supposed to wave us goodbye as we set off but the bad weather was still stopping us from flying to Hercules Inlet. We drove Mia, Gravy and Bec to the airport and my departure demons started to attack. The reality of saying goodbye to Mia for at least three months hit hard. I couldn't help but think of Robert Scott and his wife, Kathleen. She had written, 'I decided not to say goodbye to my man because I didn't want anyone to see him sad.' He never returned. That night I wrote in my diary:

My heart feels like it's been wrenched out of my chest – I love Meez so, so, so much. For half an hour after we got back to our hostel, I couldn't stop crying, no, bawling. Every memory of her – our little walks along the water, the Swarovski crystal necklace she gave me, looking at our bed in the hostel reminds me of cuddling up to her, having the key in my pocket reminds me that she always kept it 'cause I would lose it, my folded clothes – everything I look at reminds me of her and it makes me

**want to cry. She is by far the most incredible part of my
life. Every experience we share together is always so
rich – everything without her loses its vibrancy.**

Just before Mia left she gave me a necklace with a red Swarovski crystal shaped in a heart. This good-luck charm ensured I kept Mia's heart near mine – she was with me every step of the way. Having been stuck in Punta while she was with me wasn't a problem; I loved the downtime with her. But without Mia, the place felt completely empty. The only good thing about missing her so much was the motivation it provided to nail the expedition and get back home quickly.

Once everyone had gone, things with Jonesy got a bit rough. But I knew I had to get past all that if we were going to succeed in our quest. The days stuck in Punta began to mount up. Each day, my diary entries were pretty similar: 'Delay, delay, delay. Still stuck here in Punta. There is constant tension bubbling with Jonesy and me.' Unfortunately, we needed to stay pretty close to the phone in case a short weather window opened up and we were able to fly south. This meant we were stuck with patting the stray dogs and going for endless walks through the cemetery. I preferred to be alone, but we ate together and went on the occasional walk together. At times we discussed the saga, other times we screamed at each other about it:

'F★★k Jonesy … I can't believe what you did behind my back.'

'I'm sorry, Cas.'

The apologies didn't help.

Chapter Ten

THE RASTA NORWEGIAN

Jonesy and I had been the first team of the season to arrive in Punta Arenas but we knew others wouldn't be far behind. It was the centenary year of Amundsen's and Scott's South Pole expeditions and many would be attempting to follow in their footsteps, though no-one we knew of was attempting the unsupported return journey like us. That was pressure we didn't need.

After getting acquainted with our hostel, the dogs and the cemetery, our next port of call was to visit the office of Antarctic Logistics and Expeditions (ALE), who would be flying us down to Antarctica and would provide the logistic support and safety back-up we required. The outside of the office looked just like any normal building. We stood on the quiet street and knocked on the door. There was no answer. Then with a sudden burst the door swung open and the place was absolutely buzzing with activity. Pretty much the entire team that was going to be running the base at Union Glacier was frantically getting ready for the season. There were the owners barking orders, operations staff guides, machinery operators, medics, cooks, kitchen hands, comms staff – you name it, they were all there. The busyness inside seemed so out of place for the sleepy town.

We sat down for our briefing with Peter McDowell, one of the co-owners of ALE, who was an outspoken, gregarious Aussie and a born storyteller. He'd been involved in the company for over twenty-five years and was not afraid to tell us that he'd seen plenty of young fellas (like us) arrive at the start of the season with big, bold objectives only to be very quickly shut down by the uncompromising white demons in Antarctica.

'Struth, some people come down here with no bloody idea I tell ya. No idea. What are they expecting? A holiday? The difference is that on a holiday you put on weight and on a true expedition you lose weight. Just last season one bloke put a knife through his hand while slicing cheese in his tent. A few years before him, a bunch of ladies lasted only a couple of days, bit cold for them. Or the Koreans, the one I saw at the end was going to need a skin graft. Or the ...'

Peter was enjoying sharing his horror stories and seeing right through our poker faces. Changing topics quickly, I asked if there were any other interesting expeditions going on in the area.

He walked out of the room and came back a few minutes later carrying a lever-arch folder with '2011–12 Expeditions' written in thick black pen on the spine. Moving his reading glasses onto the tip of his weathered nose he began rattling off some other trips happening in Antarctica that season.

'It sounds like it's going to be a busy year,' Jonesy said.

Peter kept going through the list until he paused and said, 'Oh, and there is a solo Norwegian – Aleksander Gamme – planning on doing what you two clowns are setting out to do.'

Our jaws dropped, we both stared at each other and simultaneously spluttered, 'What?!'

'Yeah, Aleks is in town right now and is going to be flying down with you guys.'

Peter kept talking but I didn't hear him. A thousand thoughts were running through my mind at once. I think I was in shock. After years of preparation and conveying to sponsors and the media what we were attempting to achieve we found ourselves once more in a race – something Jonesy and I didn't like. Hearing about this Aleks guy gave me a bad feeling of déjà vu.

There was also something kind of spooky about it. Just over a hundred years earlier, in Melbourne in 1910, the *Terra Nova* was being prepared for an imminent journey into Antarctic waters. Captain Robert Falcon Scott was on board in his captain's quarters. His fingertips, suffering nerve damage from a previous attempt to reach the South Pole, held a telegram:

Beg to inform you Fram proceeding Antarctic – Amundsen

This simple message from the scrupulous Norwegian explorer set the scene for one of the greatest races in history. Scott was livid and his men shocked as the media jumped on the news – it was now a race to the Geographic South Pole. At a time when the Ford Model T had just hit production lines, Charles Kingsford-Smith was still in school, Americans had only recently stood at the North Pole and few knew of Mount Everest, the jewel of geographic exploration – the South Pole – had not yet been attained. Both of these men were determined that they would be the one to claim rights to that jewel.

Scott's launching pad for Antarctica was Melbourne, ours was a small town at the bottom of South America. We had no telegram, but it was just as devastating to learn that a blond, Viking-like Norwegian polar guide was there to beat us. We learnt that he had followed all our preparations, training, modifications and knew of the gear we were taking thanks to Facebook and the internet. We'd never heard a word about his intentions before then and I couldn't understand why he had kept so quiet. Walking out of ALE's headquarters, we immediately organised to have dinner with Aleks. We wanted to suss out his plans.

Later that evening, we walked into a bar and were greeted warmly by an oversized smiling version of Sideshow Bob from *The Simpsons*. He had a muscly frame, and steely eyes of determination. Before we met him we had planned not to become too friendly too quickly, but that wasn't possible. We bonded with Aleks right away. Yes, he was there to attempt the same unsupported return journey and, no, he had not informed us of his intentions. Yes, he had followed our preparations but he didn't see it as a race. After sampling a few local lagers, he gave us perhaps the kindest compliment any Norwegian can offer: 'I have been watching your progress online. You boys seem much more Norwegian than British in your preparations, those guys have been making the same mistakes for over a century. You are very well prepared and I think you're going to make it.'

We laughed about how fat we were all looking, told stories about past adventures and pretty quickly realised we all had a similar outlook on adventure. One topic that we dug into was the meaning of an unsupported expedition. Unlike many other sports or hobbies that have central bodies like the International Sailing Federation or the World Chess Federation, no such authority exists for adventure or polar travel. The closest we have is a privately run website – adventurestats.com – which outlines some rudimentary definitions. As a result, there is no centralised definition for the 'rules of polar travel'. What does unsupported really mean? How is unsupported different from unassisted? As a result, each year expeditions throw terms and words around that suit their marketing and media interests. After the conversation bounced round for quite a while, Aleks made the comment that we should be the ones defining these terms. After all, we were the ones out there doing these trips so it made sense that we should be the ones discussing and setting a benchmark for what's what.

I agreed with Aleks to an extent. One of the beautiful things about adventure is that there are no rules. Adventure is an activity with an unknown outcome. By adding rules and definitions it makes adventure more like a sport or competition. For me, that isn't what it's about. Adventure is so much more than that – it's a journey, an unknown journey that evolves and shapes as time goes on. Having said that, there are very few expeditions that are self-funded. Most rely on funding both pre- and post-expedition from sources such as sponsorship, media deals, private donations, book sales and lectures. It is only fair that stakeholders can assess by what means the expedition was attempted and how it differs from what others have achieved. If we followed Aleks's ski tracks is this support? How about if we had our flags flown to the South Pole for photos there? Using a toilet at the South Pole Base?

The night with Aleks ended well and we all headed back to our hostels, ready in case there was a 7 am flight call. Not surprisingly, the call never came. So, the next day, after having spent the previous ten days not doing much exercise at all, we went in search of a gym. After a couple of hours of cardio, we weighed ourselves on the changing-room scales. For the first time in my life I weighed over 102 kilograms and Jonesy was a whopping 106 kilograms. We had to get out of there and start trekking before we put on too much extra weight and ALE charged us excess baggage!

Finally, after twelve days in Punta Arenas, the 7 am call came. We had our last shower, ate our last fruit salad and slipped into our fresh thermals and clothes. We would be wearing them for a very long time.

Chapter Eleven

READY, SET ... DELAY

Even when we actually boarded the plane there was still a fair bit of uncertainty as to whether we would take off or not. Mark, the meteorologist, didn't think the weather would stay clear enough for the journey but the crew at ALE had calculated otherwise. I have to admit I was a bit nervous about it. We were flying in what looked like an antique. The Ilyushin had been designed in Uzbekistan in 1976 and made a military Hercules look small. You could have fitted a couple of buses in the windowless belly of the plane, no worries. They obviously weren't too fussed about decor in the Soviet Union back then – there were exposed wires and pipes, the control panels looked like they'd be more at home in a World War II Spitfire, the toilet was a bucket, and the seats were ripped and squashy like a Datsun 510 from the same era. Our sleds and equipment were strapped down behind us with cargo netting and if there was a problem most of the emergency signs were in Russian (as was the pre-flight safety brief), which wouldn't have been much help.

We were on board with Aleks, two Spanish blokes and about twenty others who worked for ALE. The crew of the Ilyushin were contracted by ALE for the Antarctic summer. When they were not flying over the Drake Passage, they transported all kinds of crazy stuff around the world. Their last job before meeting us in Punta Arenas had seen them fly an elephant from Africa to the backyard of a wealthy oil Sheik in Saudi Arabia. They also did plenty of relief work throughout Africa and the Middle East. I couldn't help thinking about some of the other stuff that might've been flown around the globe in this very plane. I was told the 'unofficial' company byline was, 'If you've got the money, we'll fly it – no questions asked.'

They were good to their word. For A$150,000 they would fly a private expedition to Antarctica. Not many others would do the same. As I clicked on my seatbelt and looked around at the dangling wires, a conversation I'd had with Jonesy's brother, Andy, who flies Tiger helicopters for the Australian Army, popped into my head. 'I'm more worried about you guys arriving in Antarctica in one piece, than the actual expedition itself,' he'd said. Not what I needed to think about at that moment!

As the heavy doors slammed shut, any chance to reconsider the flight was gone. Thank God for the earplugs that had been handed out to compensate for the non-existent soundproofing. The engines roared and our heavily laden beast of the sky lumbered down the runway. It didn't feel like it was ever going to take off. With no windows to judge whether we were in the air or not, after a couple of minutes I decided we must be airborne.

Jonesy and I shared a smile. Aleks was sitting opposite us and to be honest I was still wrestling with my feelings towards him. Even though we'd all talked about our trip not being a race I had the feeling I was at the starting line looking over at another competitor. I had to try to shake that off. The four-hour flight from Punta Arenas down to Union Glacier in Antarctica passed without incident and I spent much of the time anticipating the weeks ahead, thinking about the preparation we'd done and wondering if it would be enough to see us succeed. Before I knew it, the Russian comms operator signalled to all of us to strap up as we were preparing to land. I registered the same nervous look on the faces of the others on board, after all, it's not every day 180 tonnes of Soviet metal slams down on an blue-ice runway. I've always wondered what keeps planes up, but now I was even more interested about how a plane of this size stops on ice without fishtailing out of control. I shouldn't have worried, the crew gently placed the plane on the ice and we hardly felt a jolt. I've experienced much worse at Sydney's Kingsford-Smith Airport. It felt like we rushed along at quite a speed for the length of the five-kilometre runway. The momentum finally stopped and we all let out a relieved giggle and cheer. Finally, we were in Antarctica.

Once the doors opened, we stepped out and were immediately slapped in the face by the -30° Celsius temperature, and the 30 kilometre per hour wind bit through our clothes. I snapped into the 'thirty rule' which Matty had drummed into us while we were at Iqaluit. I could almost hear her voice: 'When it's -30° and the wind is blowing at 30 kilometres an hour any exposed skin will get frostbite in thirty seconds.' Jonesy and I 'buddied up', checked each other's faces to ensure we were covered and only then let ourselves take in our surroundings. It wasn't just the cold that took my breath away. I was here! Glistening mountains surrounded us. Being early summer, the sun sat low on the horizon, with the odd wispy cloud drifting by in the pale blue sky. The dry snow underfoot crunched like styrofoam. Sure it was cold, but where the Arctic had felt like a one-two punch in the face that also winded us, this was more like a slap.

This is how Captain John King Davis of the *Aurora*, who dropped Mawson at Commonwealth Bay, described his arrival in Antarctica:

> And the air! I had never breathed such a cold, dry,
> exhilarating draught before. As I filled my lungs
> with it I felt eager to perform feats of strength,
> prodigies of endurance. It made your senses tingle.
> You were ready to jump out of your skin!

Amen to that! Jonesy and I were taking in huge lungfuls of the stuff, and it had the same effect on us.

We were greeted by a gaggle of Norwegians, Russians and people who were used to living in the high Canadian Arctic. In contrast to these snow leopards, we felt like the Jamaican bob-sled team at the Winter Olympics, two tubby Aussies who were trying to remain calm and look cool. The first challenge was not to slip on the blue-ice runway – we wouldn't have been the first. Just the season before an Italian adventurer had slipped when walking away from the plane, fallen over and was packed back onto the Ilyushin with a slipped disk in his back. Game over.

We didn't have to linger long, as we were soon bundled into these souped-up Icelandic vehicles and transferred to the Union Glacier camp. These beasts would've had Optimus Prime standing to salute, they were that impressive. They had massive tractor tyres, more flashy dials in front of the driver's seat than in the entire Soviet plane and they were raised so high that we almost needed a ladder to step up into them.

Once in camp, Jonesy and I began sorting our bags into a shapely mound. We accounted for all twelve of our North Face duffels (we'd consolidated down from the sixteen we left Australia with) but couldn't find our five food boxes. The panic started to rise but we calmed down and talked it through. We knew we'd seen them being loaded onto the plane, but after ferreting around the piles of equipment that had been unloaded and not seeing them, we started to get more than a little nervous. We called Steve Jones, the operations manager for the Union Glacier Base. Steve was a skinny, well-spoken Brit, with a dry sense of humour and a great knowledge of adventure. He was a good bloke and would be one of the key 'go-to' people for us when we were on the ice. He came to lend us a hand and he couldn't find them either. The comms team radioed the packing staff in Punta to ask whether the food had indeed been loaded onto the plane. It had. They said, 'We packed it into the belly of the plane.'

Steve's face went an ashen white as he replied, 'What! We weren't told anything was packed into the belly, we didn't check that area of the plane!'

It was too late. The Ilyushin was already on its way back to Punta Arenas. Someone made a half-hearted joke about the frequent flyer points those bags could have earned but, seriously, it was no time to joke. Without that food, there was no way we could start the expedition. We had to wait for the plane to come back, and considering our own flight had been delayed for twelve days, we weren't feeling very good at that particular point. If the food took that long to get back, we'd be destined for failure before we even began as it would only leave us seventy-five days to make a return journey. No way would that be enough time. There was a flight scheduled for the next day and all we could do was hope.

The reason we were so concerned about timing at this point, was because we knew that the final flight out of Antarctica before the onset of winter was 26 January. If we missed that flight, we'd either be stuck in Antarctica for the winter, or we'd need to pay a ludicrous sum of money to charter a flight to extract us. Plus I knew that Mia wouldn't be too thrilled if I missed our wedding!

We spent time checking and repacking our gear to stay busy, but we were good to go as soon as that food arrived. We had to watch

Aleks pack his food into his sled and then we helped him carry his gear to the Twin Otter that would fly him to the starting line at Hercules Inlet. Jonesy and I stood numbly waving goodbye as we watched his plane take off. Those bitter thoughts came back, it wasn't enough that he was born on skis and had been a polar guide for ten years, now he was getting a crucial headstart on us also.

Once Aleks's plane was out of sight I felt quite depressed. Even though Jonesy and I were in camp with a bunch of great staff we both felt flat, isolated and alone. Jonesy was even worse than I was, because in the rush to get ready when the flight call finally came, he'd left a good-luck-charm necklace his mum had made him for the trip back in Punta Arenas. I guess the one positive of not being dropped at Hercules Inlet with Aleks was that we would be able to set our own pace without thinking we should try to keep up.

The next day, Jonesy and I sat in the mess tent drinking tea and whispering encouragement to the weather to stay clear as we stared out into blue sky. With fingers and toes crossed, we waited not-quite-patiently. I pictured Aleks skiing under these blue skies and was jealous I wasn't out there skiing south myself. The hours ticked by with no word, then suddenly Steve burst through the door and exclaimed, 'The Ilyushin has touched down!'

That was it. We jumped up and went to work energetically packing the vagabond food into our sleds. If that wasn't enough to lift our spirits, the plane had also carried Jonesy's missing necklace over to us. It was a good sign, if you believe in that stuff. Steve offered some advice as he helped us get organised.

'Don't forget to have fun out there,' he said with a sly smile on his face.

That was the same thing Matty had told us up in the Arctic. If there was one thing Jonesy and I were good at it was having fun in the outdoors, so surely that wouldn't be so hard.

'No problemo!' we replied, like two naïve children heading off for their first day of school. Steve introduced us to the Twin Otter's Canadian pilot, a bloke who had a thick goatee, grease-covered overalls, and a pot belly that would make any elephant seal proud. With all our gear on board, we were ready. The pilot spun the propellers of the Twin Otter to give it a kick-start, and we were on our way.

It was only a thirty-minute trip from Union Glacier to Hercules Inlet on the coast of the Antarctic continent. It was noisy on board, and hard to think about much but the hypnotising drone of the engine, and there wasn't much change in the view. To be fair, when we circled above our landing it didn't look any different from the floating ice shelf or the continent proper. Everything was covered in a thick layer of white snow. The Kiwi duo, Kevin and Jamie, had told us to make sure the pilot dropped us as close to the actual coast as possible as it had taken them two days of walking from where the plane had dropped them on the ice shelf to get to the official start point. It made sense. You wouldn't start a marathon a few kilometres before the start line and it was no different here. The pilot brought us in nine kilometres from the coast and that seemed good enough to us. We clambered out of the plane, shook hands with the pilot and co-pilot and the co-pilot offered us a few words of encouragement.

'Just remember, we're only a phone call away.'

Those words would play on my mind throughout the journey. It was a nice sentiment but far from the reality.

Arriving at Hercules Inlet, the beginning
www.casandjonesy.com.au/extremesouth

PART II
CROSSING THE ICE

'The only way you're going to do it ... is by doing it.'

PETER TRESEDER

PHASE ONE
Survival

DAY ONE

Once the Twin Otter had disappeared over the horizon, the silence echoed loudly in my ears. The sun sat fat and low against the deep blue of the sky, and ice crystals the size of ball bearings danced along the icy ground. We were on the Ronne Ice Shelf on the coast of Antarctica and beneath our feet was the Weddell Sea. Everywhere I looked, there was ice, ice and more ice, broken up only by a few distant nunataks (exposed areas of rocky peaks). Jonesy and I – and Aleks, somewhere in front of us – were now perhaps the most isolated people on the planet. We hooked ourselves up to the sleds, and without fanfare or any dramatic statement, took our first steps towards the South Pole. Eight kilometres to our south we could see the steep icy slopes rearing out of Hercules Inlet. That was the direction we were heading.

It was great to be on the trail and moving south. This is what we had worked so hard for and there were a few exultant shouts to the sky from both of us. We were bloody well here doing what we'd put our minds to. Every now and then we'd bump our ski poles together like two blokes clinking beer glasses in a pub celebrating the victory of their favourite footy team. It had been such a long journey just to get to this point. Although nervous and intimidated by the surroundings I couldn't wipe the smile off my face. But my excitement was tempered by the thought of what we'd face in the next few days. I had to admit I was horribly worried. We were going to be travelling through some crevasse fields and the terrain was steep climbing out of Hercules Inlet. On the positive side, the weather was brilliant with endless blue sky (if a tad chilly at –30° Celsius), our sleds were moving well, and because visibility was as far as the distant horizon, we were able to navigate off the jagged mountains and nunataks that dotted the icy landscape and didn't need to stay fixated on the compass. Once we were away from the coast, we'd leave these mountains behind and travel over vast plains of endless Antarctic wilderness, but for the moment I was enjoying the familiarity of the landscape, which didn't seem too different from the Arctic or parts of New Zealand we'd visited.

One of the gifts that Antarctica offers the intrepid explorer in summer is twenty-four hour sunlight, which is great for travelling, although not the best for sleeping. The sun rotates around your head like a big halo. With no sunsets, and no difference between night and day, our strict routine would be our only reference point to let us know days were passing. This early in the season, the sun sits quite low on the horizon, and even though it's clearly visible, you get no warmth from it. We knew that in these first few weeks it would take close to an hour to warm up the inside of our tent with the stove before we could safely take off our gloves. But as the season progressed and the sun rose higher in the sky, the tent would trap warmth like a greenhouse. We'd even heard stories of people sleeping on top of their sleeping-bags just in boxer shorts. Unfortunately, the luxury of a warm tent was still quite a few weeks away for us and we had to make do with what we had. We'd had so much practice in Iqaluit and New Zealand setting up the tent, getting the stove running and refining our camp life that on the first night of the expedition we attacked it like it was just another drill. We started a ritual that stayed with us for the remainder of the journey. We timed how long it took me to get in the tent and start the stove (first night: thirty minutes) and the time it took Jonesy to cover up the snow flaps, cut some snow blocks to melt and make sure everything was packed up outside (first night: eighty-five minutes). By the time Jonesy entered the tent, my goal was to have a few litres of water melted, our wet clothes hung up and a warm drink ready to put in his hands. For the entire expedition, all cooking was done inside the tent between our two sleeping mats. Just like any project manager working on a construction job, we'd identified the tasks that took the longest to complete (the critical path) and got started on them first. Snow melting took 2.5 hours each night, and gave us enough water for dinner, breakfast and drinks the following day – about ten litres in total.

On that first night, Jonesy dived into the tent covered in icicles and started what was to become his expedition ritual of ripping off his boots and balaclava while I worked to get dinner on. To my surprise, attached to the meal bag was a note from back home. When I read it out, we both got teary. Ever since I've known Jonesy, he's suffered from horrendous claustrophobia. As soon as he got inside the tent he almost had a panic attack and needed to remove his headwear, neckwarmer and any clothes that clung tightly to him. I thought I'd seen him at his worst while in the kayak cabin on the Tasman, but this was coming close.

From the moment we stopped to set up camp for the night, everything was go, go, go. We had two skeds to do each night: a short one with the ALE staff at Union Glacier, where we fed them basic information including the latitude and longitude of our campsite, along with the number of hours and distance travelled, and a much more in-depth sked with Bec. Jonesy relayed all kinds of information back to Bec in Sydney – our position, a daily summary (hours skied, distance skied, hours slept, the time it took us to break and set up camp, food consumed), strategy (expected versus actual progress), scores for our physical, mental and fatigue states, detailed information on how the equipment was holding up and any RFIs (requests for information) from the previous evening. This might seem overly militaristic, but one of the lessons we learnt from the Tasman was that relaying this information to a third party who was detached from the day-to-day grind, really helped us to keep perspective on different facets of the expedition and allowed them to objectively track how we were progressing physically and emotionally. This sked took anywhere between fifteen and sixty minutes depending on the number of RFIs that we had to go through.

That first night, we were tucked into our sleeping-bags about four hours after we'd stopped skiing for the day. Not a bad effort, but we knew that we needed that time to improve. Crawling into my sleeping-bag would become the most anticipated moment of each day. Prior to leaving, we'd loaded some movies and television series onto our iPods – *True Blood*, *Californication* and, my favourite, *Flight of the Conchords*, just to name a few – so we had those to occupy us when we needed a distraction from the pain of blisters, ice burn and the mental fatigue that comes from walking for hours in a white-out. We didn't bother watching anything that first night, but we both scrawled in our diaries before placing sleeping masks over our eyes to block the light, and shoving earplugs in our ears so we couldn't hear each other snoring. The twenty-four hour daylight was going to take some getting used to, but we were on the ice and things were looking good.

DAY TWO

Jonesy's never been a great morning person. On previous expeditions he was always pretty grumpy until he had a coffee in his hand or we were out of the tent and moving. On this trip he made a real effort to be more pleasant in the morning and for some strange reason took over the responsibility of disarming the alarm when it beeped so rudely. On our second day he sang out, 'Casa ... rise and shine!', in the most positive voice he could muster, and he kept this going for most of our time on the ice, even when his voice was more pained than positive.

Sleeping inside the tent was horribly similar to the long cold nights we'd spent up on Baffin Island. The condensation from our breathing froze on the tent walls forming a thick coating of delicate hoar frost. After a while, it looked like hundreds of Antarctic-dwelling spiders had woven feathery, icy webs, their intricate branches dangling from the tent walls. As we slept, gusts of wind would rattle the tent and dislodge the build-up. I'd forgotten the shock it gave when this happened. I'd be dozing, when suddenly there'd be a dump of ice and my face would be splashed by freezing droplets. The effect was almost as dramatic as if someone had thrown a bucket of water at me – I never got used to it. When we woke, the hoar frost had to be brushed off the walls and tent zipper to stop ice showering onto our dry clothing.

It was a blustery morning and without thinking I ran out of the tent to do my first shit in Antarctica. It was something I never quite mastered the art of in the Arctic, and here I was thrown out of whack by the sudden urgency of the situation and forgot rule number one – be prepared! I ripped my trousers down round my ankles and immediately felt the ice crystals scald my fat, naked butt as the uncaring 50 kilometre per hour wind whipped them straight at me. Without being too graphic, let's just say I tried to punch it out as quickly as possible but some things can't be hurried. When the time came to wipe, I found myself in a bit of a predicament. For starters, I couldn't remember which pocket

I'd shoved my two pieces of toilet paper into, and then I realised that I'd forgotten to bring the shovel and hadn't prepared snow blocks to wipe up after the toilet paper. My hands were freezing as I waddled back to the tent with my pants round my ankles to get the shovel, cut some snow blocks and faffed around trying to find the toilet paper. Due to our weight restrictions, we could only afford to bring two sheets of toilet paper per person per day. If we needed more (which we always did) we cut and shaped snow blocks to wipe up. By the time I'd located it, I couldn't feel my digits and I had no idea what was going on back there. I used one sheet for the initial wipe, then some crystally snow that caused my bum to bleed, then the final sheet to dry myself and clean up. My fingers were too far gone to pull up my pants so I jumped into the tent screaming and yelling, which sent Jonesy scuttling away as he tried to avoid my naked flailing legs. After a few minutes with my hands near the stove, blood started to rush back into my fingers causing extreme pain – the kind of pain that ice climbers refer to as the 'screaming barfies' because, basically, you want to scream and barf at the same time.

My abysmal ablutions performance was enough to prompt Jonesy to be super organised. He prepared himself perfectly. Toilet paper: check. Snow blocks cut out of soft snow: check. Clothing sorted: check. He waltzed out uber confident and did not disappoint. Every thirty seconds I called out from inside the tent: 'How you going, Jonesy?'

'All good mate,' he replied in a calm, authoritative voice.

I had a long way to go to match his effort.

It took us almost three hours to break camp on the second day, and I knew we would have to improve on that also. I've said it before, but with polar travel, every minute spent not skiing or resting is time wasted. We were both feeling pretty stiff from the previous day and somewhat anxious to get out skiing. The plan was always to ease ourselves into the expedition, and so we were taking our first steps for the day at 10.30 am. We were aiming to ski between six and eight hours a day in the early part of the trip and build it up from there. From prior expeditions and the wisdom of other adventurers, we knew it was important to let our bodies acclimatise to the cold and physical exertion. We were following the lead of people like Jim Shekhdar and Jon Muir. Shekhdar, who rowed across the Pacific, and Muir, an incredible Aussie adventurer who'd hauled sleds to both Poles, walked across Australia and climbed Everest, had averaged three hours per day in the first week of their expeditions so as to allow their bodies to adapt to the stress of expedition life.

It was one thing to understand the importance of allowing our bodies to adapt, but there was no way around the necessary hard yakka we had to put in. Initially we divided the day into six one-hour hauling sessions with a ten-minute break at the end of each session. In that ten minutes we left our skis on and pulled our sleds up beside us. We'd throw our big, puffy down parkas on over all our clothes, zipping them up quickly to catch as much warmth inside as possible. We'd then shovel food from our snack bags and try to scull half a litre of water. One lesson we learnt from the Tasman was the importance of variety. When the scenery doesn't change much it's important that food adds a bit of spice. Mia had ensured that each snack bag had different lollies, nuts, biscuits and chips. The three litres of water we carried sat snug in bottle pouches in an attempt to prevent them from freezing up as the day progressed. But no matter what we did, ice floated in our bottles after a few hours and we ended up with ice-cream headaches when we drank it quickly. If any clothing or gear needed to be adjusted it had to be done in one of our ten-minute breaks.

After the first shift on the second day, we were well and truly off the floating ice shelf and our journey across the continent proper had begun. We started climbing the vertical icy inclines that we'd seen when the plane dropped us off. They seemed much higher from ground level. As the terrain steepened, the skins on the bottom of our skis had trouble gripping the icy slopes, so we took off our skis, strapped them on top of our sleds and strained in our traces pulling the weight. There was no sign of Aleks Gamme on the horizon.

For the first time since we'd stepped foot on the ice, we flicked on our iPods and listened to music as we trekked. We had a whole combination of podcasts, music playlists and audiobooks, ranging from the ABC's Richard Fidler to Hamish and Andy. Mia had compiled six playlists with all my favourite music (leave 'Home Among the Gumtrees' and 'Eye of the Tiger' alone, all right!). We also had all the Harry Potter books, Peter FitzSimons' *Kokoda* and a biography on Steve Jobs to keep us entertained. When the going was tough or the end of the day was too far away, music was the answer – it was our performance-enhancing drug. We'd sewn pouches onto our base layer to keep the iPod battery warm next to our skin and had the cords running up the inside of our clothes to our ears. The biggest problem I had was that the earphones kept falling out. (My earlobe shape wasn't what the good folk at Apple had in mind when they designed their earphones – it's an inherited thing, my mum has the same problem.) It became incredibly frustrating because earphones are impossible to put back in while wearing big mitts. I needed to stop, faff around with my bare hands and then, once I'd located the earphones, slide them back under my beanie into my ill-fitting ears. Adding to the complication of the whole exercise was the ice that started forming on my goggles, which meant I was hauling blind. The whole in-out-stop process continued all day and started sending me mad. As I walked I kept pondering and working through solutions for how I could keep them in. Tape? Bracket? Clip?

And the earphones weren't my only problem. This may sound ridiculous, but we were finding a whole heap of teething problems in just trying to listen to music. The moisture-management strategies we'd learnt from Matty in Iqaluit meant that we were constantly zipping and unzipping the pitzips under our arms and the main zip on our shell-wear. However, one thing we hadn't trained with in Iqaluit was using our iPods. The breeze had picked up, so I tried to do up my main zip but it was getting stuck on what I initially thought was ice build-up. I was wrong, it was my iPod cord. The zipper teeth gnarled the cord and severed one of the earphones. I got really disappointed and angry at myself. Neither of us could afford to make these kinds of mistakes on an unsupported expedition.

When the one living earphone was finally nestled back into my ear, my thoughts ran wild. It felt like another hill-training session back home. Not being on skis meant the same muscles were burning, our calves flamed, glutes were yelling and our butts tightened. In a way, the familiar pain was comforting in this unfamiliar environment. We strained and heaved, trying to edge our 160 kilogram loads up the incline as our lungs burnt with each in-breath of the cold air. We couldn't see the top of the incline and were resigned to putting our heads down and plodding on while staring at our strange shadows.

On a long bushwalk or paddle, whether it's in the front of your mind or lodged deep in your subconscious, you get pretty used to your own shadow; it's like looking into a mirror. However, with all the polar clothing and the fur ruff on my head, I cast an unfamiliar shadow on the snow in front of me. It felt like I was projecting someone else. I became transfixed with its outline, and was somewhat confronted when I realised Captain Scott's shadow would have been eerily similar. The penny dropped and this was the moment I truly became aware of where we were and what we were setting out to achieve. I didn't feel comfortable with this strange shadow person and I distanced myself from it by giving him a name – Polar Dude. I thought about how Scott's expedition turned out. I thought of Mia and the fact I was so far away. I thought of Kathleen and how Robert Scott had never come home to her. I started to cry.

I had to force myself to stop focusing on my shadow and to concentrate on what I was doing when I was confronted by a crack in the ice running perpendicular to our course as far as the eye could see. It was only a small one, maybe 30 centimetres wide, and Jonesy and I gave it a powerful prod with our ski poles to ascertain whether the bridge of ice that had formed over the crack was solid. We proceeded over it without incident. These cracks became more frequent as the day progressed. Some were micro-cracks, others were indents in the snow as wide as a road. Each time we approached one, we'd probe it with our ski poles and find the bridges over these crevasses were rock hard and solid, so there was nothing to worry about.

After a while the relentless plodding had started to feel familiar. I was no longer being as careful or as attentive as I needed to be. I was trying to calculate the number of steps to the Pole, when my leg punctured through the snow and I plunged downward. I might have screamed, but as suddenly as it started the falling sensation stopped. I looked down. I was suspended above a gaping chasm, my legs dangling beneath me. The trace-line back to my sled had prevented me from falling further, and for the first time that day I was thankful for the weight of it. A shaft of light reflected off the contorted wall of the crevasse for a short distance before disappearing into the earth's bowels. I took a deep breath to calm the rising panic and shouted for Jonesy.

We were both shaken by the incident and in the fall my ski pole had snapped. From then on, each slight depression in the snow transfixed me with fear. Another crevasse? It was similar to being on a bushwalk and almost stepping on a snake – after doing it once, every stick or root seems to slither. Now I wondered if every depression in the snow was going to swallow me up. I thought about the emotional toll that trudging through the heavily crevassed Beardmore Glacier must have had on Scott and his men and I felt a connection that I hadn't experienced before. It wasn't a good feeling though. I felt a sense of vulnerability, intimidation and anger.

One fall was enough for me. Again I was angry at myself. In Antarctica, there is no room for complacency. On our first full day of travel, I'd broken a ski pole and an earphone cord and had very nearly lost my life in a crevasse. If I continued this way, we'd have no gear left in a month's time and perhaps I would be dead. We set up the tent in near silence as I grappled with my frustration towards myself. In the tent that evening, I taped a ten centimetre-long aluminium splint around the ski pole and it was back to working order, but the repair was a constant reminder of my carelessness.

Video journal – Crevasse!
www.casandjonesy.com.au/extremesouth

DAY THREE

What a f**king hard day.

It started off oh so brilliantly when I tore the leading snow flap on the tent ... Dickhead. The rest of the day really didn't pan out much better. Our progress was slow and I just found myself falling behind. I think yesterday really took it out of me. Listened to some tunes for about half the day and it's great how some of them really took me down memory lane.

Guts are playing up a little because of the high-fat diet.

Had a minor disagreement about direction today on the trail. Normally I'm the one who struggles to express his point of view.

Cas really picked up more of the slack today – he led for about two-thirds of the day – what a champ. By the end of the six hours we were both shattered. To add insult to injury the ground is so hard we had to cut blocks for the tent – we only did the front half and then had to fix the snow flap OUTSIDE in the COLD with WIND. I could only manage a couple of stitches before I'd have to re-warm my hands in my crotch – took sixty mins to complete.

Cas broke his harness (not his fault) and repaired that in the tent and devised a cool iPod earphone holder!

This expedition is never calm, there is always something to do ... maintenance, fixing stuff, even

everyday tasks are so hard. Sitting in the tent we grunt
like wild animals with all our movements.
Fur ruff freezes like a wet matted dog.

Day Three was tough. The wind had picked up from the south blasting at 60 kilometres per hour. It buffeted our tent, which violently protested against the assault. Welcome to Antarctica! We'd been lucky for the first couple of days, as the wind had been quite benign, but now the niceties were over.

Antarctica is regarded as the windiest continent on earth. During Mawson's stay at Cape Denison he recorded winds of up to 320 kilometres per hour:

> Having failed to demolish us by dogged persistence,
> the gale tried new tactics on the evening of May 24
> [1913], in the form of a series of Herculean gusts. As
> we learned afterwards, the momentary velocity of
> these doubtless approached 200 miles [320 kilometres]
> per hour.

The winds in Antarctica are consistently driving from the elevated interior of the continent, off the Polar Plateau towards the coast. This turbulent air is caused by the build-up of high-density cold air over the plateau, which sits at an altitude of 2800 metres. Gravity forces the cold air down the ice slope like a giant stream and, consequently, we would be dealing with fierce headwinds all the way to the Pole. The chief meteorologist of Douglas Mawson's expedition to Commonwealth Bay, C. T. Madigan, wrote in 1913:

> For nine months of the year an almost continuous
> blizzard rages, and for weeks one can only crawl

about outside the shelter of the hut unable to see an
arm's length owing to the blinding drift snow.

These powerful winds strip away the snow from the surface of the
ice shield and expose the old, blue ice. This is why we thought
the hard-wheeled POWs would work so effectively, as we were
expecting hard ice underfoot, and for these first few days we'd had
just that. Kevin and Jamie had warned us that the wind always
sounded more angry from inside the tent, than from outside. They
were right, the noise inside was like a train rocketing past, and to
make things worse, the wind kept trying to escape under the tent
floor, causing it to buck like a bull.

We started our daily routine barely able to hear ourselves
think. Snow melting, breakfast on the boil, toilet time ... After
my previous efforts, going to the toilet made me nervous and
now with the wind raging outside I was truly terrified. I neatly
folded my two sheets of toilet paper, put them into the thigh
pocket of my GoreTex pants and was fully dressed for the ground
storm with my goggles on when I headed out. The sleds were
covered by windblown snow and I looked up and spotted the
moon dazzling above in the bright sunshine. I squatted as close to
the back of the tent as I dared so as to still get protection from the
wind but not mess on the tent and tried to do it as fast as possible.
I had more luck than the day before, but my fingers froze like
Calippo iceblocks and the screaming barfies followed once I got
back into the tent.

We kitted up in full Darth Vader face attire to protect us
from the conditions outside. Every inch of our skin needed to be
covered or frostbite would result far too quickly. In these most
hostile conditions we each wore a Neoprene face mask and goggle
combination that made sure no wind could hit our face.

After a nervous, 'Well, I guess it's now or never', we dismantled the tent and hit the trail as quickly as possible. As is often the case in Antarctica, the wind was blowing its top off, but there wasn't a cloud to be seen. Travelling in these windy conditions sapped even more of our energy than usual. Breaks were much more difficult and the wind carried away any words that we tried to exchange. In these conditions we skied one behind the other – partly because the sled in front provided a little windbreak for the second, and partly because it gave the trailing person a break from navigating responsibilities, and they could tune out for a bit.

By the end of the day I was struggling like a drunkard, from exhaustion. From the start of the journey, Jonesy had an extra ten kilograms or so in his sled and I still battled to keep up with him. Right from when we'd had our problems in Centennial Park, Jonesy made it very clear that the weight we were hauling was team weight and that we'd distribute it so that we were both working as hard as each other and moving at the same pace. This was very different from many other expeditions, as it's a very male thing to want to keep an equal weight in the sleds, but we tried to take inspiration from American writer Jack London who said:

> when two men go together along the white silence, it
> is not important that one works more, and the other,
> less. The thing that matters is that each of them
> should do everything in his power.

Well, we were doing everything we could to move forward. We'd covered a solid 11.4 kilometres in six hours of skiing so we were pretty chuffed about that considering the conditions.

Towards the end of the third shift, the shoulder strap of my harness pinged under the enormous strain of the sled. There was no way I could keep on hauling with it the way it was so we whacked on our parkas and tried to repair it quickly. The fiddly work meant we had to take off our thick mittens to tie the shoulder strap to the waist harness, and the thin Polypro base-layer gloves we were wearing provided little protection against the cold. Jonesy did his best to shelter my hands from the wind but my fingers fumbled more and more as the blood and tissue in them froze solid. It was a downward spiral, as my fingers got colder they became less dexterous, which meant the repair took longer, which made my fingers worse. Just as my fingers felt like iceblocks that were about to snap in half, I tied the last knot. I hoped it would last out the day until I could do a proper repair in the tent that night.

Later, after we'd finished dinner and Jonesy was doing the sked with Bec, I worked on my earphone solution. I had a few spare hair ties, and taped one to the top of each earphone and then hung the tie over my ear. You beauty! I tested it out with a little head banging in the tent and it seemed to work but the next day would be the real test. Before I fell asleep I taped my heels as a precautionary measure because it felt like hot spots (a precursor for blisters) were developing.

DAY FOUR

CAS DIARY ENTRY – 2 NOVEMBER 2011

Woke up this morning to raging wind outside, 50 to 60 km/hr – blowing everywhere. Very difficult conditions. Today was very much a 'what are we doing here?' day. There is nothing sexy about this – it's just ugly. First session I was in the lead and felt great! Knee still holding

113

up. Music worked! Big thing today is that I've developed two massive blisters on my heels and one of them has popped. So angry at myself for not addressing it earlier. Biggest motivator was thinking that if Mawson could travel with his soles falling off, then I can deal with this. This afternoon weather closed in – high winds, now white-out outside – tent very cold, hard to dry stuff tonight. At end of day today, EVERYTHING was wet – all clothes, both sets of goggles – shocking moisture management. Couldn't see anything by end of the day. Also, absolutely buggered. To fix blister, set up tent after 3.5 hours to put dressing on – took 1.5 hours to get back on the trail. Starting to comprehend the enormity of what we're embarking on – very intimidating. The amount of repairs to equipment and our bodies that we've done over the past four days I expected for the whole trip! The Al Pacino quote from *Any Given Sunday* on my iPod kept me going today – JJ and I will FIGHT for those inches. I'm in quite a down mood today, really struggling.

JONESY DIARY ENTRY – 2 NOVEMBER 2011

What a prick of a day. (This is going to be a common entry.)

I still can't decide whether this is harder than or the same as the Tasman. Each day starts the same: either you think you'll enjoy it and you don't, but at least you're in a better frame of mind, or the day is a bitch.

I think we have to realise that yet again we are sneaking quietly across the back of this vast continent, if we think otherwise she'll chew us up.

Had a pretty good day today but there were a lot of downs. I dragged myself out of it by thinking of people (girls) back home – past, present and future, and devising a keynote in my head. Cas had a really down day. After 2.5 hours he said he had bad blisters so we made the decision to push on for another hour, put the tent up and treat them ... hopefully we will be treating them right from here on in.

I can't get over that I am skiing in just a thermal and jacket. It's freaking freezing though.

Bec let us know today that we are actually meant to be averaging 15 km/day not 12 km/day (for this first section) – we need to catch up and soon.

DAY FIVE

Being in a white-out is like skiing through a milky soup, kind of like avgolemono soup (that's for the Greeks) or chicken and sweet corn soup for everyone else. There is no horizon and it's very easy to get disorientated, some people have even felt motion sickness, as it plays on your sense of balance. It's eerie, silent and at times feels incredibly claustrophobic, as if the world was being sucked into a vacuum around us. For Jonesy it must have been really tough, but I didn't talk about it with him because I didn't want to put that notion in his head if he wasn't feeling it already.

Once again, we skied one behind the other. Skiing in front is much more difficult as the lead person is breaking new ground while the other follows in their tracks. We swapped the leads after every break. Having no point of reference other than staring at the compass can get really disorientating. After my first few leads,

I found it easier to set a bearing then keep my skis parallel, rather than staring at the compass the entire time. In theory, each ski should keep the other in check and if both are parallel, you should move in a straight line. We'd made compass mounts out of old sled runners from Matty's shed while we were in Iqaluit. The compass sat 30 centimetres in front of my belly button so that I didn't need to hold it and could have both hands on my ski poles.

Even though we were undertaking this expedition together, we were starting to feel the isolation of not being able to interact as much as we had on other trips. Most of the paddling we'd done together had been in a double kayak, where no matter what the conditions were like we were able to share a laugh and a chat. Same on bushwalks and in canyons. Down in Antarctica, both the wind and the distance between us made it difficult to chat. It was lonely and felt more like a solitary pursuit than a joint expedition. I wasn't going to count Polar Dude as my travel buddy, that's for sure. By the end of the fifth day, we'd done a much better job of managing our clothing and covered our biggest distance yet, a whopping 12.8 kilometres.

DAY SIX

Jonesy has never been the best sleeper, and the twenty-four hour light started really messing with his sleeping patterns. When our alarm went off on the sixth day, he looked absolutely exhausted, but we rolled out of bed and into the morning tasks, which by now had become routine. The visibility when we started hauling our sleds was slightly better – we could probably see about 40 metres ahead.

On the trail, Jonesy and I felt a responsibility towards one another when we were out leading and breaking a path. We were always trying to put in 110 per cent, not wanting to let one another down. I questioned whether I'd feel the same motivation to push so hard if I had been doing the expedition solo, like Aleks. I didn't think so. The motivation not to let my best mate down was a big driver. We were constantly distributing and redistributing weight between the sleds to ensure that we were travelling at the same speed for the same effort. I'm embarrassed to say how tempting it was to say nothing when I felt that Jonesy's sled was heavier than it should be. I never let it go on for more than a shift ... maybe two – but, honestly, never longer than that. It just wasn't right.

DAY SEVEN

The first day or two of the white-out was almost fun – it was something different and posed another challenge for us – but after three days in a row it was getting pretty tiring. Progress was slower, life in the tent was colder and navigation took much more concentration. None of it was helped by the fact that my stomach didn't feel right. Although we'd increased the calories we were eating for a few weeks leading up to the expedition, our bodies hadn't adjusted to the 6000 calories we were trying to consume. When I woke up on the seventh day I felt a bit funny, and tragically I had to abandon all the lessons I'd learnt over the previous few days and make a mad dash outside. We tried as best as we could to eat everything we were supposed to, but the calorie overload was a shock to our systems and gave us both massive, runny diarrhoea.

We were one week down and only 80 kilometres into a 2200 kilometre journey. My feet were aching, blisters on my heels stung, I had the runs and felt emotionally isolated. It was completely overwhelming and doubt started to creep into my thoughts. I couldn't help but question the enormity of what we were trying to do and how far we had to ski. I was really down. Each step had been so hard fought, so laborious, how the hell were we meant to keep plugging on for 6.6 million of them? (I figured this out in the first few days of trekking – three steps per metre multiplied by the 2,200,000 metres total distance.) It wasn't a good place for me to be so I tried to take comfort in the fact that if we could bumble through these steps, we'd be making history by completing the longest unsupported manhaul of all time. There is something incredibly motivating in working towards a goal with some real significance, albeit a little confronting. We would be travelling further than Fiennes, Stroud, Muir, Hillary ... It'd be putting our achievement right up there. My mantra for the rest of the day was 'make history', and it helped keep me focused.

I'd had a bit of a cold when we'd started the expedition, and with the exertion of the previous couple of days, it seemed to be getting worse. I was constantly coughing and spluttering as we plugged south under the drab, overcast sky. The cough wasn't annoying me too much; it was the runny nose that was the real nuisance. The snot clogged up my face mask and by the end of the day it froze on my face like armour. But it wasn't just the physical demands that were dragging us down, some of our communication from back home wasn't helping either. Satellite phones are a two-edged sword. On the plus side, they can facilitate the flow of vital information such as medical advice and weather updates, and speaking to family and friends back home often picked up our mood incredibly, if they said the right things. Unfortunately, without meaning to be, some people were absolutely terrible to speak to. Here's a tip: if you ever get a call from someone on an expedition, keep it light, cheerful and interesting. Is that so hard?

Some of the information that Bec passed on didn't do anything for our morale and was hard to deal with on the ice. One example was when a mate of ours who'd offered to do our website suddenly went quiet. The website was hugely important to our expedition because it was a way of keeping people informed and allowing them to feel they were part of our journey. Bec told us that the website wasn't being updated and that our mate wasn't returning her calls, emails or texts. The rational side of my brain was telling me not to worry and to focus all my attention solely on the mission at hand, but the other side of my brain was much more difficult to tame. Bec absorbed some of the website load even though she'd never done anything like it in her life. She started uploading photos, videos and kept Facebook and Twitter active while sending out the occasional e-newsletter. She told us she had it all under control to ensure we'd stop worrying. We just had to let it go.

DAY EIGHT

JONESY DIARY ENTRY – 6 NOVEMBER 2011

Scrap that last entry – today was tough.

There is so much snow falling as I write this. Outside we have about eight inches – one foot of snow has fallen and it's big fluffy powder. We're sinking in and making next to no progress. Today in seven hours and ten minutes, we made 9.5 kilometres. Pathetic, but it's all we can do ... just keep plugging away and not give up.

Dragging the sled when you're leading through this soft stuff is the hardest thing that you could possibly imagine – chafe, blisters, the feeling that you're crushing your insides – it's horrible. Why, oh why did we decide that this would be fun?

One thing that I spent a lot of time thinking about and it got me through a lot of the day was planning Cas's bucks night and wedding speech. I don't know if I'll be best man but I hope so.

Each morning was a bit like the expectation you had as a kid on Christmas morning imagining what presents would be waiting. We'd peel our sleeping masks off slowly and gingerly pick the earplugs out of our ears while anticipating what the day had in store. While our eyes took a bit of time to adjust to the bright yellow light inside the tent, our ears registered either a positive ('Mmm ... tent's not flapping, wind is less') or a negative ('Grrrr ... it sounds crazy out there') right away. On the eighth day, once my eyes began to focus, I realised there was a dull flat light coming through the tent, not the bright light that would've meant conditions outside had cleared. Damn! It was another day of white-out. When the sun is hidden by the clouds it makes -20° Celsius feel even colder than it sounds, and by the dull light I knew it was going to be one of those cold, wet days.

As we skied south into the gloomy white-out the snow kept falling and it was like it muffled and soundproofed everything. If we'd been sitting in a log cabin sipping tea, it would've been incredibly calming, almost meditative, to watch the snowflakes float through the air. But skiing through it is just heavy, brutal work. If I grunted or spoke it seemed so loud because everything else was so silent. Jonesy was out in the lead and as I drew up next to him after the second shift, I could hear aggressive desperation in his voice.

'Geez mate, is there any point to us travelling today? We're making less than 1.5 kilometres an hour.'

'What choice have we got?'

We did have a choice. We could set up the tent, stay inside and say conditions were too tough. But we both knew this was a loser's attitude and doing that would surely mean only a one-way trip to the South Pole. That's not what we were there for. If we wanted to have any chance of completing the return journey we had to keep on plugging away. We knew from Robert Scott's diary that he'd faced the same conditions and we knew we couldn't afford to give in:

> I never had such pulling; all the sledge rasps and creaks. We have covered six miles, but at fearful cost to ourselves ... Can we keep this up? It takes it out of us like anything. None of us have ever had such hard work before ... our chance still holds good if we can put the work in, but it's a terribly trying time.

Scott was right, it was a terribly trying time. After eight hours on the trail we stumbled around the tent securing the guylines and pegging out the vestibule. Jonesy started rambling on in a South African accent, like Leonardo DiCaprio in *Blood Diamond*. Jonesy has an incredible memory for movies and while he was acting as Danny Archer in one particular scene he delivered all the dialogue in his thickest Saffa accent:

Archer: 'T.I.A., right M'Ed?'

Maddy (to Archer): 'What's T.I.A.?'

Archer: 'This is Africa.'

'No, Jonesy, this is Antarctica!' I replied before laughing.

We'd found a phrase that stuck instantly. From then on anything unexpected that was thrown our way – bad weather, gear breaking, unexpected crevasse fields, strange infections – we'd dismissively shrug and say, 'Uh ... T.I.A. I guess.'

It was good to laugh for a change. We hadn't been doing much of that in these early days. Later, while the stove was roaring away, I caught Jonesy by surprise with a question that had been bothering me:

'Mate, if these conditions stick around for much longer and if it's looking like we can't ski all 2200 kilometres, what do you think is more important – reaching the South Pole or treating this expedition with the same attitude as the explorers a hundred years ago and just trying to push as far south as possible, then returning to the coast, even if that means falling short of the South Pole? Like Shackleton on the Nimrod expedition, who got to within 180 kilometres from the Pole and turned back.'

Jonesy thought for a moment. 'I assumed if things weren't looking good on the outward journey we'd just stop at the Pole like the other teams. But you're right, it's not like an ocean crossing between two land masses or standing on the highest point of a mountain, out here it's a GPS waypoint in the middle of nowhere. Pretty arbitrary, really. I reckon our goal was to get back to our start point in the true spirit of those pioneers a hundred years ago.'

The more we talked about it, the more passionate I became. I kept raving on until Jonesy reminded me that we *weren't* doing that, that we *were* going to make it to the Pole, and that we needed to sleep so we could get up the next day and keep going. I think we both drifted off full of new resolve that we hoped would last a while.

DAY NINE

JONESY DIARY ENTRY – 7 NOVEMBER 2011

What a f**ked up day. 7.2 kilometres in 7.5 hours. Spilt my hot chocolate everywhere. WTF.

On the trail today we had really bad conditions underfoot, so soft. Meant we moved at less than one km/hr – ARGHH!

Finding the motivation to get out of my toasty warm sleeping-bag and face the day ahead seemed to be getting harder and harder. I wondered if we'd ever see the sun again. I laboriously crawled out of the tent to go to the toilet and then somehow managed to poo on the side of my boot. Awesome! By the time I was done, it'd frozen solid. I tried in vain to wipe it off with snow, but the only way was to pour hot water on it and use a wet wipe to clean it up.

Normally, music helped when things started out badly, but without any sun for the previous five days we hadn't been able to charge our iPods, and we both knew they were going to die any minute. Sure enough, by the end of the first shift, both ran flat, which made the day go on forever. It was incredible how much listening to them helped with the monotonous slogging. Aleks had told us that he had four iPods with him because without them he'd go nuts. At least Jonesy and I had each other, but even then the silence could be deafening.

Our sleds were getting lighter as we were using up supplies, and in theory our bodies should've started adapting to being on the ice. But our progress was getting slower and the soft snow wasn't helping. And the sleds didn't *feel* any lighter, that's for sure. We were constantly straining in our harnesses, leaning so far forward it felt like we were trying to kiss the tips of our skis. Over the previous few days we'd been thinking of ways we could improve our speed. I suggested that we lighten up the lead sled to break trail, so that the heavy sled could trail behind in its track. It kind of helped, moving our average from just under one kilometre per hour to just over. It was really disheartening to make such slow progress, but emotionally I was doing okay at this point. Jonesy, on the other hand, seemed to be really struggling.

After doing eight hours on the trail, we erected our tent. Just as we started doing a sked, the sun broke through the clouds. It was the first time we'd seen it in almost a week! Our moods rose with the sun ... that is until Jonesy accidentally spilt his full mug of hot chocolate all over everything. He went berko. He was frothing at the mouth and punching the ground, which is a pretty extreme reaction to spilling a drink, and I think we both knew it wasn't the hot chocolate he was angry about.

DAY TEN

The sun was beaming under a blue sky when we woke, but our tent was shaking violently in the 50 kilometre per hour wind. We scoffed our oats saturated in dehydrated butter, and reluctantly put on our battle gear to face the windstorm outside. Even with the strength of the wind, so much snow had fallen over the past week that these gusts were having trouble blowing it away to reveal the more solid ice that was buried far beneath.

Jonesy seemed to be having a better day, so he took the initial lead and began to tear away from me from the start. I was struggling. I woke up with a headache, my body was feeling heavy, fragile and I was completely intimidated by the unrelenting gale. My goggles fogged up quickly and I tried yelling to Jonesy to slow down. He couldn't hear me above the roaring wind and failed to look back to see how I was doing. He just kept pulling away and I got more and more angry. By the time the end of the shift came he was a little black dot and it took me close to ten minutes to catch up to him. As I pulled up close I yelled angrily above the wind:

'Bloody hell, mate, bit irresponsible don't you think?' I spat out my words in a most irritated tone so he knew how pissed off I was.

'What do ya mean?' Jonesy replied.

'You haven't looked back in over forty minutes and I was battling big time. My sled's heavier than yours. What if I'd needed to stop? Tearing ahead in these conditions is bloody dangerous.'

Jonesy started yelling and was quite aggressive, hurling a whole heap of abuse at me about how his sled was still heavier than mine. It was our first real fight of the trip and meant we were both in a foul mood for the remainder of the day. By the time we got in the tent later we were still quite negative and short with one another. We'd managed to ski a measly eight kilometres and were beginning to feel beaten and sorry for ourselves.

Fighting is so oppressive. It's not like when you have a bad day at work or a disagreement with your boss and you can go home, have a bitch to your partner about it and leave the problem there. On a trip like this it affects the entire day – you can't escape the other person. We found if we didn't address the problem or, more to the point, put ego aside and just apologise, the negative mood lingered. After about half an hour of us both being pretty curt with one another in the tent, Jonesy apologised and pretty soon we were back to normal.

DAY ELEVEN

My cold was really starting to bug me. In the tent it was bearable, but on the trail it was a real nuisance. Unlike Jon Muir on his 1998 Icetrek expedition, it wasn't what I wanted. He'd had quite a bad flu, but seemed to revel in it, it added to the challenge apparently.

I wish I was that tough. Unfortunately, I'm a classic man-flu victim and without Mia around to offer me sympathy and a cup of tea I felt pretty sorry for myself. And this cold refused to go away – I guess skiing for eight hours a day in -20° Celsius temperatures wasn't exactly what the doctor would have ordered. The most annoying thing about my runny nose was the constant flow that leaked out under my face mask. We'd modified my goggles by sewing a fabric nose flap to them so I could blow my nose 'bushie' style and sort it out, which was fine, but when I wore the complete face mask the snot would run over my lips and pool near my chin before it leaked out and froze.

Jonesy and I were absolutely shattered by this point. Conditions on the trail had been marginally better, but the snow was still soft underfoot. By the end of our eleventh day of skiing my body was screaming with exhaustion and I was forced to set up camp on my knees. We'd been pushing hard for almost two weeks and I'd started thinking about the phrase Matty McNair had hammered into us while we were in Iqaluit: 'You need to eat before you get hungry, drink before you get thirsty, take off your jacket before you start sweating and stop before you burn up 80 per cent of your energy.'

Her wise words were haunting me. We were burning what felt like 180 per cent of our energy and still falling ridiculously behind schedule. The problem we faced was that if we wound back to the mythical 80 per cent figure we'd be staring at inevitable failure. This was the nature of the expedition we'd set ourselves, we were going to have to give 110 per cent the entire time. There was a reason other strong teams had failed. We always knew what we'd proposed was right on the boundary of human endurance – was it even possible? If the conditions we were experiencing continued, probably not. Only time would tell. What we needed to do at this point was to try to stay in the game.

It's all well and good to realise we were digging deep into our energy reserves, but to ski over 2000-odd kilometres over a three-month period, there needed to be an element of sustainability to what we were doing. I guess the 'art' of adventure is knowing where that zone of sustainability lies without having to go to the breaking point to know that you've gone too far. There are so many changing factors on an adventure that make it difficult to calculate whether you're too far short of your limit or whether by extending further than you thought possible, you'll discover new limits and personal boundaries that you never knew existed. You would never find these without pushing, and yet you have to find the line so that when you push yourself, you survive, and don't go too far.

Jonesy summed up our situation in his diary: 'We push too hard, we fail. We push too little, we fail.' We were both wrestling with our limits, and complicating this was the fact that we both had different breaking points. Every evening we hoped that the conditions would get a bit easier and that our bodies would start to settle into the battering they were receiving. And on a trip like this it wasn't just physical boundaries that we had to worry about, mental attitude was just as important. We were still bothered by our mate letting us down on the website and that night after all the critical info was run through during our nightly sked, Bec brought up the fact that she had been working longer hours than originally discussed and didn't feel that we were remunerating her fairly.

I understand that people need to be paid for their efforts. Jonesy and I had made a recent choice to become 'professional adventurers' and along with that decision came complications and challenges. We were no longer just two mates heading off for a weekend of climbing, canyoning or bushwalking, then going back to chat about what we'd done at the pub and regaling family or anyone else who cared to listen with our antics. Prior to our Tasman crossing, we were naïve amateurs trying to be 'professional', and everyone who was involved in that project was doing it because they believed in the pure adventure of the objective and the passion with which Jonesy and I pursued it.

Everything changed when we decided to attempt a big Antarctic expedition. In order to raise the funding to do so, we needed to get serious and pursue the path of professional adventurers. Ranulph Fiennes, the greatest living explorer according to the *Guinness Book of World Records*, was asked about his motivation for going on expeditions:

> Because it is my job. It's the way I make my income. It is a fact that the origin of it all was to make an income. Then I began to like it very much. I was fascinated by each problem and the knowledge that human beings hadn't solved this particular problem before.

And if that didn't make the purist in me squirm, how about this comment from Fiennes: 'I go on expeditions for the same reason an estate agent sells houses – to pay the bills.'

Fiennes accepted that money was important early in his career. Back in the Heroic Age of Antarctic Exploration, going on an expedition was a paid job. Scott offered Mawson not only the guarantee of being part of the final Pole party but also £800 payment (that's A$90,000 in today's terms) for two years' work – not bad considering the average wage at the time was the equivalent of A$17,000. I was conflicted about the marriage between finance and the purity of an adventure. To me, adventure is much more than a job; it's a lifestyle, an attitude towards living. Is it wrong to derive income from your passion? From pursuing exploration?

The key to any success is preparation. For us, preparing for Antarctica meant thirty hours a week of physical training. Tyre-dragging was key — it wasn't fun but it was the closest we could get to dragging a heavy sled.

P.O.W. = Pulk on Wheels. Sadly, epic fail.

LEFT: At the media launch of the Crossing the Ice expedition on a temporary ice rink outside Sydney's St Mary's Cathedral with two You Can patients. Thinking about young people like Jess and Tom and their battles with cancer provided a huge motivation for us to keep pushing in Antarctica.

BELOW LEFT: Trust me, Jonesy will eat anything when he is hungry.

This is what training in the snow in Australia looks like. Very different to the conditions we would face on the expedition. Mia was with me every step and even learnt to ski at the same time.

A training run in the Arctic:
all the food, fuel and provisions
needed to survive for a month.

ABOVE LEFT: Life inside our tent.
For three months it was our bedroom,
laundry, kitchen, bathroom, study.

RIGHT: Training on Baffin Island in
the Canadian Arctic Circle. Bit cold
for a swim, though! The air
temperature was −34 degrees Celsius.

Modifications to our equipment and clothes seemed never-ending. Here we are attaching skins to our skis and sewing fur ruff onto our shell jackets. The support that was offered to us by friends, family and via Facebook was incredible.

ABOVE: After four years preparation, the core team finally arrived in Punta Arenas, Chile, our launch pad for Antarctica: Bec, Jonesy, me, Gravy and Mia.

LEFT: Every food item needed to be repackaged, which saved us both time in Antarctica and 12 kilograms in wrappers.

RIGHT: Two tubby Aussies on the coast of Antarctica: I weighed 102 kilograms and Jonesy 106 kilograms. Moments later the Twin Otter left us and the silence was deafening.

RIGHT: Ploughing through deep soft snow, which was to become the longest, unbroken unsupported trail in polar history.

MIDDLE: Navigating off our compass. The compass holder we made in my parents' garage held up well in Antarctica.

Crossing a delicate snow bridge over a crevasse.

Pulling a 160-kilogram sled with a 80 kilometre per hour headwind tore our bodies apart.

LEFT: In the first month, the hoar frost on the tent walls and sleeping-bags made life miserable. Our only safe haven was inside the bags.

MIDDLE: Burying our Gateway Cache, I really didn't think we were ever going to see it again.

Tent life: Dehydrated ice-cream and drying a frozen balaclava.

Sastrugi.

Dear Cas & jonesy this is my encouragement for you:
"If life give you lemons you make Lemoade"
have a great trip from 4RB (Bobbi)

ABOVE LEFT: Cameron the Cache Marker at the Centenary Cache. He did a good job of protecting our food and fuel.

ABOVE RIGHT: The messages in our daily food bags from Aussie school kids were incredibly motivating and helped inspire us to not give up.

With any paid job, there are parts that you love and parts that you don't. Unfortunately, this was one such area I didn't want to deal with. I thought we'd settled on a remuneration package with Bec before we left and that Jonesy and I had been more than fair. I wasn't happy that she wanted to talk about it while we were sitting in a tent on the ice, 1000 kilometres from the South Pole; the discussion seemed to tarnish the pristine environment outside our tent. She knew what we were going through and how much energy was going into pushing out our pathetic mileage each day. Although Jonesy was doing the sked, I angrily snatched the phone off him and told Bec that it was something we couldn't deal with out on the ice. If she wanted to do less hours, she should do less hours.

DAY TWELVE

Our twelfth day saw us plugging away with next to no visibility and a nice brisk 25 kilometre per hour breeze in our face. Conditions underfoot still hadn't improved and our progress remained pitiful. My blisters were worse. They made me wince for the first five minutes after each break, but once I got going they didn't seem to slow me down. The weather was really wearing us down; the wind howled and the soft snow made each metre a battle. After our fifth seventy-five minute session, Jonesy was well and truly done in and I wasn't far behind.

I thought he'd lost it completely and was hallucinating when he yelled above the constant screaming of the windstorm, 'I think there's someone behind us.' The sudden sound of his voice broke the silence and caused me to lose my rhythm. It was ridiculous that he thought he could see a person between the ever-swirling snow drifts. I was sure Aleks had to be in front of us and no-one else was out there, right?

'Where?'

'Behind us, just over there,' Jonesy was like an excited kid but I was agitated that this was costing us skiing time.

I stared out towards where Jonesy's clumsy mitt was pointing, but couldn't see anything at first. Then, like a ghost in between the plumes of drifting snow I saw a shadowy outline for a brief second before it was hidden away by more snow.

It *was* a person! Was it Aleks? If so, how had we got *in front* of him? Seeing someone else out there was so unexpected and bizarre. For a moment, I questioned whether we'd both gone insane. The cold quickly put an end to us standing around talking about it. In order to keep warm we kept plugging on for another thirty minutes until quittin' time. When we stopped for the day, we thought we could see a red tent a few hundred metres behind us, but with the sun positioned as it was, it was difficult to tell.

We whacked up the tent nice and efficiently, but spent another ninety minutes outside building a snow wall on the windward side of the tent. During the previous night's sked, Steve had warned us that the wind was building and was likely to peak the next day at close to 90 kilometres per hour – a terrifying storm force. The last time we'd experienced wind with that ferocity we were strapped to the cabin floor of our kayak as we were thrown around in a ten-metre sea. Two-storey waves pushed the kayak under so we were completely submerged. The memory of that terrible night still haunts me. A wind this strong back home can snap an old-growth tree like a twig and rip the roof off a house. We were going to have to bunker down with only our tent between us and the extreme weather. I was scared. If our tent was damaged – or even worse, blown away – we wouldn't last long.

To build a wall, one of us cut blocks the size of a fruit box with the snow saw and the other started piling these blocks on top of each other. The ground in Antarctica is kind of similar to the consistency of styrofoam, and the jagged teeth of the saw slid through the snow efficiently – but at the end of a long day it was still exhausting work, and if we could have given it a miss we would have. When we'd finished, the wall stood as high and as wide as the tent. Inside we flopped down on our sleeping mats not able to move for a while.

Incredibly, because of the wall, the tent stood dead still and the fly didn't flap at all, even though on the outside of our little wall it was now roaring above 50 kilometres per hour. I felt pretty chuffed that our effort had been worth it and our wall had worked. We crossed our fingers that it'd hold up as the storm intensity built.

As I began stripping off my clothes, I noticed that my inner thighs were speckled black and blue with fluid building under the surface. That's weird? I needed to address this straightaway – we couldn't afford serious injury or infection to develop. We took a photo and sent it through to Dr Glenn, as well as to Dr John Apps, the doctor at Union Glacier. Both came back with a different diagnosis and different suggested treatments. Dr Glenn was sure it was chafe and was keen to treat it like any other chafe – reduce the friction by using Vaseline or Sudocrem (our old favourite from the Tasman, which we generously applied to our rumps multiple times each day). Dr John, however, was convinced it was a cold injury. Initially we agreed more with Dr Glenn because both Jonesy and I found it hard to believe that an area as well covered as my inner thigh could suffer from the surface of the skin freezing. One of our major goals of the expedition (apart from wanting to achieve the unsupported return journey and not returning home wanting to kill each other) was to avoid any cold injuries like frostbite, and to avoid blisters. With both these ailments we knew prevention was much better than trying to treat them on the trail, and with all our preparation there really was no excuse to 'waste' time having to manage issues such as these. We'd heard of other polar travellers sustaining nasty frostbitten *outer* thighs because of the cold wind hitting an area where there is not much padding between the skin and the outer garments. To combat this, we thought we'd been really smart in sewing PrimaLoft (kind of like synthetic down) patches onto the outer thigh area of our fleece pants to create a little more insulation. We'd never heard anything about the inner thigh! This type of cold injury wasn't common for explorers of yester-year because, back then, the clothing was looser fitting and their jackets often went down to their knees, which added more protection. We were walking into 90 kilometre per hour winds with only a thin layer of thermal, a layer of fleece and a GoreTex outer shell. It obviously wasn't enough.

I coated my legs with Sudocrem and then Jonesy and I went about making dinner and getting settled in. Even though the tent was still, the howling wind never stopped. We could hear it roaring and with the knowledge that it was expected to build to hurricane force, combined with the way we were feeling, it wasn't a tough decision to make the call that Day Thirteen would be our first rest day. After our sked, we called Aleks's satellite phone and were surprised when he told us it *was* him behind us. Somehow we'd passed him in poor visibility and hadn't realised. Judging from his tone, he wasn't too happy about it, but we didn't ask too much about why, we didn't have to. Aleks may have had much more experience on skis but it definitely wasn't easy skiing in the current conditions so he would have been battling as much as we had been.

DAY THIRTEEN

Ah ... the sweet bliss of being able to stay tucked in our sleeping-bags and not having to get out of the tent. We were both obviously exhausted because we didn't stir until 10 am. The sun was beating down on our tent, and with the snow wall funnelling the wind around us it seemed like a nice day outside – but when I popped my head out the rear vestibule, my beanie almost got ripped off from the blast! I didn't know if Aleks was still around, but I wasn't going to be able to check. We spent most of the day dozing, watching some movies on our iPods and drinking cups of tea. We also decided it'd be a good day to dump our first cache.

Our initial strategy was to dump four lots of six days worth of food and fuel on the outward journey at latitudes 82, 84, 86 and 88 degrees south (about 230 kilometres apart). Assuming the journey to the South Pole took fifty days, this would give us a tight thirty days' food and fuel to get back to the coast. Feeling the weight of every gram on our sleds on the soft snow, we made the call to drop three days' food and fuel weighing almost ten kilograms, earlier than planned. By mid-afternoon the wind had died down, so we used snow blocks from our wall to build a pyramid, which we topped with an orange flag. We buried our provisions beneath and named it the Hidden Cache, because it was unplanned.

Trying to calculate how much food to leave and the timings of the drops was one of the challenges of making the return journey. The implications of the decisions we made now could impact on our survival in a few months, just as they had for Robert Scott. The more we left now, the lighter our sleds would be and the faster we'd move, but if we left too much we'd run out and not have enough to get back. It was a critical decision and one I hoped we wouldn't regret like Scott had.

After spending a day resting in the tent, we both felt revitalised physically and mentally and all was looking up, until our sked with Bec. We were on the sat-phone for sixty minutes dealing with still more issues: the website, the ongoing challenge of balancing Bec's work hours and other requests from sponsors. By the time we'd finished, we were both over it. We needed all the help we could get for such a huge expedition and I was thankful to everyone who supported us, but sometimes I wished that all we had to concentrate on was the mission itself.

DAY FOURTEEN

The good vibes from our rest break had completely evaporated by the time we woke. We both had an atrocious night's sleep, due to a combination of our bodies being used to the exercise and the stress of what was going on back home with our support team. The operational pressures were really affecting us. Four years before when we'd been on the Tasman, Captain Pat had kept us insulated from operational challenges, like sponsor requests, and media and stakeholder issues that popped up when we were at sea. In a weird kind of way, Pat was like a gander fiercely protecting his gosling at a pond, something we'd only really started to appreciate since we'd been in Antarctica.

The moment I stuck my head out the tent door I cringed and sunk back into my sleeping-bag for a few more minutes. It was snowing heavily causing a complete white-out, and adding to the nastiness was a headwind blowing 70 kilometres per hour. We got ourselves ready with full face masks to combat the vicious conditions, only to find our goggles fogging up within the first half-hour on the trail. Because of the snow, conditions were 'wet' and before the end of the first shift my goggles were completely frozen over except for a tiny pinprick clearing in the bottom left-hand corner. Jonesy's were much the same.

I've always been a pretty positive person. Most of my mates and family would call me an optimist, but I wasn't then and hadn't been for weeks. I was carrying a lot of negativity and my outlook remained dark. Reading through my diary entries makes me cringe and I have to ask myself, 'Was it really that bad? Why didn't I write about the fun or the beauty or some of the more positive experiences?' The truth is, there was nothing positive about these early weeks. It was grim and brutal and if we weren't stuck in one of the most isolated places on earth, I think we would have found a very fair excuse to call an end to the expedition. At this low point, for the first time in my life, I felt that I was getting a glimpse of what depression must feel like. In the past, I'd been pretty dismissive of this mental illness. I had a 'c'mon mate, chin up, life's not that bad, just smell the roses' attitude. What a wanker! I can see now how insensitive that was. The oppressive white-out and the feeling of isolation and futility in what we were doing was seeping into all aspects of my being. It was totally consuming me. I was experiencing the same depression polar explorer Apsley Cherry-Garrard described in his account of the Terra Nova expedition:

It is curious to see how depressed all our diaries become when this bad weather obtained, and how quickly we must have cheered up whenever the sun came out.

The tops of my thighs hadn't responded to the balm and we both knew now that we were carrying cold injuries on our legs and our sides and I had a huge ulcer on my lip which I kept biting. It made eating even more unpleasant and meant another part of my body was aching. To make matters worse, the edges of our Therm-a-Rests had developed slow leaks from being pressed against the heat shield around the stove. We didn't have time to repair the leaks so that meant we'd be getting up every couple of hours to blow air into them. Jonesy's diary summed up how we were feeling as we drifted off to sleep:

> **As I lie here the sound of snow falling against the tent attempts to lull me to sleep. So soft, so innocent and yet the very bane of our existence. This weather is killing our trip ... got the weather update and yep, it was shit again. We have at least another two days of this!**

DAY FIFTEEN

The alarm buzzed, and we got ourselves ready to face another ruthless day similar to the day before. Strong winds and zero visibility. Every little task inside the tent was proving harder due to the fact that I now had pus-exploding cuticles that were very sensitive. I think having worn latex gloves to keep the sweat from penetrating our insulated gloves was the cause of this most recent problem. It was a typical case of addressing one issue and causing another, and it seemed to be happening often. T.I.A., I guess.

It was a massive grind of a day and after nine miserable hours slogging south, we only had 10.2 kilometres to show for it. We'd been out there for two weeks and for ten of those days we'd had to face white-outs and blizzards. The biggest shame was that we'd now passed the grandiose Patriot Hills mountain range (which was apparently quite beautiful), but we'd seen nothing, just endless white – like swimming through a bowl of milk. If the weather did clear up (and it didn't feel like it would) all we'd see now would be endless plains of nothingness until we were halfway to the Pole and got close to the Thiel Mountains. I had my fingers crossed that we wouldn't still be marching in a white-out at that stage. Scott described a white-out in his diary of 26 November 1911:

It is always rather dismal work walking over the great snow plain when sky and surface merge into one pall of dead whiteness.

In the tent, we hung up our day's clothing, which were frozen at first, then dripping wet once they thawed. It was strange being inside a tent no bigger than a single bed and not being able to see each other among all the wet clothing hanging from our line. It was almost like being in a rainforest with vines hanging down. After our sked, we asked whether we could have a chat with Steve, the operations manager for the Union Glacier Base, to see if he could give us some advice on how we could improve our progress.

'Hello boys, the conditions you are experiencing are atrocious. How you feeling?' It was good to hear his voice but I wasn't going to beat around the bush.

'Absolutely buggered,' I replied. 'Is this weather normal?'

Steve jumped in positively, 'Not at all. This is the worst weather in November I have ever experienced, it's very unseasonal. Looking at the hours you're doing and the progress you're making, you're doing great. I think your strategy is spot on, just try not to burn too much energy. Summer is on its way, and when it comes you'll need every ounce of reserves then. The biggest thing I'm actually worried about is the state of your inner thighs. You really need to stay right on top of them and do everything you can to avoid them getting infected. Injuries like the ones you are carrying have ended more than one expedition in the past.'

Taking some comfort from his encouragement I asked, 'Have you got any ideas on how we can improve our progress?'

'No … not really. I know it probably doesn't feel like it, but you're doing a great job. Many other teams would've quit by now but you guys are sticking with it. Just keep plugging away.'

We hung up the sat-phone and took some consolation in knowing that even though we felt like crap and our progress was abysmal, we were actually doing alright.

DAY SIXTEEN

The morning of the sixteenth day had me cursing our expedition again. The zippers on the tent's inside fly had frozen while we were sleeping and when I'd worked up the courage to go outside, I realised I was stuck inside the tent. In a drowsy state, Jonesy came up with the brilliant idea of placing the stove close to the tent wall to unfreeze the zip. Unfortunately, tents are made of highly flammable material and the heat of the stove burnt a hole in the tent door in an instant. Seeing the hole quickly grow was like being slapped in the face with a wet fish. It was incredibly stupid! One of the big dangers we faced was a tent fire and here we were starting one willingly. Damaging or destroying our tent was my worst nightmare and it almost came to life. Without shelter and protection from the elements we'd be dead as soon as we stopped moving. Fortunately, the hole was only the size of a fist, and there was one plus: the heat had unfrozen the zip.

Over the previous two weeks we'd learnt the lesson that sled hauling today is as brutal as it was a hundred years ago. We had the blisters, aching muscles and cold injuries to prove it. Satellite phones and fancy technology are no help with pulling a heavy sled.

In fact, with these constant white-outs, even if we'd hit the EPIRB (a device the size of a mobile phone that you activate when there is a serious emergency), nobody would have been able to reach us. The ground conditions meant no plane, helicopter or rescue crew were coming if there was an emergency. It was sobering to know we were completely on our own.

On top of the white-out rendering our vision pretty useless, the terrain we were hauling over was not just a flat snow-covered surface like an ice rink, it was closer to a four-wheel drive track. It's hard enough just trying to move an inch in those conditions, let alone with a huge sled behind you. The bitter, unrelenting headwinds gouged the surface of the ground and formed long, deep grooves and ridges called sastrugi – the infamous and dreaded sastrugi. Travelling on the irregular surface formed by these icy ridges of windblown snow can be very tiring, and it increases the risk of breaking equipment – often these ripples and waves are undercut and the surface is hard and unforgiving. Imagine walking over the peaks and down into the valleys of a gigantic lemon-meringue pie, that is kind of what sastrugi look like. These fields slowed our progress even further (which hardly seemed possible) like natural speed bumps. If the sun had been out and we weren't each dragging a 150 kilogram sled behind us, we might have enjoyed the experience and marvelled at some of the truly magnificent shapes that the sastrugi took on, like pipeline waves on the ocean moments before they're about to break. For now though, in the white-out, we could not make out these contours and it often meant our skis would hit a knee-high wave of ice and either stop abruptly or cause us to lose our balance and fall over. The tips of our skis and poles became like the tentacles of an octopus, helping us to feel our way forward.

By midday we'd averaged just under one kilometre per hour, slower than a nine-month old baby crawling along a floor. Pathetic!

The amount of energy we were expending for the mileage we were covering was soul destroying. After standing around for a few minutes getting cold and talking about whether our efforts were futile, we justified to ourselves that our time was better spent addressing some of the repairs that were piling up. After only three hours hauling and 2.9 kilometres progress, we set up the tent feeling beaten. No amount of coaxing covered up the feeling of having given up too early. I felt terrible.

The amount of time we were spending repairing broken equipment and tending to our bodies was steadily increasing and some of the non-critical repairs had started to bank up. We spent the afternoon addressing these and although repairing gear took away from rest time, there was something really enjoyable about it. I think it was the resourcefulness of looking at a problem, laying out the limited spares and tools that we had and figuring out a way to fix it. Jonesy seemed to enjoy sewing more than I did and I was better with 'hardware' problems like broken ski poles, holes in sleeping mats, issues with the stove, etc. He sewed a patch over the hole in the tent door, which took close to 1.5 hours, while I splinted a broken tent pole and plugged up the hole in my leaking Therm-a-Rest. In preparing for the Tasman, our electrical engineer drummed into us that the success of the expedition was more an exercise in maintaining our systems and equipment than paddling. This approach saw us repairing every piece of gear that showed signs of wear and tear when we first became aware of it, and that same attitude needed to be applied on the ice.

I spoke to Mia after our sked and the wisdom and encouragement she passed on was motivating. I'm not sure how she was doing it, but she seemed to know the exact thing to say to make me feel better. Over the previous weeks there had been times when I'd needed her to tell me to 'just harden up', and other times she must've heard in my voice the need for sympathy. After hanging up the phone, I decided that we'd quit too early that day and I told myself that I didn't want to have that thought again for the rest of our time on the ice.

DAY SEVENTEEN

When we woke up on the morning of the seventeenth day, the inside of the tent seemed brighter than usual and we couldn't hear the wind. Before I even lit the stove, Jonesy unzipped the rear vestibule to check the conditions and sang out, 'Wahoo, it's blue sky outside!' We hadn't had a sunny, low wind day since Day Two, which was over two weeks before. We were stoked.

We packed the tent in high spirits and got on the trail quickly. Unfortunately, the friendly weather hadn't changed the conditions underfoot and progress remained slow. I took the first lead, and as Jonesy pulled up to me after the first shift he said out of nowhere, 'I nearly had an orgasm!'

'What?!' I laughed, half-thinking he meant he was excited about the good weather.

'For some reason the way these PrimaLoft pants were rubbing on my old fella was different and while I was skiing I almost ... well ...'

I couldn't stop giggling as we shovelled snacks down in our ten-minute break.

After Mia setting me straight the night before, I really tried to judge the day's performance not by the miles that we covered, but by the quality of the hours we slogged out on the trail. Giving it everything we had for nine hours, even though our progress remained pitiful in the soft snow, was liberating. At last I started to feel a sense of accomplishment. We finished the day 9.4 kilometres closer to the South Pole and didn't have to deal with crazy winds or a white-out. So all in all, it was a pretty good day (and almost a really good day for Jonesy!).

When we were settled in our tent, Jonesy called a good mate of ours, Turnbull. He was so excited to hear from us and couldn't believe we were calling from Antarctica. His obvious joy to talk to us really cheered Jonesy up and put him in a good mood for the rest of the evening. Small things like this made all the difference to our morale and our progress.

DAY EIGHTEEN

JONESY DIARY ENTRY – 16 NOVEMBER 2011

We are running out of time and if the ground doesn't freeze we will battle to even do a one-way to the Pole. F**cking low ...

Four years ago, we found ourselves smack bang in the middle of the Tasman Sea, stuck in a giant whirlpool going round in circles for fourteen days. Up until then, we'd had some trying times but our progress had been solid. The frustration of the current and headwinds conspiring to block our passage to New Zealand was devastating. It wasn't so much the obstacle blocking our path that destroyed our morale, it was the feeling of helplessness. 'What to do?' we kept asking ourselves. It was an intimidating feeling knowing that the toils of our efforts made no impact on getting us closer to New Zealand. There were days where we'd paddle for twelve hours and make a minuscule ten kilometres progress, only to drift backwards for 30 kilometres during the night. Out of pure desperation, we made the call to paddle 150 kilometres back towards Australia – using the currents and wind to our advantage – and then come back for another shot having positioned ourselves further south. It worked, and a month later we came ashore on a New Zealand beach.

A similar feeling of helplessness was gripping us now, but it was far worse because we didn't have the luxury of being able to paddle our way out of our situation. We were down to two options: keep pushing on regardless of our progress or wait for conditions to improve, which would commit us to failure. I've always felt in control of my life and destiny, through discipline and hard work I can get through anything. But this was different. I found it hard to accept that we weren't in control of the situation, and it was Antarctica that was calling the shots and dictating whether we were to succeed or fail.

I was struggling with this vulnerability, and the fact that Jonesy was stronger than me on the ice started to niggle again. Thanks to our six months of training, I at least had dealt with this before, but now it was more than ego that was being affected. I just didn't know how far to push myself and I couldn't use Jonesy as a marker. In the past, I knew that my breaking point was well beyond other people's. I've been the one waiting for others to catch up, taking weight from their pack or offering them some extra food or clothing. Now, being the weaker one, I didn't know how to gauge where my boundaries were, and how hard to push. I was the weakest link holding us back. I found it tough to accept this, knowing that when I was spent at the end of the day, Jonesy probably could've kept going. His sled was heavier and yet I was moving slower and holding him back. It wasn't good, and mentally it started to work me over and make me resent Jonesy. Not a good thing when it was just the two of us, a whole lot of ice and a long way to go.

The skin on my frost blisters started to scab and some bled. Steve had warned us about this and I had to do everything I could to avoid an infection, forcing me to spend twenty minutes ensuring the wounds were clean and the dressings were doing their job. Although they looked hideous they weren't too painful, but with our limited provisions of antiseptic cream there was the risk they could get really bad really quickly if I wasn't careful. As I was washing my underarms with warm, soapy water, Jonesy read out the day's total mileage, ten kilometres in nine hours of skiing. I blurted out what I was really thinking:

'I hate this place.'

As soon as I said it I wished I hadn't. It wasn't fair on Jonesy. I stared up at a quote written on our tent wall that said, 'Treat each other with respect, and no whining!' Too late. I knew better than to whinge like a little brat and I apologised, but the damage had been done. That night morale was low and I was stuck in my head thinking negative thoughts and wishing I was anywhere in the world but in a cramped tent in Antarctica.

DAY NINETEEN

Just before I'd gone to sleep, I told myself I had to wake up with a different attitude. On Day Nineteen I opened my eyes before the alarm had a chance to shake me from my slumber, and enjoyed lying there in my fluffy, warm sleeping-bag for a few moments, mentally preparing for the day ahead. Conditions underfoot probably hadn't changed much but at least the weather sounded less hostile. Two hours after the alarm buzzed, we shouldered our harnesses and set off on a bearing of 130 degrees. I should explain. The Magnetic South Pole is different from the Geographic South Pole, the one we were marching towards at latitude 90 degrees south, longitude zero degrees. Unfortunately, compasses don't point to the Geographic South Pole and that required us to take into account close to

50 degrees of magnetic deviation and ski on a bearing of 130 degrees. The South Magnetic Pole is constantly shifting due to changes in the earth's magnetic field. It's currently bouncing around mid-way between Adelaide and Antarctica and is expected to reach Australia sometime in the next couple of hundred years. This is predominantly due to polar drift. Interestingly, Aussie polar explorer Sir Douglas Mawson led the first expedition to reach the Magnetic South Pole on Shackleton's 1907 Nimrod expedition, which at the time sat well and truly on the Antarctic continent.

From the moment we started out that day my sled was a real pig, and all my good intentions about staying positive were immediately forgotten. It seemed to have a mind of its own and kept pulling to the left like an excited dog searching for a good tree to pee on. Apart from it pulling on my back awkwardly, it was also making hauling heaps more difficult because it was going off course and ploughing through the virgin snow on either side of our ski tracks. Initially I thought the root of the problem was my harness, but after jiggling and looking at it I realised that wasn't the issue, it was the sled. I couldn't work out why. After about an hour of being completely frustrated by the situation, I decided to move some of the load inside the sled from one side to the other. Bingo! Problem solved. In packing the sled we needed to ensure that most of the heavy items were down the bottom to help prevent the sled toppling over on the rough sastrugi, but I had now learnt the hard way that we had to be mindful of the weight distribution from side-to-side as well.

It'd taken me until this point, but I'd just started to be able to consume all 6000 calories that we needed each day. Jonesy had been inhaling his daily provisions for a couple of weeks, but the breakfasts and dinners had been defeating me and I'd been giving a decent cup's worth to Jonesy who would happily finish them off for me. That didn't surprise me. On expeditions, food has often been a massive motivator for Jonesy. Whether it was scoffing food during the breaks on a bushwalk or dreaming of the piles of food he'd eat when we returned, food is pretty much always at the forefront of his mind. Today he told me he'd spent a good few hours designing recipes and had been dreaming of food all day. Fortunately I hadn't had any similar cravings yet.

DAY TWENTY

CAS DIARY ENTRY – 18 NOVEMBER 2011

And we just keep plugging away – more like grinding actually. It's not pretty, enjoyable or meditative like paddling – it's just hard. Had a wig-out where I questioned everything today – is it our fault? Our sleds? Our fitness? Not pushing hard enough? For the first half of the day I really battled … Spoke to Meez tonight – her advice is always so wise and supportive – 'I am so proud of you and just want you to do your eight hours a day and stay positive.' First fifteen minutes before we get up is the hardest! Still haven't figured out whether it's better to have face to the wind or bum to the wind when going to the toilet. With the progress we're making, just can't see how we can be thinking about the return journey – I'm scared of failure. I'm scared of letting our stakeholders down. I hate the thought of not achieving what we set out to do. But I'm also accepting of it. We have done the preparation and are doing everything we could be asked to do. Although knee is holding up – it gets sorest at end of day and walking around camp. So sick of goggles fogging up! They dry nicely when you put them up top of sled. Fur ruffs on hood and mitts are frozen.

Had a really low morning, almost felt like I was about to break.

Soft snow again is killing us.

Just made 11 km.

Talked to Mum and Dad and Mia.

Achilles aching, ankles starting to hurt.

Need a break.

Mexican Chicken.

Things were looking bleak. Our daily average was sitting at approximately 9.5 kilometres, which meant we'd only covered 180 kilometres over the previous three weeks – that's half the distance we planned for in our worst-case scenario. I'm a bad loser. I don't readily accept failure. I'm not one to indulge in excuses and am quite a harsh judge on myself and others. And this was really pissing me off. All our effort counted for nothing. And it wasn't just me I was worried about. Because of the 'professional' nature of this expedition, I was feeling an enormous pressure not to let down the people who had put their faith in us and helped pay our way. When adventure is a hobby, you head out and the objective is to have an adventure, a pursuit with an unknown outcome. However, this expedition was different. Jonesy and I had stakeholders who had backed us emotionally and financially, and with their time as well. Some were investing in a successful outcome, and the way things were going they weren't going to get one. With a company, management have a responsibility to provide an adequate financial return to shareholders and regardless of their good intentions or effort, if they fall short of expectations they are dragged through the coals. Same with professional sportspeople – if they're not scoring goals or hitting runs, they're outta there. I was feeling this same accountability. Without their funds and investment in us, we'd be doing bushwalks in the Blue Mountains or paddling along the east coast of Australia. I was having trouble accepting that no matter what we did, it looked to me like we wouldn't meet their expectations, let alone our own. Feeling this pressure can be (and has been) a fatal attitude while on an adventure. Without naming individual polar expeditions, there have been a number of elaborate stories fabricated throughout history that have been used to justify failure. Others have pushed too far past their limits, losing their lives because the pressure became too much – I didn't want to do the same.

Perhaps one of the most spectacular examples of this kind of pressure was evident back in 1968 when the *Sunday Times* in London put £5000 up for grabs for the first person to sail single-handed and non-stop around the world. One of the entrants, Donald Crowhurst, a businessman with financial woes, set off ill-prepared and encountered immediate problems with his boat, his equipment and his lack of ocean-sailing skills and experience. In the first few weeks he was making less than half of his planned speed. He didn't have the skill to sail the complex tri-hulled boat at anything near its optimum speed while navigating a course to reach his circumnavigation waypoints. According to his logs, he gave himself only 50/50 odds of surviving the trip. Crowhurst had to choose whether to quit the race and face financial ruin and humiliation, or continue into the treacherous Southern Ocean to an almost certain death in his unseaworthy, unsafe boat. Over the course of November and December 1968, the hopelessness of his situation pushed him into an elaborate deception. He shut down his radio, planning to drift in the South Atlantic for several months (while the other boats sailed the Southern Ocean), falsify his navigation logs, then slip back in for the return leg to England. Finishing in last place, he assumed his false logs would not receive the scrutiny of the winner's. For a time it looked like his plan might have worked, but the pressure and shame became too much and he ended his life by jumping off the back of his yacht.

Having read this story prior to our Tasman crossing, I could never fathom what would be going through the mind of such a man. I'd dismissed Donald Crowhurst as insane. But now I could feel the creep of understanding. Pride can make you do many things. Using the excuse that the weather was unseasonably bad or that I simply wasn't tough enough to achieve what we set out to do seemed like pitifully inadequate excuses for failure. As I took each painful, grinding step forward, knowing that somewhere Aleks Gamme was doing the same but with more skill on his skis, my mind started to run away from reality. I felt a shame coming over me – perhaps we couldn't do it, and maybe this Norwegian could. What elaborate story could we manufacture to lessen the harsh judgment of others? I slogged on slowly under clear skies and into a 20 kilometre per hour headwind until I realised what I was doing – I was making excuses.

I felt angry at where my thoughts were taking me and had to get back to basics. Both mine and Jonesy's goggles were fogging up constantly, but we'd figured out a couple of ways to semi-unfog/ unfreeze them. The first method was to tuck them into our shell jacket with the outside lenses of the goggles touching our thermals (for some reason if they are the other way round it didn't work), the second was to place them under the yellow sled cover directly facing the sun (with the sun now higher in the sky this became more effective). Both methods took about an hour to de-fog the goggles and the job was enough to distract me from my Donald Crowhurst madness.

The soft snow was making every part of our bodies work harder. We had to lean so far forward in our harnesses to plough through that it aggravated Jonesy's Achilles heels, which caused him a heap of grief. I was glad my knee was holding up but the conditions meant I felt a twinge every now and then that was enough to worry me. The whole experience at this point was f★★ked.

DAY TWENTY-ONE

What a difference a day can make!

CAS DIARY ENTRY – 19 NOVEMBER 2011

Record day! It just goes to show that when conditions are firm we CAN make the miles! My spirits were booming all day, it felt so good to be skiing for the first time this trip. In hindsight, it's actually been a beautiful thing to see Antarctica slowly move into summer. Conditions are now almost bordering on pleasant in the tent, on the trail and during the breaks (today we actually had a break where we didn't put our down jackets on!). After the second shift I said to JJ, 'Why don't we aim for nine hours skiing today?'

Jonesy had the shits big time today. He had been struggling to keep up during the second shift. He had a bit of a whinge about his sled being heavier (which it is by about five kilos) and that I never thank him for carrying more weight. We then swapped sleds for his last shift and I made a real effort to stick on his bum for the entire hundred minutes, which actually wasn't too hard 'cause there isn't too much difference in the two sleds' weights. I think the point was made that it was more him being tired and in a shitty mood rather than it being the weight. We gave each other a cuddle at the end of the day and made up.

Were on the trail from 9 am to 7 pm ... big day but gotta get used to it. If we wanna do the return we gotta start pushing now – can we push for two months? I don't know, but the way I'm feeling today is that I want to go all fifteen rounds.

JONESY DIARY ENTRY – 19 NOVEMBER 2011

What a great day in terms of mileage ... we made 19.8 km – WTF! That is almost double what we've been averaging.

It started off interestingly with me singing Beyonce to Cas, as per Mia's instructions. [*Note from Cas: Yes, it was 'All the Single Ladies', and yes, he did do the dance as well.*] We packed up, cooked breakfast – always takes ages to make. Spilt fuel in the tent – Cas was pouring way too quick.

Nine-hour day. On the trail the surface was increasingly firm and Cas set off with a cracking pace. I could barely keep up all day. I think he forgets or takes for granted that my sled is much heavier, anyhow we pressed on.

This trip is DO-ABLE!! If we make 10 nm to 82 deg we'll be there in two more days!

Had a major argument with Cas at the last break.

I hate it how I have to say sorry first. He's *never* wrong.

DAY TWENTY-TWO

After our great progress the day before, we were all fired up to attack while these good conditions lasted, and there was a sense of excitement and urgency as we packed up the tent and sleds. We were hoping that if the conditions were the same we could ski for an extra hour and try to smash our daily mileage record.

We should've stayed in bed! Somehow, during the night, the ground had gone from firm to slushy and soft. Our skis were sinking down fifteen centimetres into the snow, and our sleds ploughed deeply. Adding to the confusion of it all was the fact that weather conditions weren't too different from the day before. Sure, the wind had picked up a little and was probably blowing 40 kilometres per hour for most of the morning, but the clear blue skies were very similar. We were both devastated. Without mentioning it to one another, we knew we were teetering on a very fine line, with the return only just being possible. A few more crap days and we'd be forced to concede defeat and either turn back before reaching the Pole or commit to a one-way journey. If the conditions improved it was still *maybe* possible that we could attempt the full return, but only just.

As we slogged on through soft snow drifts, I started planning my wedding speech. It was crazy to think that within a few weeks of leaving this desolate frozen continent we'd be in Thailand celebrating my wedding. I let my mind roam and allowed myself the indulgence of visualising hot sand pressing up between my toes, suffocatingly humid air filling my lungs and the freedom of not having to wear gloves … ah, the warmth. I could almost smell the Singha lager when I was snapped back to reality and realised Jonesy was getting too far ahead. After catching up to the rear of his sled, I went back to thinking about my wedding speech. What is it that I love about Mia? Seems like a silly question to be asking about the woman you're about to marry, but actually pinpointing individual traits and parts of her personality that are unique (and trying to avoid all that clichéd corny stuff) proved harder than I expected. I guess it's like seeing a Ferrari drive down the road and saying, 'Wow, nice car,' without actually thinking about what makes it so special. I really enjoyed playing this game and knew one of the biggest challenges was going to be remembering the things I came up with so I could write them in my diary later that evening.

After I was all Mia'd out (oops ... I might get in trouble for that one), I started thinking about Mum, the other most important lady in my life. If it hadn't been for her constant belief in me there is no way I would've found myself down here on such an expedition. Throughout my life she was always in my corner – like when my fifth grade teacher told her that if she didn't take me out of school as soon as I was old enough and enrol me in a trade, I'd end up in prison. Mum not only rejected his advice, she continued to believe in me. Whether she was patiently teaching me my nine-times table on our way to diving lessons or helping us modify our gear for this trip, she was always there supporting whatever I did. Thinking about how much of a pivotal role she'd played in my life made me cry under my goggles, but also made me put in that little bit of extra effort. For some reason, Antarctica was making me much more emotional than normal. Not much fun for Jonesy, that's for sure.

DAY TWENTY-THREE

A really bad night's sleep taints everything. The sled covers and tent fly were flapping wildly in the wind and even with earplugs jammed in as deep as they'd go, the noise *still* kept me awake. The alarm went berko at 6.30 am and although we both wanted to sleep in, we managed to slowly extract ourselves from our sleeping-bags and light the stove. Those first couple of minutes each day, before we had the stove roaring and cups of tea in our hands, just weren't getting easier. Even in the twelve measly hours we were camped in one spot, it was crazy how the wind-whipped snow buried our sleds and the structure of our tent caused long, dainty, finger-like plumes on the downwind side of the fly. My first duty outside the tent each morning was to dig out the sleds and bring them up alongside the rear door vestibule to make the process of packing them a smidgen faster.

The strong winds of the previous few days had carved some interesting sastrugi into the icy surface. This meant there were beautiful shapes to look at once we got underway for the day, but the chopped-up surface wasn't so pleasant to haul our sleds over. It felt like we were hauling through a potato field. The sled constantly got caught on the knee-high bumps and mounds that made for very jerky progress. It also meant that we had to concentrate on carefully placing each ski to avoid falling over. The wind continued to build throughout the morning and we were forced to wear our full face-mask system, hoods up, heads down as we plodded forward. Even though we weren't feeling too much stronger, we'd built up the days to six ninety-minute sessions, which is three hours more skiing than we were doing at the beginning of the journey. I felt much better about that!

After yet another tough day on the trail, I gave Mia a call. She'd had a really bad day at work and though she tried to hide it at first, she started crying. All I wanted to do was comfort her but I couldn't because I was in a tent in the middle of Antarctica. The normal world seemed so far away and, for Jonesy and me, reality was focused on the weather and staying alive. Explorers before us, like renowned Australian naturalist Charles Laseron, knew this feeling of alienation well and wrote about it in his book, *South with Mawson*:

> Day by day the outside world faded further from our thoughts. It was indeed hard to imagine we had ever been puppets tied to the routine of cities. Even thoughts of home came as memories of a remote past. We lived in a world of our own, a primitive world, in which the only standards were efficiency and utility.

Back home, though, life was going on as normal and it was hard trying to keep up with it all from the other end of a phone line. We craved to hear all the little details that we would completely disregard if we'd been at home. I was desperate to hear about Mia's regular daily life, and – not for the first time – I found myself asking, 'So, what did you have for breakfast?' I just felt so alone, I might as well have been on Pluto, and the thought of English Breakfast tea and Vegemite on toast was somehow incredibly comforting.

DAY TWENTY-FOUR

CAS DIARY ENTRY – 22 NOVEMBER 2011

We finally made it to our planned cache destination at 82 degrees. Woohoo! We're both absolutely buggered and I've developed bad chafe on my balls and groin. It made me limp all day. The sad thing is that conditions were pretty good today and we still made crap mileage. I'm feeling very doubtful that we're going to make it back here. The way we're going, we'll be lucky to reach the South Pole. I'm missing Meez and family more than climbing – eighty-day expeditions are very long. For the Tasman, we were prepared for thirty-five to forty days – this trip is definitely a different league. It's quite lonely too; hours on the trail are like solitary confinement, hardly talk all day, no opportunity to have deep chats.

Was so tired today on the trail – I think the both of us are knackered from the last few weeks. Made our cache today, which we filmed. Decided to sleep in tomorrow, we need the rest.

Gamme – awesome bloke, chat, mentoring us. Invite to Sydney, party in Punta.

Getting so hungry ... thought about food for ages.

Chatted in tent about rationing.

Heels a bit better.

Both of us woke up hungover from the weeks of hauling. I was a bit grumpy, didn't feel like talking much and the first 'real conversation' we had was me asking Jonesy not to put powdered milk in my tea until it had brewed.

'Sure mate,' Jonesy replied just as tersely.

The kettle boiled and much to my disbelief, I saw the steamy water being poured into my mug, which already had a spoonful of powdered milk in the bottom.

'Bloody hell, Jonesy. Now it's going to be weak as puddle-water,' I said, pretty irate.

'Sorry Cas, I forgot – I'm still half asleep,' Jonesy replied rubbing his eyes.

He looked like a lost, starving puppy that had been smacked for eating scraps out of a bin and I felt terrible. He tried to remedy the situation by adding his teabag to my mug, but the situation was irretrievable. I should've been much more understanding, he hadn't done it on purpose and all he was trying to do was speed up our preparation time in the morning. If I ever treated Mia like that back home, I'd deserve to have the tea thrown in my face. I guess it shows how edgy we'd become and how the tiniest, most innocent act, could make the other flip. Back on the Tasman Sea, one thing that frustrated me more than anything was the slurping noises Jonesy made while eating in the cabin – it drove me crazy! Knowing this, Jonesy had been making a real effort to eat quietly in the tent – something I was aware of every time he armed himself with his spoon, but something I hadn't thanked him for yet.

Conditions overhead were once again stunning. Blue skies and a low 20 kilometre per hour wind greeted us as we stepped out of the tent, but our progress remained painfully slow due to the soft snow that was lingering underfoot. Up until then, we'd been quite lucky in that neither of us had any chafe between our legs. Considering the weight we'd piled on pre-expedition, I'd kind of expected our stumpy thighs to rub, causing friction and problems. And, as I'd expected, my luck on that issue ran out. Without wanting to get too graphic, let's just say my bait and tackle were being munched by my fatty thighs, and every step was rubbing my groin raw. I tried straddle-walking like a cowboy, but that somehow made it worse. I tried rubbing Sudocrem and Vaseline on everything, but that only resulted in my fingers freezing. Similar to the blisters that had appeared on Day Four, this problem came out of nowhere and caught me by surprise.

I tried to take my mind off the pain. On previous trips, I'd always done a lot of thinking. I'd reflect on the past and dream about the future. My mind would be constantly active and I'd often find it hard to switch it off. If I wasn't thinking about the past and present, I'd be analysing our progress, doing sums on things like required daily average, food rations, etc. I'm somewhat jealous that Jonesy can turn his mind off for hours at a time. He can put his head down for half a day with no music and just Zen out. Granted, he's often thinking about food, but he can also just quiet his mind and lose hours at a time. For some reason, on this trip I found it hard to think deeply about life. Maybe it's because the going had been so bloody tough and all my energy was being focused on propelling myself forward. I was hoping that would change soon because that deep thinking is one of the reasons I like expeditions. Life back home is often too hectic and I am better at reflecting when I am away from everything. And let's face it, you can't get much further away than Antarctica.

Skiing into our campsite that night, Jonesy and I gave each other a high five. We'd crossed over the 82-degree line of latitude and we were both stoked to have reached such a massive milestone. Reaching 82 degrees meant that we could drop another three days worth of food and fuel to pick up on our return. We cut snow blocks the size of eskies and proudly piled them up like an Egyptian pyramid towering just under two metres high. Along with the fuel and food that we'd later refer to as the Gateway Cache, we buried a few extra items of clothing that we hadn't been wearing and some spare tools – all in all offloading close to ten kilograms. We drove our Bunnings bamboo pole deep into the pyramid and our homemade orange flag fluttered on top.

After our sked, Aleks called us and Jonesy had a great chat with him. I could overhear some of it and Aleks's tone was friendly. 'I'm

Norwegian, I was born skiing in these conditions ... but you guys are Australians and you're doing so well – I'm very impressed,' he said to Jonesy. He ended the conversation saying his dream would be for us all to finish together. It was a wonderful thought, but we were so far away from it actually happening, it was almost dangerous to think about.

DAY TWENTY-FIVE

By this stage in the expedition, we felt that we had well and truly earned a sleep-in (or, more importantly, knew that we desperately needed one), so on Day Twenty-five we didn't stir until 8 am. After a good night's sleep both of us were noticeably chirpier, and got stuck into our morning tasks with much more energy than we'd exhibited in a while. The sky was clear but a 40 kilometre per hour wind had whipped up while we slept. We felt sure that all this blue sky and wind would have blown away the fallen snow – but, no, conditions remained soft.

The chafing between my legs was getting worse, and from our very first step I knew I was in for a very long day. The only positive was that dropping off our last lot of provisions had made a real difference to the weight and speed of our sleds. The little pyramid that marked our cache got smaller and smaller as we skied away from it. I couldn't help but feel we were never going to see it again – how could we possibly ski the required 2000-odd kilometres to get back here in the time we had left? We only had three months in total, just over a school term, only a quarter of a year, and it was already taking so long, we were almost a month down. The distances were mind-boggling and given our progress, it seemed unlikely we could do it.

Jonesy was leading the second shift and I was close behind him, staring down at the back of his sled, when … BANG! Jonesy stopped suddenly and I crashed into the back of his sled and fell on my side.

Jonesy looked around and shouted over the wind, 'Are you alright mate?'

'Yeah,' I replied, kind of annoyed at him for stopping so suddenly and *very* annoyed at myself for getting so close.

I picked myself up and stood next to him. He'd stopped for good reason. Carving a line as far as the eye could see was an odd indent in the snow that was as wide as a bus lane. Flashbacks to my fall on Day Two flooded my mind. Not another crevasse! This one was a monster. There seemed no way around it, so Jonesy probed the 'edge' gingerly and started skiing over it, thinking light thoughts all the way. Once over, he called me across. My heart was pounding as I gingerly made my way towards him. On the other side we continued on for another ten minutes until break time. Thirty minutes into my lead during the next session I saw the same snakelike indent in the snow in front of us. This time it looked less like a crevasse and more like a … no, surely not – it wasn't a crevasse, it was a vehicle track! Out there in the middle of nowhere, we'd come across the tyre impressions left by a vehicle. We were beside ourselves with excitement. Other people did exist in this barren frozen wasteland!

'I wonder if it's from this season or last?'

'Yeah, me too,' Jonesy replied. 'But with all the snow that's come down, surely any old tracks would've been covered up by now.'

Seeing the tracks really lifted our spirits and had us asking all kinds of questions back and forth all afternoon. Our progress for the day was a whopping 18 kilometres, and the combination of covering some decent distance, seeing some evidence of human life and having a sleep-in meant we were both in the best mood we'd been in for ages. This was more like it!

While our stove was melting snow and I was writing in my diary, Jonesy was giving himself a bath. We had two 'methods' for washing ourselves in the tent: one involved using a Wet One, starting at the head and working down (very important that you get the order right with this method); the other involved using warm water poured into a ziplock plastic bag, half a block of soap and a chamois. The second was Matty's preferred method and although it was more refreshing and more sustainable – in that you weren't disposing of the Wet Ones – the chamois was already getting pretty smelly and we weren't too sure how hygienic it was anymore. We did try to make it a priority to wash ourselves most nights in order to minimise the risk of skin infections, but with our Wet One supply dwindling, and our chamois smelling a little worse for wear, well ... let's just say that some nights I wished we'd thought to pack air-freshener.

DAY TWENTY-SIX

The alarm buzzed and I rolled away from it, unable to face the day ahead. I'd hardly slept the night before – my inner thighs, groin and balls were an absolute mess, and the stinging and sharp jolts of pain had kept me awake most of the night. We packed up camp under clear blue skies and tame headwinds and started marching south. Ever south! Each step felt like it was causing more and more damage to my testicle sack. It felt like someone had sandpapered my scrotum and then covered the raw skin in chilli paste. I took some comfort in talking to Polar Dude who had no feelings, no pain, no emotion. I had a conversation with him out loud in my semi-delirious state caused by all the pain and discomfort. Jonesy must have thought I'd gone crazy. It made sense in my diary:

> **My shadow, my friend – it keeps me company all day. I look at it and sometimes talk to him. Who are you? Who do you want to be? My shadow is exactly what previous explorers' shadows would've looked like. The explorers a hundred years ago would've suffered all the same issues we're facing – cold injuries, chafe, blisters, etc. – technology doesn't help these.**

Pain back then was no less or more than it is today. The consolation we had was satellite contact with doctors and the hope that diagnosis and treatment helped the ailments heal faster and more effectively. I don't think explorers were made tougher back then, or that their pain threshold was higher. I watched as Jonesy pulled ahead and I asked my Polar Dude shadow how he was feeling towards Jonesy. He was neutral. I, on the other hand, was feeling bitter pangs of jealousy at how strong he was looking on the trail, and even more so because his groin was healthy and painless. I brewed in my delirium and tried to work myself up to loathing. Sometimes anger can be a good driver, especially when every step was causing excruciating pain.

By the time we'd got inside the tent that evening I couldn't wait to get my pants off, but once I did I was horrified by what I saw. Things had definitely deteriorated throughout the day. Around each of the hair follicles, pus-filled pimples ranging in size from the tip of a ballpoint pen to welts the size of blueberries covered my scrotum. In between the outbreak, the skin was a fiery red colour and the painful itchiness came in waves. Like with any chafe, I was trying to reduce the friction by using Vaseline and Sudocrem, which to our knowledge was the best treatment. The way we'd been pushing our bodies over the past month was all too much, I was breaking down. But if we wanted to stay in with a shot at the return journey, we had no choice, we had to press on. We just didn't have time to take rest days.

Once Jonesy jumped in the tent and dinner was rehydrating, we sent images of the outbreak to Doctor John at Union Glacier and our doctor on standby in Sydney. Both quickly diagnosed it as folliculitis, a condition that starts when hair follicles are damaged by friction from clothing and blockage of the follicle. It wasn't chafe at all! Adding to the mess, the damaged follicles were now infected with a bacterium called *staphylococcus*. Great. I had to start a course of antibiotics immediately, try to reduce the rubbing, keep the area as cool and unsweaty as possible and apply Betadine liberally.

It is one thing dealing with blisters that cause discomfort on the trail, but as soon as we entered our safe haven, our tent, all was fine and forgotten. This was completely different – the folliculitis was attacking me constantly, whether I was walking, sitting or trying to sleep. I just couldn't escape it. The pain was just as bad in the tent as it was on the trail and the discomfort meant I slept fitfully. I could not rest even in my safest of safe places – my sleeping-bag – because it trapped too much moisture. I had to try to sleep with the infected area exposed to the frigid air. It wasn't a great sight, let me tell you.

DAY TWENTY-SEVEN

I woke constantly throughout the night, partly from sleeping with my groin uncovered and partly from the pain and itch. I found applying Betadine to the affected area helped soothe the pain and took away the worst of the itch. By morning I was feeling marginally better but I was enormously irritated that we hadn't brought more Betadine. I was holding in my hand a small bottle of liquid that if applied generously would help fix the infection in a matter of days, but we only had fifteen millilitres to last us the entire expedition, so I had to use it sparingly. Knowing how many tools, spares and first-aid supplies to bring with us was an incredibly delicate balance. Some items sit down the bottom of the sled for the entire expedition and are never touched, while others, like the Betadine, were woefully under-provisioned.

In getting ready for the expedition, one of Jonesy's responsibilities was to prepare the medical kit, while I focused on the tools and spares. Jonesy examined the kits from many other expeditions and spoke to a number of doctors. Given the isolation and remoteness of the expedition, most medical professionals wanted us to fill the entire sled for just-in-case situations. This wasn't practical and Jonesy had to make some tough calls on what to include and what to leave out. We had items in the kit for the severest of conditions – hardcore antibiotics, morphine, all the stuff we'd want if either one of us was right on the edge, knocking on heaven's door, but it seemed to me we were short on treatments for certain everyday injuries and infections. The problem with this approach was that by not having the medical supplies to address these 'tame' issues when they first popped up, ailments worsened quickly. Somehow antifungal powder and cream didn't make it into the kit and this was a major reason why Jonesy's toes were starting to fall apart like they were – there was cracking between his toes, and lots of pus. Similarly, my groin would've been well on the way to mending if we'd had more than the tiny bottle of Betadine. I started a course of antibiotics after breakfast and hoped that they would kick in quickly.

During the first break of the day, I discovered a note attached to my F.I.R.S.T meal-replacement powder from one of Jonesy's mates. Jonesy asked me to keep it so he could add it to his collection of personal notes that were starting to fill up a snack bag. After I finished the contents of the ziplock bag, I went to stuff it into the sled-cover pocket but the wind whipped it out of my mitt and it flew away before I had time to register it'd even gone.

'Er ... Jonesy,' I screamed above the howling wind.

'Yeah, mate?'

'Um ... you know Marshy's note that you asked me to keep?'

'Yeahhhh.' He could see where I was going.

'Well, the wind just ripped it out of my hand and I lost it. I'm really sorry, mate!'

I could tell that he was pissed off. It's little things like this that can just make you snap. He went really quiet for the next few hours and I felt terrible. There was nothing I could do. Adding to the tension was the time pressure we were under. We both felt very lonely.

CAS DIARY ENTRY – 25 NOVEMBER 2011

Bodies are really taking a punishing – are we going to keep on pushing? We're only going to know if we push too hard ... Solid day today but we need better than solid days.

DAY TWENTY-EIGHT

JONESY DIARY ENTRY – 26 NOVEMBER 2011

What a f**ked up day.

When the alarm went off on the morning of the twenty-eighth day, I felt like death – my head throbbed and I was nauseous with fatigue, I'd slept terribly again due to the agonising pain in my groin. Neither of us were up for talking as we prepared breakfast and packed our sleds. Fortunately, conditions were calm and if I hadn't felt so depressed and ill I might have been able to take in the beauty of the long cirrus clouds stretching through the endless blue sky. As it was, I could barely grunt. After half an hour skiing next to each other and sinking in the soft snow up to our ankles, I finally found the energy to speak. But the question that had been on my mind from the moment I woke that morning wasn't very positive:

'Jonesy, why the hell are we doing this trip? What's driving us?'

'I've been trying to answer that same question myself, mate.'

'You know what?'

'What Cas?'

'I'm disgusted to say it ... but being down here feels like a job.'

And it did. For the first time ever I wasn't getting the feeling of freedom and personal fulfilment that normally came from pushing myself, being resourceful and relying completely on myself and Jonesy. This time I was more motivated by the fear of failure than by the love of being out in the wilderness. I'd never felt that way about adventure before. I also felt so accountable to all the people back home who were supporting us financially and emotionally. If we had a rest day I felt it needed to be justified. On previous trips, rest days had given us some of our most memorable experiences – like the time we got stuck on Deal Island in the middle of Bass Strait when we were paddling across it. My memories of the Tasman are less about the paddling, and more about the way we pushed ourselves and the wildlife we experienced. Similarly, on bushwalks it was often the views and breathtaking landscapes that motivated me, or the people we met and the campsites we visited, as well as the insatiable appetite to discover what's around that bend or up the top of that hill. In Antarctica those elements of the adventure didn't exist, or at least hadn't up to that point, and I was struggling to find motivation in the unchanging, never-ending, raw nothingness.

Jonesy was feeling much the same. 'We may as well be locked in a white room with fluorescent lights and have to walk twelve hours a day on a treadmill,' he said.

We didn't talk much after that, we were both in a bad head space, and so we just trudged on, keeping to our routine. Jonesy was limping most of the afternoon. By the time we set up the tent and he started to take off his boots I could smell the putrefaction of his pus-bulging toes. His toenails were wobbly and about to fall off, and he needed to lance his ballooning digits. As soon as he popped them with a safety pin, mustard-coloured goo oozed out, and he then squeezed every last drop of pus out of each toe. Once he'd done that the pain subsided. He also removed the orthotics from his boots to reduce the pressure on his toes.

After dinner was cooked and our sked completed, we tucked ourselves miserably into our sleeping-bags. The waves of pain from my groin hammered more frequently than ever. I knew I was in for a long night.

DAY TWENTY-NINE

And sure enough I winced my way through the night – rolling from one side to the other, trying anything to reduce the pain. It was my fifth night of next to no sleep. The uncompromising ravenous infection finally became too much. When the alarm went off, I broke. Completely out of control, I began crying like I had never cried before. Sitting cross-legged in the tent, tears washed down my face. I looked down helplessly at the mess between my legs. We had only covered ten per cent of the total distance we needed to cover and I was completely broken. The tears were letting out a whole mixture of emotions – recognition that I'd pushed myself too hard, that my body could not go on, that we'd failed in what we'd set out to do, that we'd let our stakeholders down … and while all this was going on inside the tent, the sun beat down cruelly with no wind – taunting, almost laughing at us. I felt embarrassed and that I was letting Jonesy down. Why had this happened to me? Jonesy tried to comfort me by placing a hand on my shoulder as it rose up and down with each sob. It was a kind gesture, but made me feel more inadequate. I felt alone. Jonesy was still trying to stay positive about our chances of the return which made me feel even more distant from him. Was he not understanding what I was going through? No-one back home understood either.

At the time I didn't remember this quote from Apsley Cherry-Garrard about Robert Scott:

> He [Scott] cried more easily than any man I have ever known. What pulled Scott through was character, sheer good grain, which ran over and under and through his weaker self and clamped it together.

I just hoped that, like Scott, my inner strength would pull me out from this dark place I was in.

CAS DIARY ENTRY – 27 NOVEMBER 2011

The pain/itching/discomfort of my groin finally beat me. Last night I only got about four hours' sleep because it kept waking me up. I woke up this morning feeling absolutely horrible. I knew we'd pushed too hard – I was breaking and I started crying and crying and crying all morning. I just couldn't control myself. The pressure of taking a rest day versus pushing on became too much – I know by taking it, it's a step towards failure and a commitment to a one-way trip (if we're lucky). I can't believe I cried so much – the only reason I can think of is that it was a breakdown, my body just can't handle the strain I'm putting on it, I need to ease off. By taking this rest day I feel like I'm letting Jonesy down, letting Mia down, and letting the people who have believed in us down. I feel completely disconnected from everyone at home. They just don't understand what we're going through. It's so easy for them to say, 'You're doing really well – you can do it', or 'We believe in you'. Just because we've pulled some trips off in the past doesn't mean we can do this as well. I guess the only person back home whose advice I appreciate is Mum telling me, 'Keep it in perspective. You've got a great life ahead of you with Mia – just come back safe.' Each time she tells me this it's like a pressure release.

JONESY DIARY ENTRY – 27 NOVEMBER 2011

Rest day.

I think that the dream may be over.

I have never seen Cas so low. Even on the Tasman when he flew off the handle and punched the kayak wall. This is different (MELTDOWN).

He looks beaten.

After years of dreaming, visualising and committing every cell in our bodies to this goal, it was being torn away from us. I was disgusted in myself for not having the eye-of-the-tiger approach and keeping on fighting, and felt guilty that I was forcing my problems on Jonesy – without me, he would've been so much closer to the Pole. I started to justify our failure to myself:

> **We've had to push so hard to keep one foot in the door with the return, but with the ten-day delay in Punta and three weeks of blizzards, snowfall, etc., we need to realise that what we were embarking on was at the limit of the possible – we needed a few things to go right from the start and they didn't.**

I kept saying this to myself over and over – it wasn't our fault, we did what we could – but it only made staring at our failure marginally less oppressive. I lay on my sleeping-bag staring up at the tent ceiling for most of the day. Every now and then I'd try to escape by watching a video on my iPod, but I couldn't concentrate so I turned it off pretty quickly. Occasionally I'd start sobbing uncontrollably, unable to hold back the tears.

This was the rawest and lowest anyone had ever seen me in my life and I felt embarrassed. I was into the third day of antibiotics and sparingly applied the precious Betadine a few times during the day. I kept repeating the mantra, 'Please God, oh please let the antibiotics start to work their magic soon.'

It was an equally difficult situation for Jonesy. He felt helpless and was questioning what he could've done differently. Sure, his toes were giving him grief, but he could've been out there skiing if it wasn't for me holding him back. We talked a little throughout the day, but mostly we just stewed in our own thoughts. Jonesy wrote in his diary:

> I'm really worried about Cas, I have never seen him cry like this and be such a wreck. Is it that he has pushed too hard QED [as demonstrated], or are there a number of factors that have contributed? His life back in Sydney is so much happier now than before the Tasman. Is it too big a difference? Has it destroyed some of that iron will? I don't know how to pep him up … everything I say is wrong.

I only found out after the expedition that Jonesy had given some thought to whether or not my head – or more to the point, my heart – was really in this trip. It was something I was truly concerned about leading up to the expedition, but I knew I wouldn't know the answer until I was in Antarctica. Had I lost my hunger to keep fighting? Life back home *was* good. Mia, work, friends, family – everything was in such a good place and I didn't have that same anger motivating me as I did prior to the Tasman. Should I just quit and go home? Mia and my family would love me just the same. However, something deep inside me rumbled and even in the dark place I was in, I still couldn't entertain the notion of quitting. It's never been in my vocabulary and I didn't want that to change. Out of nowhere I started visualising a conversation with my future children. Would I have to tell them I quit because it got too hard? What example would that be for them?

Any thoughts that we were in a race with Aleks were over – for us it was now a matter of survival. Sure, we talked about him and wondered how he was progressing – as I'm sure Scott and Amundsen talked about each other – but that is where it ended. We didn't have the energy to 'race' someone else. The competitiveness

I had felt on the plane never really followed me onto the ice. As I broke down physically and mentally I knew the real fight was going to be with our own minds and bodies, managing our limited provisions and trying to push out maximum mileage without burning up all our energy. I was trying to find some strength within to refocus our objective. The return was unobtainable, but perhaps reaching the South Pole was still an option? Although 800 kilometres seemed like an *impossibly* long way.

Video journal – Breakdown
www.casandjonesy.com.au/extremesouth

DAY THIRTY

CAS DIARY ENTRY – 28 NOVEMBER 2011

We made the call to spend another day in the tent resting up, hopefully allowing my crotch to improve with the antibiotics. It's heaps better, but still inflamed. How to know when to push on/how much to rest up? There are no easy answers out here – it's not black and white. Today was JJ's day to realise the return journey is slipping away ... he started crying.

I've sewed a G-string into my boxer shorts to help keep balls up and forward – fingers crossed it works. Feeling much less fatigued – what a shame groin isn't feeling more recovered. Very typical of the cruel nature of this trip – no wind for the last two days – fingers crossed it's like this tomorrow.

Rest day number two.

Bit of a low day in the tent.

I can't stop thinking about the return journey and really want to do it because other than this trip, I've really got nothing else going on in my life. My parents are overseas. I'm estranged from my family to a degree. Apart from Louisa, Aidan and Cas, I'm not really close to too many people – I'm quite alone. So I feel like a failure here is a reflection of a failure of my life.

The thought crossed my mind of a solo push (back to the coast) once we hit the Pole if Cas isn't up for it. He did promise that if we are in good nick when we hit the Pole to consider a supported return journey.

Had a chat to Eric Philips – his gut feeling is that the trip is slipping away but to wait a few more days to make that decision.

Had a chat with Cas about parents, his take on my life and he wasn't far off with some of his theories ... I had a good cry about it. So jealous of his relationship with Mia – at least if we fail he has that support. I don't have much.

Last night, I couldn't sleep till 2.30 am – thinking about the situation – quite tired today. Fixed Therm-a-Rest and made Cas a neck buff, he made a G-string undie attachment.

It's so cruel, outside it's a beautiful day – almost like the Blue Mountains – I was outside with trackies and black jumper and it was pretty good ... ears were a bit cold though.

> **Had a chat with [Justin's sister] Louisa last night and I really miss her. It sucks that I keep calling her at work and can only spend a little time chatting. Cas wants to dump some food to lighten the load, I've convinced him to hang onto it for a few more days ...**

With another rest day and some improvements in the groin situation, I started thinking about solutions to at least one of my problems. One of the issues that caused my follicles to get 'agitated' was that the boxer shorts I was wearing just weren't holding my balls forward during the hours skiing on the trail. I needed to make a pair of briefs – but how? Our sewing skills had come a long way over the previous six months, but the thought of making undies in the middle of nowhere seemed impossible. Jonesy and I laid out all our spare material on the tent floor, and considered what clothing we could chop up. We realised pretty quickly that we didn't have enough material to make a brand new pair of undies. The idea of a 'ball-sack sack' had merit a few days ago, but just wouldn't work. We thought and thought and ... bingo!

Why not use my boxer shorts for the scaffolding, and sew something on the inside? After playing with a few different designs, pinning them in and testing whether they were effective in holding my scrotum out of the way of my legs, we thought we had it. We sewed my current neckwarmer buff into my briefs as a G-string. I went for a walk outside with my newly fashioned underwear and it seemed to work. I'd never worn a G-string before and can't really understand how people find them comfortable, but anything that would save my balls was worth a shot. For the rest of the afternoon I was excited about testing it on the trail. Having some kind of hope to grasp onto made such a difference to my mood. I was eager to get going again.

DAY THIRTY-ONE

I woke up at 4.30 am with itchy balls that kept me awake until 6.30 am. Jonesy had found it difficult to fall asleep and had laid awake thinking into the wee hours of the morning. The alarm went off at seven and we pressed the snooze button twice before finally getting up at 7.30 am. After the G-string breakthrough, I was especially focused on protecting my scrotum from further damage. With a plan to deal with the rubbing sorted, I also had to address the amount of heat and moisture that would build up down there. I'd been trying to keep my inner thighs warm to help the blisters on the inside of my thighs recover, but today my goal was to address the main problem (my balls) and see if the frost blisters could handle being a little cooler without my insulated PrimaLoft pants.

After so many days of skiing through white nothingness, it was a day of stunning blue sky, and it was actually quite enjoyable to get back on the trail skiing. Conditions underfoot were similar to our last day of skiing, but we were making heaps better progress. The skis and sled were still sinking into the snow by about three centimetres, but that was much better than it had been. We were able to ski side by side again and had some great chats – embarrassing girl stories, cadets, schoolies, who was in what rugby team and stuff like that. My most embarrassing moment was vomiting on the bus next to my date at my Year Twelve formal and Jonesy's was … well, you can ask him about that.

The rest days had done wonders for our bodies and our minds and we ended up doing our biggest day to date – 21 kilometres. We were both in relatively good moods and set up the tent quickly. I jumped in, put on the stove, took my pants off and then, to my horror, saw that the inside of my thighs had taken a real beating. The frost blisters were almost black, my inner thighs were purple and the skin was very sensitive. Wearing less clothing on my lower body had definitely taken a toll on my inner thighs but, on the positive side, my scrotum hadn't deteriorated any further throughout the day. When Jonesy jumped in the tent, I showed him my legs and we started talking about how every decision we made in Antarctica often has massive implications and repercussions, 'consequential living' we termed it. We'd address one issue, and the solution to that problem led to another issue. It was a never-ending seesaw battle of our bodies against the unforgiving elements.

Scott was once quoted as saying, 'Misfortunes rarely come singularly.' Tragedies in the outdoors are seldom caused by a stand-alone incident – it's a cumulative effect over time. We call it the domino effect. Often you can handle a situation when one or two things are out of whack and not going as planned, and these should be viewed as warning signs. The serious problems arise when multiple issues line up.

After dinner, Jonesy was kind enough to let me chop off the bottom of his fleece pants to make chaps for my thighs. We figured this might be a solution to keep my groin cool and my inner-thighs warmer. What a sight I'd become – here I was skiing across the frozen plains of Antarctica wearing a homemade G-string and chaps like a Texan cowboy!

DAY THIRTY-TWO

I woke just after midnight *again* from the discomfort radiating from my groin. I fumbled through the med-kit, popped a few Panadol and was relieved to nod off back to sleep pretty quickly.

By the time I woke in the morning, it was the best night's sleep I'd had all week. Conditions outside were similar to the previous day and we were able to ski next to each other again. For most of the day, Jonesy entertained me with his most hilarious pick-up stories. It's funny, I thought we both knew most things about each other, but clearly not! Some of his stories would make Tucker Max raise an eyebrow; they were so incredible, they were bordering on fiction. But truth *is* stranger than fiction. Jonesy wrote about the conversation in his diary:

> **Cas seemed to be hurting so I told him some of my dodgier sex stories. I think that they really entertained him but I'm pretty sure they also disgusted him. Perhaps telling him those stories wasn't such a good idea if I want to be his best man!**

Towards the end of the day, I told Jonesy I wasn't enjoying the trip. It wasn't like I was telling him something he didn't already know, but his response was something new. He was quiet for a few seconds and then replied thoughtfully, 'Even though you're suffering now, Cas, you need this trip.'

He was right. I did need it. 'Extreme' adventure had taken me on some wild rides over the previous ten years. It had taught me who I am and had given me worth in this world. Our trip to Antarctica gave me the clarity to realise that reaching the South Pole would close a chapter in my life. If I didn't try I'd always be left dreaming, wondering. I have such a special bond with Mia and know for sure that marriage and family is what I want more than anything in life. I didn't want to risk that or be away from her for trips like this again. Richard Weber wrote in his book *Polar Attack*:

The more I'm away, the more I miss Josee and the kids. The longer you live with someone, the more they become a part of you - and the more you miss them when they aren't there.

I second that!

After 19 kilometres we set up our tent and I called a mate of ours, Tink. Some people we'd spoken to were so motivating and encouraging (like Turnbull), others less so. This was one of those others. Initially Tink was fun to talk to, but then he started questioning whether we were trying hard enough, 'Can't you guys just put in another 10 or 20 per cent?' Jonesy was fuming when I passed this bit of feedback on. I'm sure Tink was just trying to motivate me, but it didn't come across like that. People back home struggled to understand what we were going through. The only people who could possibly understand are those who have been to Antarctica, and that's not many. Their point of reference might've been a tough hike for their Duke of Edinburgh or school camp, where they were pushed for a week or two, but none of our mates had spent months being pushed to the absolute limit of their being in the most inhospitable conditions imaginable. They just didn't know how hard it was.

After dinner, we committed ourselves to the one-way journey by dumping three days' food to lighten our sleds. It was roughly the same place that Chris Foot and Mark Langridge had made the same decision on their separate expeditions. We didn't build a cache, we just buried it unmarked. The weight of our sleds was still tearing our bodies apart and we needed to do everything we could to make the journey to the South Pole more attainable. I was keen to dump six days' food, Jonesy didn't want to dump any, so we compromised. Up until then it'd been all talk, but now this was the line in the sand – we saw no point in burying it as a cache and building a cairn on top of the food, there was no chance we'd ever be back here. Even though I thought we'd made this decision as a team, unbeknown to me Jonesy was holding onto the remote possibility that the return was still attainable. His decision to dump this food unmarked meant his intention was to potentially allow enough food for only one of us to get back to the coast. If he had belief in both of us, the cache would've been marked clearly for our return. By agreeing to dump this food, Jonesy was leaving the door open for a solo return trip. I didn't know it then but it was clear when I read his diary later: 'it still leaves six days' rations if one was going solo'.

PHASE TWO
Breaking Through

DAY THIRTY-THREE

We all have different triggers, a massive one for me is sleep – not enough, and I really feel it – for Jonesy, it's food. Once again I woke at 4 am from the pain in my crotch, and lay there contemplating the day ahead. It was the first day of December and the first day of summer, I wondered if it would bring anything new.

Stepping into the harnesses at 9.15 am, I was feeling a little more positive and not as physically depleted, despite the lack of sleep, and I started appreciating the stark beauty around us. The snow underfoot was compact and right from the start we were making solid headway. With a rich blue sky above and good visibility, the clouds dazzled. The air was so crisp, pristine and pure, I wanted to bottle it up and drink it. In every direction there was plain upon plain of icy white nothingness, but on this day it didn't make me feel lonely, but oddly lucky. Sure, on the Tasman we experienced isolation, but even when we were smack bang in the middle of it people were 'only' 1000 kilometres to our east or west. Here, we were completely alone ... and I kind of liked it. For the first time in weeks, there were different shades and shadows to marvel at – the sastrugi were delicately carved and clouds of varying shapes and sizes marched across the sky. After a few hours, I realised that my groin hadn't been bothering me as much and instead of being in my own world of pain, I was able to focus more on the world around me. It was the last day of antibiotics and with the chaps and drops of iodine, it finally felt like full recovery was a real possibility.

We had an in-depth chat about the end point of the expedition. Jonesy still had his heart set on trying to push back to Hercules Inlet, and with my groin starting to feel normal again, I was also pretty keen on turning around once we reached the South Pole. However, I was hesitant to commit to a specific distance or target. I really liked the idea of being picked up on the way back from the Pole, even if we only made it a few hundred kilometres north. The Thiel Mountains sit halfway between the Pole and Hercules Inlet, and we started thinking of it as the 'middle ground' for our arbitrary end-point target. I could feel that my objective was shifting from a specific distance or location, to being motivated to stay in the ring for all fifteen rounds, regardless of where we ended up. Jonesy, on the other hand, needed a definitive goal to aim for and this started to cause some friction between us.

Essentially, we now had different objectives – mine was more about surviving until our food ran out, while Jonesy's was to get to a certain point (whether that point was the Thiel Mountains or Hercules Inlet). Both objectives required different strategies, mine more conservative, Jonesy's more aggressive. Neither was right or wrong, and they both seemed to be in the spirit of Captain Scott and his fateful march. Whether you consider him a hero or a highly flawed and incompetent leader, he was a man who didn't give up until the very end. If we were going to fail, this is the message that we wanted to send to the world – we weren't going to give up either. The thought of not being a quitter was a massive motivator for the rest of the day.

I was so relieved that the G-string I was wearing worked well. At the end of the day, I lovingly washed it in my left-over 'bath' water, wrung it out, then pinned it up at the top of the tent to dry. Jonesy got irate that my undies were now touching his balaclava and started obsessing that some of the water off them might drip into our kettle. I told him that I'd wrung them out and that they wouldn't drip, but there was tension in the tent until I moved them over to my side of the clothesline.

DAY THIRTY-FOUR

Sure enough, the marching clouds that had entertained me the day before were frontal, and as we woke and poked our heads out of the tent we were greeted by thick cloud cover. As soon as we started hauling, we noticed a few millimetres of light snow had eliminated any glide and made for tough pulling. The conditions also made skiing tricky as there was zero contrast between sky and earth and the diffused light cast no shadows, making it impossible to see sastrugi and other bumps in the ground. Our progress was laboriously slow and by the end of the day we were both exhausted. On the plus side, my feet and legs were nowhere near as sore as they'd been in the first couple of weeks and although fatigued they weren't aching, and best of all my groin felt almost better! Wahoo! Those previous ten days had to be up there with the most uncomfortable of my life. With my balls almost back to normal I could start thinking about other stuff while I was skiing, rather than just focusing on how to cope with each painful step. Although the snow that had fallen hampered our progress, I enjoyed marvelling at the frost flowers that had bloomed on the backs of the sastrugi. From a short distance they appeared furry, but up close they were exquisitely intricate and symmetrical. Inside the tent, the grunting noises we made while trying to remove our multiple layers of clothing sounded like a Wimbledon final between Maria Sharapova and Venus Williams. I've always thought the grunts on court seemed excessive at times, but when we tried changing in silence it was remarkably difficult. There was actually a ridiculous amount of core work involved each night in the tent – crunches, sit-ups, twisting and turning. The noises didn't seem to annoy either one of us, in fact they made us giggle – so the grunts continued.

With Betadine supplies at critically low levels and my groin on the mend, I started using hand sanitiser to clean the area each morning and night. It wasn't as effective as the Betadine, but still did a great job of drying the area and addressing the bacterial infection, but, yes, it stung like hell.

DAY THIRTY-FIVE

The dreary conditions cleared through the night and we woke to blue skies and winds of up to 25 kilometres per hour. We were both immersed in our morning routine, and as I was lighting the stove I glanced up and noticed that Jonesy's eyes were plum red. I told him, and he thought it was from skiing too long without his goggles. He was feeling pretty tired but fortunately his eyes weren't painful, which would be a classic indication of snow blindness. For the first night in two weeks I'd finally slept through without waking, so while Jonesy may have been feeling a little flat, I was in a brilliant mood. Life was starting to feel better and I felt more positive than I had all trip. The wind had dropped off enough for us to hear each other, and while we packed our sleds we talked a little about rationing food for later in the trip, but didn't come to any hard and fast decisions.

During the day as we heaved and hoved our sleds through the multiple sastrugi fields, I passed the time describing to Jonesy some of my favourite rock climbs in the Blue Mountains. I got pretty detailed, right down to the individual moves through the crux of each climb:

'Mr Magoo at Diamond Falls is my nemesis! Arghh … I've cruised the bottom two-thirds of the climb through the crimpy crux where you've got a small right foot that you bump up through a series of crimps with an edge no bigger than …' And on and on I went describing every little detail, foot placement, where you had rests, etc. I guess for me, talking about climbing was like Jonesy talking about food, it was my happy place. It made the sessions fly by, and by the end we'd clocked up our biggest day yet – 24.5 kilometres! Perhaps what was better than the actual mileage was the fact that we both felt like we could've kept on going for a bit longer. My diary entry was almost upbeat:

That's how we SHOULD be feeling at the end of each day, not crawling around the tent in pain. Since the last rest day five days ago, I've been feeling better and better and better each day – stronger.

We were learning that when in Antarctica on a three-month expedition, you just can't force the miles when conditions or people aren't up to it. When things improve you need to crank it up a notch, just as you need to ease back when things are crap. We needed to move with the heartbeat of the place, not fight it.

Just as I was about to jump in the tent to get the stove cranking, Jonesy yelled out excitedly, 'Look, plane!'

'Where?' I quizzed, my eyes searching the sky.

'Over there, over there!'

Sure enough, way, way up high there was a plane flying in what looked to be the direction of the South Pole. To think that there were *people* inside that warm cabin.

'I wonder if they can see us? What do you reckon?'

'Nah, they're too high up, all they'd be seeing is a desert of white.'

I looked around and felt the electric shock of realisation at how tiny and insignificant we were, pinpricks on thousands upon thousands of barren square kilometres. Nothing. We were alone.

As soon as I entered the tent the first thing I did (before starting to strip down) was to light the stove and get the snow melting. I got undressed, hung up my wet clothes and then called my brother Clary and a good mate from school, Nick, and asked them if they'd be groomsmen at my wedding. It felt weird to be as isolated as we were and coordinating wedding stuff. That was something Scott and Amundsen didn't have to do, that's for sure!

Jonesy was wincing and groaning as he was taking off his boots. I checked out his toes and they were looking worse than ever. I'd noticed that for the last few days they were taking a few minutes to 'warm up' when we started marching on the trail. After the calls we tucked into what had quickly become my favourite dehydrated meal of the trip, cottage pie. I rated it a 9.5 out of ten, the only thing missing was fresh, warm bread and butter to scoop up the dregs. It honestly tasted home-cooked! A theory we were both keen to test further when we returned home.

DAY THIRTY-SIX

We were both shattered after a poor night's sleep – Jonesy was waking every hour. I gingerly crawled out of the tent and was limping around like an arthritic eighty-year-old, my joints ached and my muscles were so tight. The eight and a half hours' skiing the day before had really taken its toll. While I was doing my tasks for the morning outside the tent, Jonesy was cleaning up his sleeping-bag from the first wet dream he'd had on the trip. My stomach was also feeling a bit funny and I found it hard to get my breakfast down. After a couple of hours skiing, my guts were contorting and I couldn't hold it in any longer. I ripped off my harness, whacked my big down jacket over the top of everything, then fumbled carelessly with the four layers of pants I was wearing to expose my rump in time for diarrhoea to explode onto the pristine white snow … and, yes, to bounce onto my boot. Jonesy took a sheet of toilet paper out of one of the sleds, kindly cut some snow blocks for me to wipe my bottom with and came and sat next to me on a one-metre high sastrugi. We chatted while I finished creating a mess and then he handed me my allocated sheet of toilet paper and the snow blocks he'd shaped for me. Man, had we become close!

As we skied further south, we noticed that the fields of sastrugi had grown in size from toddlers to teenagers. We'd ski for kilometres over a relatively flat surface, then they'd crop up in fields out of nowhere. These fields ranged in size from small little outcrops to larger than an eighteen-hole golf course. Even though pulling through the sastrugi was a real nuisance, I couldn't help but appreciate their beauty and lose my thoughts in their incredible shapes. If it was warmer and not so isolated I'd want to spend days walking through these fields admiring, photographing and being absorbed by their beauty.

Each day was starting to follow a similar rhythm – the first few sessions were a little slow, but in the afternoon we'd get stronger and stronger, and in the last session of the day we'd often cover our best miles. By the end of Day Thirty-six we'd smashed our record and clocked a whopping 26 kilometres! Our result came at a price though. We were exhausted and I felt we were probably pushing too hard. Since my breakdown and the two forced rest days, we realised we'd now entered what we were calling the 'sustainability phase' of the expedition, and that the way we were feeling the previous day was how we were meant to be feeling. I was stoked we'd hit our biggest day, but disappointed that we didn't have the discipline to stop earlier so we weren't as tired. We had to be smarter.

DAY THIRTY-SEVEN

Conditions on Day Thirty-seven were beautiful – blue skies and a gentle 15 kilometre per hour headwind. We took two hours to break camp and were able to ski next to each other for most of the day, which made the time much more enjoyable. In our second session we discussed food rationing, and it became pretty clear that we were coming from two different points of view. Jonesy wanted to be more aggressive by rationing hard now, then, if we had extra food left at the end of the journey, we could dig in then. I was more conservative, thinking we were better to eat more calories now and conserve all the fat and muscle reserves we were carrying on us for as long as possible, and then if we needed to cut back for the last few weeks, we only had to get through those weeks. I knew about the ridiculous amount of weight other teams had lost on past expeditions: Kiwi explorer Jamie Fitzgerald, for instance, had lost 23 kilograms in fifty-odd days on full rations, and that saw him get only one way to the Pole. If we lost too much weight on the journey to the Pole, our bodies simply would not be able to continue past it or, if we did, we were gambling dangerously with our lives like British explorers, Ranulph Fiennes and Mike Stroud. They called short their 1993 crossing of the Antarctic continent because they'd lost too much weight to maintain their core body temperatures even when out on the trail hauling. On one occasion,

Mike collapsed from hypothermia and only regained consciousness when Fiennes set up the tent, and shoved him in his sleeping-bag. Jonesy and I debated back and forth for a while before agreeing to compromise and ration every second day, but to monitor our bodies closely. If we appeared to be losing too much weight we'd immediately bump back up to full serves.

Regardless of what our end goal was, we'd used much more food than we'd expected to by this point and in order to satisfy either one of our goals we couldn't afford to bury six days' food and lay a cache at 84 degrees south. We were going to need this food up on the plateau. This decision meant our sleds would remain heavier and would slow our travel, but it was the safer option, allowing us more control if conditions deteriorated once again.

Tucked in our tent at the end of a ten-hour day, we spoke to Steve Jones after our sked and mentioned that although our progress had been slow we were still determined to turn around at the Pole, regardless of how far we got back north before the end of the season. The excitement and encouragement in his response was ridiculously motivating, and just what we needed to hear: 'We've all been so impressed with the miles you've been making given the atrocious conditions you've been dealt. If you turn around at the Pole you'll be setting a new benchmark in polar travel.'

On bad days, as we skied across the endless white desert, we'd mutter to ourselves about how nobody cared about what we were doing, that it didn't matter. We felt isolated and alone. Steve put it back in perspective and really strengthened our resolve that the goal we were working towards was worthy and that it was worth throwing everything we had into it. We wouldn't have put in the years of hard work and organisation and pulled those wretched truck tyres up Vista Street if we hadn't believed this, but it was a welcome reminder that recharged our energy levels.

DAY THIRTY-EIGHT

CAS DIARY ENTRY – 6 DECEMBER 2011

How long can we keep this up?

JJ's feet are a mess. Could smell pus – it looks so disgusting. Hours on the trail today were a real grind – flat light, low contrast and overcast – couldn't really see anything.

Not much wind today – in fact, it was quite warm, probably warmest day yet.

Skiing along in the flat and dreary afternoon light, I listened to a playlist entitled 'Antarctica 3' – it was one of the six playlists that Mia compiled for me before I left. At the start of each day I'd select one playlist and listen to it for the rest of the day. Listening to 'Antarctica 3', the rendition of the Australian national anthem sung at the 2000 Sydney Olympics came on. I started crying. I was skiing behind Jonesy, and focused on the Australian flag clearly visible on the rear of his sled. I was so proud. I thought about all the trips we'd done all over Australia and truly appreciated the variety of the landscapes I'd seen. I guess desolation can do that.

On the Tasman, the public were amazed that we could send podcasts and the occasional photo from out on the ocean. Four years on and technology had improved to the point where we were able to regularly send back images and thirty-second videos. With the combination of the live tracking on our website and this content, the public could follow our journey in real time. This improvement in capability was more to do with the software we were using than the hardware. We sent content through our old-school satellite phone, at a speed of 4 kilobits per second –

a fraction of the speed of a dial-up modem. Unfortunately, it dropped out often, but the mail server we were using was able to piece together the bytes of the attachment on the other end, allowing the phone to connect and disconnect multiple times when sending an attachment. In a world of high-speed ADSL, this may not seem revolutionary, but to us it was! On the Tasman, each time the signal dropped out we needed to resend the entire email attachment. It was the bane of our existence (along with sharks and whirlpools). Jonesy was in charge of uploading the data on this trip. When the technology was working, all was dandy, but every now and then the computer would play silly buggers and Jonesy's inner nerd would be called upon to remedy the situation. Sometimes this would take a few evenings of attention and would frustrate him no end.

After covering 24.6 kilometres I was relieved to be inside the tent. As I peeled my clothes off to have my nightly bath, I noticed for the first time how heavy my base layer had become. I'd worn the same Icebreaker merino thermals every day and night for close to six weeks and they'd become caked in a thick, waxy layer of sweat, body oils, dead skin and hair. And if you think that sounds bad, you should've seen my socks, which I'd started wearing inside out so the 'clean' side was next to my skin. Boy, oh boy, was it ever time to do some laundry.

When Jonesy took off his boots, the decomposing flesh smell was stronger and more potent than ever. We needed to open the doors at either end of the tent to allow the fresh cold air to flow through the tent and carry the putrid smell out. It was rank! Each night I was taking longer and longer to bathe and address my ailments, so tonight I actually timed it. Having the stopwatch ticking over probably made me address each issue with additional speed, but it still managed to soak up forty-five minutes.

Just as I was going to sleep Jonesy decided to reduce the pressure in his toes by releasing some of the pus. The smell was still lingering from when he'd taken off his boots and it was making me feel queasy. I said goodnight, which I think made him a bit irate. He wanted some help or company while he was lancing the pus but didn't expressly ask for it and I wasn't feeling good enough to offer it. I could feel a bit of tension building as I drifted off to sleep.

Video journal – Bad day on the trail
www.casandjonesy.com.au/extremesouth

DAY THIRTY-NINE

We woke to clear skies, but our minds were focused on our stomachs – hunger niggled from the moment we opened our eyes. It was our second ration day at 3000 calories (plus a few additional snacks), which meant this feeling of starvation was going to linger all day.

On the trail, my lower back was steadily becoming more painful. I felt lucky that up until this point in the journey I hadn't had to deal with any muscular or skeletal issues – I guess it was only a matter of time before one cropped up. And this one was all my fault. Over the previous week, Jonesy and I had been enjoying the improved glide so much that at the end of each shift we'd both thrust our hips forward and allow the pulk to glide up next to us or right behind us. This let us get our parka, drinks and food out of the sled without having to turn around and pull the trace-line towards us. To see the sleds glide effortlessly forward after this thrusting motion was something that would have been unthinkable a few weeks ago.

Unfortunately, my body was not used to this motion and it must have pinched a muscle or nerve. If only I had thought about what I was doing. At the time, we'd even had little competitions when we were skiing next to each other to see who could thrust the sled the furthest forward. When the pain started I felt like a goose. It was all completely avoidable and the only person I had to blame for my discomfort was myself. I was now popping two Nurofen every few hours, which seemed to help reduce the aggressive aching jabs but the general discomfort still lingered. Every now and then when I twisted awkwardly to see where Jonesy was or to manoeuvre around some sastrugi, a lightning jolt would surge through my body and my legs would buckle from the pain.

Although we were making solid progress and I was no longer having to deal with the discomfort of my inflamed scrotum, we still had to constantly fight our bodies, which – even on a good day – screamed for us to stop, set up camp and enjoy the relative warmth of our tent. But ever since Day Sixteen when we quit after three hours, I knew the feeling of stopping early was more devastating to our morale than plugging on. We just had to keep going.

DAY FORTY

CAS DIARY ENTRY – 8 DECEMBER 2011

Weird random rashes are popping up all over both our bodies – different shapes, sizes and colours ... Another grind of a day – bit more cloud cover but apart from that, same as yesterday. Can just see the Thiel Mountains off to our right. Scenery is very monotonous, nothing really changes. Lower back getting sorer and

JJ's toes still giving him grief. Meez suggested rolling on a Nalgene bottle to loosen back up – works a treat!

I am starting to hit mindless Zen out here. Hours on the trail are not bothering me and I half think that my issues sleeping are because I am not tired enough. My body and mind are restless … we can maybe, just maybe, still do this.

Over the past five days I have been slowly decreasing the weight of Cas's sled compared to mine. On the trail he seems to be getting quite tired and irritable by the end of the day. I think I need to start stepping up more on the trail. Take more weight so we can make more distance. I have to admit, I'm sick of not being able to sleep though.

Sleeping tablet taken … still not sleepy though.

I want to hit 85 degrees tomorrow – that'll be two degrees in nine days … I also want to marry a princess.

They say practice makes perfect, and after setting up camp and breaking camp for forty days, I agree. We'd managed to reduce the amount of time it took us from the moment we woke to the moment we strapped ourselves into our harnesses by over an hour, to 105 minutes. Our tasks became more clearly defined and we also changed a few things – like melting all our snow the evening before, setting up breakfast so it was waiting in the pot ready to go, and readying the hole for our toilet and the snow blocks for wiping.

For the previous five weeks, all we'd seen was endless plains of white. This day, however, we spied the distant jagged peaks of the Thiel Mountains, which instantly boosted our mood. They were too far away to change the scenery but at least they broke up the horizon. Apart from the dots on our GPS, this was the first geographic sign that we were actually making some progress and weren't just marking time on a treadmill. We weren't quite there yet, but we knew that when we drew up alongside the range, we were halfway to the Pole.

All day I'd been really looking forward to dinner. It was going to be a double whammy of our favourite food, dehydrated roast chicken and dessert. We were absolutely loving those desserts, which we treated ourselves to perhaps twice each week – it was the perfect way to finish off the day. These small things seemed to make all the difference.

DAY FORTY-ONE

As I woke up and pulled my hands out of my soft, warm sleeping-bag to light the stove, my back felt stiffer than it had all trip. Before I did anything else, I rolled on a Nalgene bottle again, which helped loosen it up enough for me to sit up, then I put my boots on and got into my chores. Day Forty-one marked our third ration day. We'd found with the dehydrated meals the best way to make ourselves feel fuller was to add plenty of water so it became a light soup, kidding ourselves that it was more substantial.

We skied along with the Thiel Mountains on our starboard side under predominantly blue skies with the odd fluffy cloud overhead. In a way it did feel as if we were out at sea and staring at land in the distance. It was nice to have the company of the rugged mountains. We skied one hour less than the day before but still managed 21.1 kilometres (the distance of a half marathon) and we crossed the elusive 85-degree line of latitude so we're officially halfway to the South Pole!

At the end of the day Jonesy and I had a bit of an awkward conversation in front of the camera. We started chatting about our friendship, and I commented that I was feeling more dependent on him than he seemed to be feeling towards me. I suppose, in a way, we were in such different places in our lives before we embarked on this expedition. Over the past four years I have become so close with Mia, and we share everything. She is privy to every thought that enters my head and vice versa. I guess with Mia not there I'd transferred this reliance onto Jonesy. However, he was the opposite – over those four years he'd become more independent. He'd been living the single life and as a result had become emotionally introverted and wasn't into sharing his feelings. In some ways we were both more distant because the expedition was so damn demanding. I started wondering whether it was us growing up or growing apart, and how much the whole Bec affair played on both our minds. At times, there seemed to be an awkwardness that had never been there before. I didn't know what to do to fix it. And I didn't know if he felt the same way.

I did know when Jonesy was getting hungry though. He didn't shy away from articulating that! We didn't add as much water to dinner so it was thicker, but as we fell asleep Jonesy was rubbing his belly, trying to reduce his hunger.

DAY FORTY-TWO

After skiing more than nine hours per day for the past week, we felt that we deserved another sleep-in, and when the alarm woke us at 8 am we both felt optimistic and energetic. It was amazing the difference a couple of extra hours' sleep made to our moods. We broke camp in a neat one hour forty-five minutes and hit the trail with a bit of bounce in our stride.

Even though it hadn't been snowing, by lunchtime we found ourselves ploughing through ten centimetres of soft snow. Where had it come from? Fortunately, due to all the food we'd eaten and the caches we'd left behind, our sleds weighed 'only' 100 kilograms each and glided better than they did at the start of the expedition despite the soft snow underfoot.

We were constantly playing number games with days, speed, food and fuel. When Jonesy was having trouble sleeping he noted in his diary:

> Scribblings in back of book – rationing numbers. I think with current rationing we can get back to Thiel but if we have time we'll have to get a resupply unless something amazing happens on the way to and back from the Pole.

DAY FORTY-THREE

The alarm woke me from a deep slumber at 7 am, but as I looked over at Jonesy I could tell he'd had another restless night, only managing to snatch about four hours' sleep in total. His body language was defeated right from the start of the day and he was in a foul mood. The fatigue from weeks of not sleeping well was starting to get the better of him. I tried to be more gentle than normal, but as we packed up our gear his temper was flaring over the smallest things. When he got his harness and compass holder all tangled around his fur ruff he completely lost it. He started yelling, cussing and stamping his feet. I have to admit, I was a bit frightened by his temper, but I think he probably scared himself a little too. I just put my head down and concentrated on moving forward.

After a while, the sastrugi from the previous few days flattened out and it felt like we were skiing on an ice rink, but with ten centimetres of soft snow on top. I trudged on and my mind wandered. I started having the most visually graphic, erotic fantasies. I couldn't escape them even if I wanted to, they were completely entrancing. Sadly, Jonesy wasn't getting any respite from his bad day. At the second break he spilt half a cup of F.I.R.S.T on his sled and at dinner he broke his spoon in half. He was just having a particularly crappy day. As Jonesy continued to stew the weather seemed to feed off his negative energy and by our final session we were engulfed by cloud. It was the not-so-perfect end to Jonesy's not-so-perfect day.

DAY FORTY-FOUR

CAS DIARY ENTRY – 12 DECEMBER 2011

I f**king HATE this place! It's cruel, unforgiving and insensitive – it gives you nothing!

Finally, with the help of some sleeping tablets, Jonesy got a decent night's sleep, and in the morning it was like the gods had passed the pissed-off-and-over-it baton from him to me. The day started out alright, but as the afternoon wore on, I got more tired and struggled to keep up.

What was really agitating me was that my body just couldn't take as much punishment as Jonesy's and was breaking down earlier. I hated hearing in his voice that he wanted to push out more miles or hours and knowing that my body just couldn't.

Having experienced the breakdown a few weeks before, I wanted to avoid having another one at all cost. I knew it would be equally frustrating for him, and that guilt is what really got me down.

I know I shouldn't be admitting this, but out there on the ice there was something deep inside me that liked to see Jonesy struggle. It comforted me and made me feel that I wasn't the only one suffering. It helped me deal with my own ailments and, in a way, gave me strength. When I've been on trips with others and there has been a group member battling with an injury or ailment, I've always wished it was me – wanting to take the pain off their hands, confident that I could deal with it better myself. But in Antarctica, I wanted Jonesy to hurt and to be the one that was slowing us down, not me. I tried to wish him well, but it was no use, these negative emotions kept bubbling to the surface.

I've always been interested in Buddhist philosophy, the essence of which is compassion – a quality I wasn't displaying much of in Antarctica. If we cannot help others or be good human beings ourselves, we should at least do no harm to others. I knew all this stuff, and back in civilisation I believed it and tried to live by it. Life back home is easy though, and it's only when you're on the edge of survival, when all the noise of city life is stripped away, that your real soul is bared – and I wasn't liking what I was seeing. In Antarctica I was being pushed right to my personal limit and I was turning my back on what I knew was right. I didn't like the thoughts I was having. They scared me.

In the tent as we were eating spaghetti bolognaise and getting ready for our sked, Aleks gave us a buzz on the satellite phone. He was chirpy and friendly as usual. He must've heard the desperation in my voice as he started giving us all kinds of motivation and support. He was like a Zen master. When Jonesy was having a bit of a whinge about the ground conditions, Aleks wisely reminded us of

Bruce Lee's philosophy of adapting to any situation. He was so right. We couldn't change the weather or the ground conditions, instead we had to work with the challenges that we were dealt rather than fighting them. He also drummed home that we'd done the hard work now and we needed to focus on the positives of being there, 'Besides,' he said, 'we've paid so much to be out here, let's enjoy it!'

Aleks did not need to be this supportive and the way our relationship was developing really motivated us to press on. It felt like the three of us were in it together and part of the same team. There was no race or competition, we all wanted the same thing: to finish what we'd started.

Aleks also suggested that we remove our insulated over-boots to help with our speed. Temperatures had improved to a balmy average of around -15° Celsius to -20° Celsius, and if we could eke out some extra miles with the same output, we were all for it. Prior to the expedition, we'd Shoe Goo'd our over-boots to our inner-boots, and for added strength screwed some short screws into the rubber sole to make sure they didn't come off. After our conversation with Aleks, we unscrewed and hacked at the glue with our Leatherman tool to cut off the insulated over-boot. By the time we'd finished with them they looked like sheep that had just walked out of an apprentice shearing shed. We were both keen to see the result out on the ice. Talking to Aleks helped me fight back some of the negative feelings I was having towards Jonesy – I had to try to channel Buddha and show compassion, to Jonesy and to myself.

DAY FORTY-FIVE

All the soul-searching of the previous day made it hard for me to sleep and I tossed and turned for most of the night. I tried swapping ends of the tent and listening to music, but my soul was restless and it took me until after midnight to finally fall asleep. I woke feeling terrible and knew I was at risk of another downward spiral if I wasn't careful. I expressed my concerns to Jonesy and although he listened, I don't think he understood the seriousness of what I was feeling. Before I crawled out of my sleeping-bag I enjoyed a couple of minutes of alone time – holding the Swarovski crystal Mia had given me and almost feeling her heartbeat through it. I missed her so much that it made me cry.

Fortunately, it was the most glorious day that we'd had on the expedition yet. Without our over-boots, the difference was immediately noticeable. From bushwalking we knew that an extra one kilogram on the feet, is the equivalent of an extra five kilograms on the back, but we didn't think this would be the case with cross-country skiing, as the foot doesn't lift during the skiing motion but shuffles. How wrong we were. By the end of the day we'd travelled faster, felt less fatigued and had clocked up a solid 25 kilometres.

Throughout the day we chatted about what provisions, equipment and spares we would add to our cache at 86 degrees south, and the rubbish that we could leave behind. Each day, we were collecting all our rubbish and stuffing it into the empty food bags, then leaving the rubbish bags at the caches to be picked up on the return journey.

That evening we removed the full-length skins from our skis and replaced them with the kicker-length ones. Skins are like a furry, carpeted surface that cross-country skiers attach to the bottom of their skis to grip the snow. They face slightly backwards, so that the ski is able to glide freely, but as you step on the ski to shuffle forward, it grips the snow allowing progress. Full-length skins are exactly that, they cover the entire bottom of the ski and provide additional grip (which is what we needed at the start of the expedition with heavier loads and the climb out of Hercules Inlet), but because of the increased surface area they are less effective at gliding forward. To overcome this, we brought half-length skins along called kicker-skins, for this point in the journey where we were hoping to get a little more efficiency from each glide. Humans traditionally don't like change and we were no different. We were excited by the prospect of moving more efficiently, but nervous that with the slick bottom of half the ski exposed we'd slip all over the fields with heavy sastrugi. Only time would tell.

As well as the skins, we also removed our oily, smelly base-layer thermals for the first time in forty-five days. We intended to drop them into the cache with our rubbish, leaving us only the pair we had on to see us through to the end, wherever that may be …

DAY FORTY-SIX

After packing our sleds, we farewelled the cache that we buried the night before. We'd called it the Centenary Cache in honour of Roald Amundsen becoming the first man to reach the South Pole a hundred years earlier to the day. Having endured forty-six days in Antarctica, I had an even greater appreciation for his efforts than I had when we began. There was to be big celebrations at the South Pole, with the Norwegian Prime Minister and eighty others making the pilgrimage to celebrate the centenary.

We did our kindergarten arts and crafts teacher proud by decorating the top of our cache pyramid with a face made from a couple of Allens snakes for the mouth, spare pink zinc for the nose and eyes. Naming him Cameron we instructed him to watch over our provisions hidden in the Centenary Cache until we got back. Anyone watching would have thought we'd gone mad as we waved Cameron goodbye.

On this day we decided to lengthen our sessions to two hours for the first three, then drop them back to ninety minutes for the final two to bring us home. The main reason for this change was that on ration days like today, we simply didn't have the snacks to split between five breaks and we thought it'd be better to eat the provisions we did have in fewer breaks. We started off well and played a game where we tried to picture where certain friends and family would be in ten years' time. It took our minds off the skiing and the time flew by. With the kicker-skins on, I found that my left foot was rolling outward and I needed to concentrate on planting my weight on its sole as it was starting to cause some pain on the outside of my ankle. That is the story of this expedition, just when you sort out one problem another can pop up out of nowhere.

It's all good and well to have grand plans, but Antarctica doesn't have an agenda, a timeframe or goals. She just is. There were a few things we could do to make the playing field more even. For one, we'd learnt that every extra gram in our sleds made a difference to our speed and every ounce we could strip from our sleds would enable faster progress. Having experienced the difference a few grams made over an entire day, we were absolutely gobsmacked that, at their final resting place on the Ross Ice Shelf, Captain Scott and his men were found to be carrying 16 kilograms of geological samples. Imagine that, 16 kilograms! Every day we were out there made that 16 kilograms seem more and more absurd. Sir Ranulph Fiennes made the comment in his book *Captain Scott* that he didn't believe this extra weight would have been a major handicap, but Jonesy and I are of the opinion that not having that weight in their sleds could have saved their lives. Scott and his men were beaten to the South Pole (just as we were about to be) and like any proud group of men felt that they needed a 'catch' or something unique from their expedition that Amundsen could *not* claim. But geological samples?

I can only guess that the point Fiennes was attempting to make was that although sled weight is important, the conditions being experienced underfoot are even more critical. From our experience, heavy sleds are no issue if conditions underfoot are firm. However, if conditions are soft it does make an enormous difference. Unfortunately, Scott and his men encountered snow flurries and blizzards on their return down the Beardmore Glacier, which hampered their progress. Lighter sleds would've helped them.

With our over-boots stripped off, kicker-skins on the bottom of our skis and lighter sleds from dumping our 86 degree Centenary Cache, we were now flying and hit our biggest mileage of the expedition − 32 kilometres in nine hours of skiing. Even more importantly, even though it was a half-ration day, we had energy left in the tank when we called it quits. The only dampener on the day was that Jonesy felt an old injury starting to flare back up again − paratendinitis in his ankle. Back in Sydney when we were pulling tyres he had this problem and the only treatment was two weeks of rest. We didn't have that luxury and so Jonesy made some inserts for his boots to raise his heels higher, hoping that would take the strain off that part of his body. He'd test it out the next day. I felt a twinge of guilt when he told me because only days before I was wishing that he was the one suffering. Be careful what you wish for! Now I was hoping for him to wake up with no problems at all. I needed him strong and I'd just have to deal with being the weaker one.

DAY FORTY-SEVEN

Jonesy and I loved our morning coffee. It wasn't anything fancy, just good ol' Nescafé Blend 43, with a generous scoop of powdered milk and a dash of sugar. But with the way rationing was working, every third morning was our coffee morning, the others were tea. Having any hot drink to start the day was extremely welcome, but coffee kicked tea's butt, and today was a coffee day.

Outside the tent, the day was overcast and a good five centimetres of fresh powdery snow had fallen gently through the night. For the first time this trip, the wind was on our backs, which was why it was snowing; the warmer, humid air from the coast had moved across the continent, frozen and fallen as precipitation. We crossed our fingers that the fresh snow wouldn't slow our progress too much, and headed off.

In the dull light of the overcast sky, we trudged and talked for hours about the Huckleberry Finn-style adventure we shared in 2001, when we became the first team to kayak the length of Australia's longest river – the 2560-kilometre mighty Murray – over forty-nine days. At the time we were young, naive insecure kids not sure of our place in the world. That trip and other early adventures helped us both understand and define who we were and how we wanted to live. Ten years on I was much more sure of myself and hadn't been finding the same dramatic revelations – more of a reaffirmation of those earlier lessons not to give up and to keep moving forward. But there was also an element of adjustment that we were dealing with, sometimes badly. I was getting married and Jonesy was still single. Things were changing and how we were interacting on the trail reflected the different stages of life we were in.

And no-one is at their best when they are hungry. It was our sixth day at half-rations and the lack of food was starting to impede our progress. Towards the end of the two-hour sessions, we found our energy would crumble and our speed wither. It wasn't helping that I'd started putting aside all my meat rations from our snack bags – salami, bacon and dried meat – to give to Jonesy on

Christmas Day. I figured this, more than anything, would be a present he'd appreciate and show him how committed I was to our friendship. I had the feeling he wasn't so sure how important he was to me anymore.

It was Jonesy's lead for the last session and I tucked in close behind him as he plodded through the last hour or so. I'd gotten used to pushing the last session out harder, and knowing that we hadn't made the best progress in the morning I was surprised by his lack of speed. After twenty minutes, I skied up next to him and shouted so that he could hear me above the music blaring in his earphones:

'Hey bro, wanna swing leads every twenty minutes for this last session?'

Seemingly a little taken aback, he replied, 'Um ... yeah, okay.'

I hit the lead and took off. After twenty minutes Jonesy skied strongly past me and continued on with added vigour. It reminded me of a fartlek training session back home. I really enjoyed us both feeding off each other in this last session and we made some phenomenal progress. It felt great to be matching it with Jonesy but he wasn't as exhilarated.

Jonesy seemed to be getting more tired and when we hit the tent each night he was withdrawn and irritated. I noted it in my diary:

He is very curt and sharp in the evenings, often makes pointed comments – bad negative energy.

It was bound to happen. It all came to a head when I was typing an SMS on the sat-phone to Aleks, which I stupidly deleted and then made the half-joking comment that Jonesy was much better at this stuff and that he should do it.

He snapped like a striking snake, 'F★★k off! YOU do it!'

His venom shocked me and I replied, 'Dude, that hurt.'

Jonesy's reply was even more startling. 'You arrogant f★★k. You always get me to do what you don't want to. Just because your life is *so* perfect …'

We were both tired and said things we shouldn't have and didn't quite mean. It all came out badly. Jonesy noted in his diary:

> **Every now and then the angry J comes out before I can stop him and he's said something in not the nicest manner. This place, the stress, the constant pain in my feet, the worry for me and Cas, the hunger, the frustration and lack of sleep is not a good environment for him (angry J). I regretted my words instantly but made matters worse by getting defensive. Anyhow I wish I could undo it all. I do love him heaps but this trip is trying to drive us apart.**

The tent wasn't the most pleasant environment that evening but in a way it was good to clear the air. We found it best to deal with this negative energy as it happened, rather than let it brew. We'd been rationing food for over two weeks and scrupulously watching our fuel consumption, which also contributed to our flaring tempers. We'd budgeted 600 millilitres per day for the first month (because we were expecting colder temperatures) and since then had provisioned 500 millilitres per day. By carefully watching our usage, we'd been consuming a mere 300 millilitres per day – it wasn't lack of fuel that would call a premature end to our expedition, it'd either be lack of food or ourselves that would do it.

Our North Face VE25 tent, fitted with solar panels, was buffeted regularly with 80 kilometre per hour winds.

Merry Christmas, Jonesy!

The only man I know who would be excited by a bag of dried meat (and yes, he also had Spam cravings).

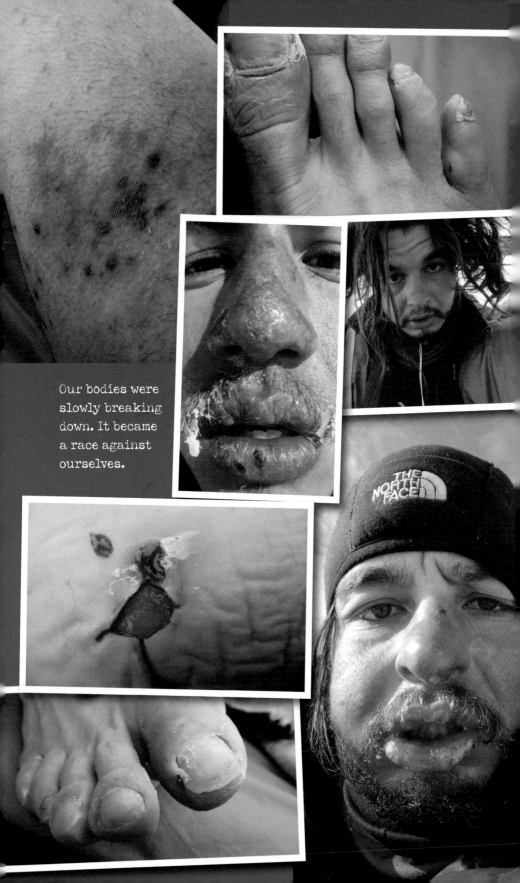

Our bodies were slowly breaking down. It became a race against ourselves.

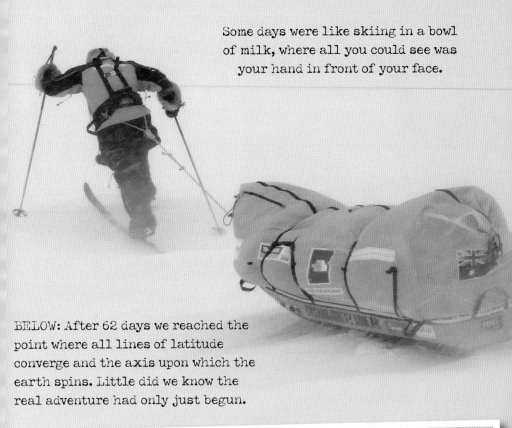

Some days were like skiing in a bowl
of milk, where all you could see was
your hand in front of your face.

BELOW: After 62 days we reached the
point where all lines of latitude
converge and the axis upon which the
earth spins. Little did we know the
real adventure had only just begun.

Celebrating the finish! Four years before, 25,000 people had greeted us at the shores of a New Zealand beach, this time there were no spectators. Jonesy, Aleks and I were greeted by a stadium of silence. We were all teary — it was one of the most incredible moments of my life.

Between us we lost 56 kilograms:
I lost 26 kilograms and
Jonesy lost 30 kilograms.

BELOW LEFT: We were stoked to be able to raise $60,000 for You Can.
They need all the help they can get to raise much-needed funds and
awareness for Australian youth with cancer. PHOTO: SIMON KERSLAKE

BELOW RIGHT: The proudest moment of my life, the thought of which
kept me going every single day in Antarctica: marrying Mia. Jonesy
was by my side as best man. It was a fairytale.

DAY FORTY-EIGHT

The tent rattled in the wind and when I looked out I could see we'd been engulfed by overcast skies. The cloudy weather over the previous few days, which had brought snow, slowed the surface and made the sleds feel heavier. Fortunately, the clouds parted around lunchtime and by early afternoon it had cleared beautifully. I loved the way the sun glistened off the coarse ice granules and threw a rainbow of colours from each crystal. They sparkled like stars on a smoky white sky, I felt like I was suspended and walking through space. As soon as I pulled my goggles over my face, I was on another planet, like an astronaut on Mars.

Our progress was slower than we'd have liked in the morning, but really picked up in the afternoon. Jonesy and I were talking more, reflecting on our paddle across Bass Strait. It was nothing compared to what we were doing now and how we were having to dig so deep. On that expedition, our rest days: non-rest day ratio was much higher, which enabled us to absorb the environments we were in. It had been less about the paddling, climbing and walking and more about the beauty of the landscapes we found ourselves in. On this expedition we were both being forced to look at the uglier sides of our character and at times that wasn't pleasant.

By the end of the day we'd clocked up our second biggest day to date, and in quite trying conditions. I jumped in the tent, melted snow and prepared dinner – *mmm* fish pie – while Jonesy was outside securing the tent for the night. When he got inside he connected the spare phone up to the computer to send a video back to base. I put the spare satellite phone in a pocket in the tent roof, warming it up for the upcoming sked calls. Just after we'd dished the fish pie into our overflowing mugs, I knocked the tent wall. In slow motion, the satellite phone fell out of the pocket, onto my

Therm-a-Rest and did a perfect somersault before landing in my partially rehydrated, practically liquid fish pie.

Aghast, we both sat there stunned and then, almost in unison, lunged to rescue the phone like lifeguards plucking a toddler from a swimming pool. I got to it first and started sucking on it to extract as much water from inside as possible. It looked like I was performing mouth-to-mouth on the phone. It might sound funny now, but losing a sat-phone at this stage of the expedition was a serious issue. It would cut our margin of safety to continue with just one working phone and we couldn't ask for another when (and if) we reached the Pole because that would completely negate our unsupported status.

After dismantling the phone to help dry it out we sat back and looked at each other in shocked disbelief. Having both dropped our mobile phones in pools and schooners of beer back home, we knew we didn't dare turn it on for at least a few days. I was surprised Jonesy wasn't more angry at me, or me more angry at myself. Don't get me wrong, I understood the seriousness of my clumsiness. There wasn't room on the ice to be a klutz but this was an accident that was just plain bad luck. And we had the second phone and our Solara tracking unit as a back-up which could send text messages to Bec back home if needed, so I wasn't going to waste energy with guilt. See, I was learning.

DAY FORTY-NINE

CAS DIARY ENTRY – 17 DECEMBER 2011

Another terrible night's sleep. Woke up feeling crap/ headache. Couldn't find my undies for half an hour so couldn't get dressed. Ended up being in sleeping-bag.

Over being here this morning. Spoke to Mum and Dad last night – good pick-up – they said we should be so proud. Beautiful bluebird day on trail – zero cloud. Really helped pick up my glum mood. Conditions underfoot firm – icy patches, more sastrugi around than last couple of days. Missed poo hole and weed on undies. Quite a hilly day – went up three big climbs – elevation 2025 metres – 800 metres to go. Bit angry at myself for listening to JJ about pushing on for another twenty mins to get to 28 kilometres – we're still in the consolidation phase, the push will come in 7–10 days, plus we need to feel as fit and rested as possible for it. Finally, finally, finally starting to feel end is in sight. It's so dangerous to play number games – but it'd be awesome if we can get to the Pole this year. Both of us are feeling a faint glimmer of hope if we get the right conditions that we might be able to do an epic push back to Hercules Inlet. Toes are definitely colder without over-boot, heels are now constantly numb. JJ is dealing with a fair amount of pain with his toes, feet, cold hands and lips – it's just amazing how he doesn't let the constant pain wear him down.

JONESY DIARY ENTRY – 17 DECEMBER 2011

Ration Day 7

Fifty days tomorrow.

We did a good day on the trail although I think that we pushed on a bit too long. I think Cas wasn't too happy in hindsight that he agreed to do another twenty mins – we did get to 28 kilometres though. 808.2 kilometres down the entire trip. The left hand toes are getting worse I have to admit but it isn't as of yet stopping us on the trail.

We did 110 kilometres in four days. That's a full degree.

Hopefully tomorrow brings a good day and we both sleep well. Cas had a bad sleep last night – this morning he was in a foul mood – swearing saying he f**king hated this place and couldn't wait to leave. On the trail his mood improved – it was too beautiful a day (windy though).

My fingers are starting to really suffer with the cold however and perhaps the altitude each day – at break it takes a lot to warm them up.

Last night playing with food bags outside – I got far too cold.

DAY FIFTY

Thank goodness – a decent night's kip! I woke up in a great mood. Fortunately, I was able to find my undies straightaway and hit the day's chores eagerly. I was looking forward to getting out skiing.

There were many more fields of sastrugi that we had to navigate through, and although they slowed our progress I really enjoyed getting lost in their beautifully sculptured shapes. Manoeuvring around, over and through these fields also broke the monotony of a day and made the skiing fun and engaging. Conditions overhead were quite volatile, dancing between complete cloud cover to bluebird sky and back again. This change also helped fight off the monotony of the landscape and kept us absorbed in the motion of skiing.

I often spent my time skiing thinking through all aspects of adventure and that day I was focused on the advances to expedition technology (perhaps the sat-phone mishap was playing on my mind) and where I think it's heading in the future. Probably the biggest assistance technology had given us on this trip actually happened before we even left Australia, and that was a deeper understanding of effective training, physiology and expedition nutrition. All the other areas of the expedition – improved communications, lighter and more efficient/effective clothing and equipment have all helped, but not to the same extent. If you were to apply this same way of thinking to a car, the big improvements have been to the efficiency of the car's engine and fuel. All the other things are nice add-ons – like iPod connectivity and airbags – but they don't help drive the car forward.

After a while I asked Jonesy where he thought expedition technology would be in ten years' time. He thought the big improvement would be in communication so that people back home could follow adventures in real time. He made me laugh when he said, 'Imagine having a small camera mounted on your head, beaming live footage back to computer screens from anywhere on earth!'

Hmmmm ... you'd have to be able to turn it off while going to the toilet, but I agreed that seemed probable. I also envisaged gear getting lighter and more efficient. What I really wanted to see was a successful version of our POW that would be a more efficient means of hauling heavy sleds over longer distances. Pulling heavy loads in cold places will never be easy and the improvements technology will bring will be incremental. I don't want these improvements to turn Antarctica into a fun park, but I would like to see expeditions getting back to the basics of attempting these journeys unsupported and ideally returning back to their start points. It was an interesting conversation and made the time pass fairly quickly, but towards the end of the day Jonesy's feet seemed to be giving him more grief than usual. I noted it in my diary that evening:

My body at day fifty is looking alright, last few days it's felt good. For the first time this trip I'm looking better than JJ with his toes and lips.

I wasn't taking pleasure in Jonesy's pain but for most of the journey so far I'd been looking at myself as the delinquent, the whining brat and the one holding us back. I was starting to see that Jonesy's body was now breaking down, that he was human and hurting. This gave me the resolve that I might just be able to hang in there.

Ever since we started rationing, Jonesy had taken on the responsibility of organising the food, dividing up portions and keeping a check on how much we had left. Apart from enjoying this task, he was much better suited to it than I was. He was meticulous in ensuring that provisions were split perfectly evenly to avoid the scenario of one person feeling hard done by. He was so careful in his work, that when dividing up snacks he wouldn't just make sure that the bags were even, he made sure each had the same number of nuts, pieces of chocolate and lollies. There is no way I could ever have shown the same level of patience, I would've poured about half a bag into another and said, 'she'll be right'. Most evenings Jonesy sorted the food in the tent, but when he tried doing it outside he got way too cold. By the time he came inside the tent again, his lips were blue and his fingers had lost their dexterity. I'm sure he had the screaming barfies as they warmed up.

DAY FIFTY-ONE

When you spend too much time with one person, it's only natural for their idiosyncrasies to grate on your nerves after a while.

Especially under these extreme conditions with broken sleep, reduced food and almost constant pain. After having spent close to a year living with Jonesy before the expedition and then not seeing another human being other than him for the last two months, well, let's just say he was definitely starting to annoy me. And I am sure he felt the same way about me. It wasn't hate or anything extreme, it was more like how I imagine an ageing married couple would feel after spending too much time together – they start to niggle each other.

Jonesy's attention to detail and my higher-level planning makes us work well as a team, but his pedantic overzealous attention to things I felt didn't make any difference was really starting to send me bonkers. An example of this was if I was leading when we were marching, he'd pay close attention to the needle of the compass and pull me up if I was drifting a couple of degrees either left or right of our bearing. I was more relaxed and had the approach of, 'Whatever, we'll go a little more left this session and a little more right next session.' Not good enough for Jonesy. He wanted us smack, bang on the bearing so we didn't have to ski an inch further than we had to. It was fair enough, and I know my 'she'll be right' approach annoyed him just as much. We had a similar fight about how much water to pre-melt in the kettle at night and Jonesy detailed his thoughts in his diary:

> **Argument with Cas this morning – he is really taking his shit sleep out on me. Again massively condescending. He asks me to be direct and say things when I feel them, so I asked on a cooked breakfast morning could we have more water melted [the night before], to which he said okay and then backtracked and said it was a stupid question.**

Although these differences in the way we approached life resulted in tension, I wouldn't want it any other way – it's what makes us stronger as a team and so we both just had to suck it up. I'd started merrily chatting to Polar Dude on the trail, and with all these little disagreements he was well and truly on my side.

We were skiing south on half-rations and though we passed some of the most beautiful sastrugi we had seen all trip it was hard to get excited, particularly at the end of the second and third sessions when I felt ridiculously hungry and low on energy. The limited rations were definitely impeding our performance. Even though we were well into the climb up to the plateau, because conditions underfoot were firm the incline wasn't as taxing as I thought it'd be. Using the word 'climb' paints an image of crampons gripping the steep icy slopes of a mountain. It was nothing like that. In fact, if you were walking the dog back home you'd almost call it flat. The gentle rise was over such vast distances that often the only way we knew we were going up was when we were travelling slower than normal or when, at the end of the day, our GPS told us that we had. This ascent wasn't just a continual rise, and throughout the day we ascended and descended over three hills. The position of the sun and the way the light reflected off the snow made a massive difference to how intimidating the rises appeared. Some looked like real hills from a distance, but ended up being rather flat when we reached them.

Skiing on a gentle hill, I felt like a vessel travelling over a frozen ocean and every now and then we'd pass frozen waves and islands of sastrugi that strengthened the impression even more. The bigger sastrugi were close to two metres tall. It was weird but some looked like enormous ears and the prettier ones like jewellery, others like shipwrecks. I've always loved photography and could have absorbed myself for hours shooting these unique creations but we couldn't afford the time. At this stage, it was all about pushing south and clocking kilometres. Despite this pressure, every now and then though the beauty would seize me and we'd set up the camera and either film or snap the shot.

We were shooting a documentary about our journey but pulling out the camera in these conditions proved to be a real challenge. For starters, it was so cold that the camera batteries need to be warmed up against our skin prior to shooting. Then we only had a pygmy-tripod that was less than one foot tall. If we wanted some height on the shot, we needed to cut snow blocks with our snow saw and then pile them on top of each other to the appropriate height. Once the shot was framed, one of us would ski through it to ensure it was composed the way we wanted, then we'd both go and hook up to the sleds and ski through the shot. This would take between fifteen and thirty minutes, which was time we could've been skiing towards our goal. Adding to the fun was that the camera body was metal and so cold it sucked any feeling you might have from your fingers. And all that was twice as hard when it was windy, blizzarding, or both (which is of course what viewers want to see!).

We made the call towards the start of the expedition that we were going to aim for 'quality' filming over capturing hours of wobbly handy-cam stuff. If we were going to shoot something, we were going to do it properly then pack the camera up and not use it for a few days. At 'night' time, I wrote potential shot lists in the back of my diary and during the day I would ski along looking for ways we could position the camera, interesting foregrounds to use in the composition and shots I'd pictured on my list. Jonesy is absolutely brilliant at cutting footage and piecing together a storyline, but he doesn't get the same level of engagement from filming, so I found myself driving this.

Once we'd finished skiing for the day, I transformed my half of the tent into a laundry, to wash my homemade G-string again. I submerged it into clean soapy water in my bath-plastic bag. Instantly the grime and dirt discoloured the water and when I started kneading them, the water turned a milky greeny-grey. Gross! You can only imagine how excited I was to put on a clean pair in the morning.

Video journal – Washing day
www.casandjonesy.com.au/extremesouth

DAY FIFTY-TWO

You know at home, when you sleep in past your alarm, as soon as you open your eyes the light has a certain harshness to it? Well, out on the ice the light was the same twenty-four hours a day, and without looking at my watch I had no way of telling what time it was. As a sensitive sleeper, for most of the trip I'd been nabbing my shut-eye with earplugs pressed in, and Jonesy had the alarm tucked under his beanie next to his ear. For some reason, for the first time on the trip, he missed the beeping and we slept way past our wake-up time. When my eyes opened naturally and I peered down at my watch I almost leapt out of my sleeping-bag, 8.09 am!

'Jonesy! Wake up, bro! We slept in!'

The amount of anxiety and worry sleeping in by one hour caused was ridiculous. We both tore through our morning tasks and were stoked to be on the trail ninety minutes after waking up – a record, and half the time it took us in the first week of the expedition – but we still felt behind schedule. We were so busy getting ready we hardly noticed the crappy weather until we stepped into our harnesses. It was a complete white-out. Damn. Typical T.I.A. We were expecting to pass through the first crevassed area in 500 kilometres and we had zero visibility with snow. I took the first lead and though it was hard going, I actually had fun navigating through rough sastrugi. Much to Jonesy's delight, I kept a careful watch on my compass for direction. At the end of two and a half hours, we stopped for our first break and I was happy to have pushed out 8.5 kilometres. I was skiing hard as I felt I had to, knowing that in a few hours the falling snow would slow our progress as it began to cover the ground. I was keen to get out as many miles as possible before this happened.

Jonesy took the second shift and right from the start he was having all kinds of problems – his goggles completely fogged up and he was uncomfortable and unnerved when he couldn't see where he was going. As a result his progress in the lead was slow as he fumbled blindly around. Not surprisingly he started getting more and more agitated. After about forty-five minutes, he skied off the back of a huge sastrugi and disappeared. He'd taken a big fall, it was like skiing off the roof of a car. I pulled up beside him and he was splayed out on his back like an angry Christmas beetle trying to right himself. He started cursing and I was worried he'd broken a bone or tweaked his knee or something.

'What's wrong mate?' I asked, unable to hide my concern.

'I've broken a f★★king ski pole. Shit!'

'It's all good – so long as you haven't broken yourself.'

'Nah, I think I'm alright.'

We whacked our parkas on and pulled the repaired ski pole, which I'd snapped on Day Two, from the bottom of my pulk. The splint on it was solid and we packed the newly broken pole into the top of my sled planning to repair it that night. By the time we were done stuffing about, Jonesy's hands had turned to blocks of ice and he was quite angry at himself for allowing that to happen. I took the lead for the remainder of the session to allow Jonesy to collect himself. When you're pushing speed and distance in conditions such as these, there's a good chance you're going to fall, it was just lucky that all Jonesy broke was one pole and not his body.

Later that afternoon, Jonesy was leading strongly out in front listening to some music when I tried to call out to him.

'Jonesy! Wait up!' He couldn't hear me above the wind, snow and music.

I pulled out into his periphery vision on his right side and yelled again 'STOP!'

I drew up next to him.

'What's up?' Jonesy quizzed.

'Check out your trail – your sled has been destroying the bridges of a heap of mini-crevasses. We're in a crevasse field.'

'Whaaaaat?' He turned around and saw the potholes he'd been unknowingly uncovering. It shook him up to know the danger we could have been in. I shuddered remembering the endless darkness when I had fallen into that crevasse on Day Two. Fortunately, the crevasses in this field were all pretty small, no wider than a foot or so. With skis on there wasn't too much risk of falling through, but we didn't know if there were bigger ones ahead. The visibility was atrocious and we had no chance of being able to make out indents in the surface of the snow that would warn us there was a crevasse beneath. It was risky, but we made the call to press on. I've heard polar travel described as 'long periods of boredom punctuated by bursts of extreme anxiety'. I couldn't have said it better myself.

After fifty-two days' skiing, the tips of our skis and poles had become extended feelers for our hands and feet. Even though they were inanimate they seemed to have the same sensitivity as my fingertips and toes. If I were to march without them, I felt like I was missing a limb. Regardless of what the visibility was like I could feel if the ski tip was floating on the edge of a sastrugi or had just bumped into one. Also making life a little easier in these trying conditions was trailing rather than leading, as the sled in front of you and the tracks it made gave enough contrast on the snow to reveal warning features. The only issue was sticking close enough to the sled and not letting it get any further than a couple of metres in front.

Marching in white-outs not only slowed our progress, but also sapped our energy because we had to concentrate so much more. Given the conditions, the sleep-in and the broken-ski-pole incident, at the end of the final session we were stoked to have notched up 26 kilometres in nine hours of skiing. Exhausted, we jumped into the tent and Jonesy wrote in his diary:

> **Well, what a shit day. I'm in the tent now, it's freezing, my toes and hands are cold, I'm hungry – dinner didn't even hit the sides. Lips, toes, hands and groin are all getting worse.**

I wasn't sure if it was the increased altitude or just the fact that we'd been thrashing our bodies for seven weeks straight, but Jonesy's extremities were being hammered and provided ridiculous amounts of discomfort to him so maybe I should have let what happened next during sked go, but I didn't.

A bone of contention over recent years between Jonesy and me has been when he unconsciously refers to things we do as a team together as 'I' (meaning Jonesy). He's also always found it hard to 'fess up when he's done wrong and take ownership, and it always gets under my skin. When describing the ski-pole incident to Bec he said: '*We* broke a ski pole today and *I'm* going to fix it.'

What made me most angry was the fact that as he was relaying this information to Bec, I had the tool kit out and was in the middle of sawing a ski peg with our ten-centimetre hacksaw blade to create a splint for the broken pole. I cut the aluminium tent peg into a 150 millimetre length and bent the edges with the pliers on the Leatherman to form a half-pipe cradle. Then placed the broken pole in the splint, clamped it tight with the Leatherman and taped it firmly with strapping tape – seemed to work a treat! We were both stressed, tired and oversensitive, so of course we had words once he got off the sat-phone. But nothing too bad.

DAY FIFTY-THREE

Fortunately the white-out had cleared and we didn't miss the alarm. Unfortunately the surface suffered a hangover from the day before and was sticky. It wasn't that much snow had fallen, rather that the crystals on the surface appeared furry and clawed at the runners on our sled, making the going hard, slow and heavy. Ground conditions were the make-it or break-it factor that would dictate how far from the Pole we'd get on our return journey.

Both of us had been enjoying the extra glide we were eking out by having the kicker-skins on, but we were becoming increasingly frustrated that the front attachment point for these kicker-skins were constantly loosening and causing the attachment to act like a wood plane on the snow's surface. This prevented glide and as soon as some snow accumulated under the skin, the effects became exponentially worse. We were having to constantly stop to dig out the snow and retighten the kicker. It was happening again and again. I couldn't believe this design flaw – bloody Swedes! They definitely didn't have their gear sorted like the Norwegians did.

This planing motion was adding additional strain to my left ankle, and I was needing to down a couple of Nurofen every few hours. By our second break, I'd had enough and psyched myself up for an on-trail repair, which I knew was going to leave my fingers numb and frozen. I whacked on my parka, pulled out the Leatherman, chopped off the metal bracket at the front of the skin and, just wearing my thin Polypro gloves, tried to screw a couple of short screws through the skin and into the wooden ski. The first couple went in great, but as my fingers numbed I lost dexterity and it became incredibly difficult. On the very last screw I felt like a bomb-disposal expert knowing that if I didn't get the screw in on this turn, my fingers would be too far gone to do any more work and we ran the risk of then needing to set up the tent, warm my fingers and finish the job properly.

'C'mon,' I whispered desperately to myself as I held the tiny screw in my numb fingers and drove the Phillips head screwdriver with all the concentration and conviction I could muster. I felt the thread catch in the wood and let out a cry of relief.

Back on the trail, my fingers took a good forty minutes to warm up, but it was well worth the discomfort as the repair worked a treat.

We were approaching 88 degrees south (900 kilometres from Hercules Inlet) and were excited to be dumping our next cache, the Christmas Cache. After eleven hours on the trail skiing, it was well and truly quittin' time. We found ourselves at the bottom of a big hill with enormous sastrugi surrounding us. It wasn't the most ideal place for a cache because if the lighting was poor on the return it would be hard to make out the shape of a cairn in this jumbled mess of ice. We decided to push on to the top of the hill and lay the cache there. Big mistake! We knew distances were proving hard to judge, but the top of the hill really only looked about a fifteen-minute ski away. We started plugging up the hill, which due to its gradient would've made a terrible slopey campsite, so even if we wanted to stop we were now committed to climbing until it levelled out. Unfortunately, it was one of those hills that never seemed to end, it just kept going and going. And going. And going. It had been a half-ration day and after an extra forty minutes, Jonesy was really hurting and lagging, it was the most I've seen him struggle all trip. He described how he was feeling in his diary:

> My extremities are going through hell – face, lips in particular, fingers and toes – the faster we get down to 86 degrees the better. I really need the sun and the altitude is hitting my fingers particularly hard. I was EXHAUSTED ...

Enough was enough, and we called a halt. We were still on the hill but it had evened out a little and would have to do. We were completely spent. Finishing late really put pressure on the evening chores and forced us to become multi-tasking ninjas. We frantically had up to three tasks on the go at any one time.

Once the tent was erected, we went through the process of examining every tool, spare and item of clothing and removing everything we didn't need for the next eighteen days, this meant only taking toilet paper, Vaseline, toothpaste and tea for the days we needed – every gram counted.

DAY FIFTY-FOUR

With the late finish the day before and the packing of our Christmas Cache, we didn't end up getting to sleep till close to midnight. The sun had remained hidden by cloud, and up on the plateau the cold was piercing – even inside the tent. It took me close to an hour to warm up enough in my sleeping bag before I could go to sleep.

We'd spent the last week climbing up onto the Polar Plateau and deep into the interior of Antarctica. It's regarded as the driest, windiest, coldest place on earth and is completely void of any life. Apart from the scientific base at the South Pole, nothing lives here – not even microorganisms – it's too cold. This place defines desolation in every sense of the word. The average height of the plateau sits at 2800 metres and it's predominantly flat, with most of the sastrugi having evened out. Robert Scott got it right when he described the place during his 1901–04 Discovery expedition:

> A scene so wildly and awfully desolate ... it cannot
> fail to impress me with gloomy thoughts.

We'd heard from a number of other teams that because the plateau is colder and higher than the ground we'd already traversed, the snow has a tendency to be more granular and prevents sleds from gliding. Glide comes when a ski (or sled) through movement melts the snow's surface, which in turn reduces friction. With temperatures of around -30° Celsius, we were concerned that it was too cold to allow glide. The overcast conditions and bitter temperatures were hard on us both, but really affected Jonesy's extremities – his middle finger completely lost feeling and his lips and cheeks blistered badly.

We waved the cache goodbye at 9.45 am and set off south across the bitterly cold plateau. We'd dropped close to 30 kilograms at the Christmas Cache, and our sleds were by far the lightest they'd been all journey. To our enormous disappointment, the sleds continued to feel heavy and our progress slow. Massive hit to morale. Not wanting to mention this to one another, we trudged on in a gloomy silence praying that it was due to the snow that had fallen over the past couple of days and not conditions on the plateau.

By the end of the day we'd knocked out a solid 26 kilometres and made the call to take the third rest day of the expedition, the first since my breakdown on Days Twenty-nine and Thirty. With this in mind, Jonesy dug into his rations after dinner – he just couldn't stop snacking!

DAY FIFTY-FIVE

Rest day! And boy did we need it. I slept well knowing that I didn't have to leap up in the morning, and blissfully drifted through until 9 am in a peaceful slumber. As soon as I woke I felt guilty for not being out skiing and that feeling lingered all day. We snoozed, watched a couple of movies and tried to keep our minds from thinking about food. We were both starving and since we weren't on the trail, needed to conserve our rations for when we were. It was hard not to think about the hunger. In a way, it was easier when we were out skiing as we had something to occupy our thoughts, but inside the tent the biggest highlight was the food. Kind of like when you're bored at home and you find yourself digging into the fridge even when you're not hungry ... or is that just me?

Apart from resting, the break gave us the time to do a few repairs, speak to family back home and send through some data for the website. We completely removed the kicker-skins from our skis and were going to rely on the scales over the mid-section to grip the snow. We were hoping this would allow us more glide on the sticky surface. Even though we'd tried to repair Jonesy's Therm-a-Rest over five weeks before, there was still a slow leak which we addressed on this rest day. By allowing Jonesy's toes to breathe all day we could already see improvement after a few hours. As with most of our ailments, if we'd given them a few days' rest they'd have recovered quickly, but we didn't have that luxury.

I spoke to Mia, but she didn't seem to be as engaged or supportive as she had been at other times. She had every reason to be resentful, and adding to that I wasn't there to help organise our wedding. It must've also been tough for her putting on a brave face with people constantly asking her, 'Isn't it hard?' I don't blame her for holding a grudge, but I hoped that things would go back to normal when I got home. And perhaps it was just me? Both Jonesy and I had become hypersensitive to the strangest things. It is tough to connect to the person you love when they are so far away.

PHASE THREE
The Push

DAY FIFTY-SIX

Odd colour poo, like oil – hope it isn't blood.

Neither of us had the best night's sleep, and woke early at 6 am to unusually warm weather (-14° Celsius) and blue skies. After our rest day, we felt that we were transitioning into the final phase of the expedition – The Push. This meant getting up earlier, finishing later and hopefully pushing out more miles. In our planning, the expedition had been broken into three phases – Phase One: Survival; Phase Two: Breaking Through; Phase Three: The Push. The boundaries for each phase were loose, however the events of the expedition had done a pretty good job in defining them for us. Phase One came to an end after we took our rest days on Days Twenty-nine and Thirty, and for the four weeks that followed we had to focus on keeping well within our limits so we could keep going. Now that we were heading into the final month, we had to push through and give it everything. Given what we'd already been through, we weren't sure if we could maintain the pace we needed, but with the distance back to Hercules Inlet via the South Pole still close to 1400 kilometres we had to give it a shot.

With out skins removed and just the patterned scales on our skis gripping the snow, the forward glide was fabulous! We could not believe the freedom and ease we experienced by not having the skins on, it felt like – for the first time on the whole trip – we were now properly skiing, not just thrashing about, and what also helped fuel our morale was that the surface was still soft and furry – imagine what it'd be like when the ground was firm! We'd decided to try and ski out the day in four 2.5 hour sessions, with a ten-minute break between each session. With warmer temperatures, we started the day without our shell layer on – another welcome change, at first. The downside of this was that as soon as a breath of wind popped up it instantly chilled us through to the bone. Thankfully, the wind stayed dormant and we were able to enjoy perhaps our finest weather all trip.

At the end of the day, before we erected the tent, Jonesy pulled out the GPS.

'Okay, okay, today felt good. Ten hours' skiing – how far do you reckon we went?' he asked.

'Thirty kilometres?'

'No – 35.4 kilometres!'

We both let out a massive whoop and there were high fives all round. We were jazzed! The only thing souring our day's miles were the longing thoughts of family back home. It was Christmas Eve in Australia and we weren't there. Jonesy's brother hosted his family's Christmas up in Darwin and Jonesy really felt like he was missing out. His family don't all get together often and he was worried about how long it would be until the next time. Mia was spending Christmas at her sister's place in Canberra and my family were in Sydney. This was one of the most emotional times, and we both felt isolated and alone. While we did what we'd done for the previous fifty-five evenings – melting snow, rehydrating meals, drying our clothes – at that exact time our families were preparing turkey and singing Christmas carols. They were a world away and the distance made me physically ache.

We also found out at sked that Aleks had reached the South Pole. He was planning on spending a couple of days resting before hightailing it back to the coast. So impressive. He had done it all alone and I was happy for him – but just a little bit jealous.

DAY FIFTY-SEVEN

JONESY DIARY ENTRY – 25 DECEMBER 2011

What an AWESOME day! If I had to re-give my mental score it'd be a solid nine!

Trail – 37 kilometres – another record in 10 hrs 5 mins!

Tomoz we'll go for 40 kilometres, but we'll have to up food intake, it's meant to be a half-ration day but more likely be a ¾ day!

Overslept by 45 mins.

On the trail I thought a lot about the doco.

Sometimes in life you can't pick the path you'll follow but one thing that you can do is make sure you live.

I want to keep writing but we're getting up @ 0615 tomoz to crank out some miles! BEST DAY EVER!

Still hungry though.

Merry Christmas! When I crawled outside I was greeted by a snowman that Jonesy had secretly made the night before. It was decked out in a Santa hat, and it set a great mood for the day. From the moment we woke, we wore red Santa hats with white pom-poms on top.

Skiing along we had a good chat about Christmas and what it actually means. I know this sounds a bit clichéd, but being on these

232

kinds of trips and feeling true deprivation reminds me of what's important in life and what's not. Missing family on Christmas Day really drove home how important they are to both of us and how we should prioritise them more in our lives. Sure it's great to be goal-driven and ambitious, but nothing is more important than spending time with family.

We finished skiing at 7 pm and notched up another record day. It's almost feeling like a different expedition compared to the first few weeks. To clock up these distances in the first couple of weeks would've taken three painful days of toil. Our strategy of doing less hours on the trail at the start was beginning to make sense: one hour skiing now saw us two kilometres closer to the Pole than one hour skiing at the beginning of the expedition.

I jumped in the tent while Jonesy finished securing the guylines and snow flaps. Straight after the stove was roaring and melting snow, I immediately set to work, blowing up balloons and hanging them from the clothesline on the roof of the tent. Jonesy unzipped the tent door and as he crossed the threshold I sang out, 'Merry Christmas Jonesy!'

'Merry Christmas Casa!'

This was going to be the whitest of white Christmases ever. We tore through our tasks then started cooking our Christmas dinner – a full serving of roast lamb each followed by dehydrated cheesecake and some pudding made by Jonesy's sister, Louisa.

Exactly one hundred years earlier, Bowers, a member of Scott's final Pole party, would have also been tucking into a special Christmas dinner with his companions:

> a good fat hoosh with pony meat and ground biscuit. A chocolate hoosh made of water, cocoa, sugar, biscuits, raisins, and thickened with a spoonful of arrowroot.

Then came 2½ square inches of plum duff each and a good mug of cocoa washed down the whole ... I positively could not eat all of mine.

While dinner was cooking (well ... rehydrating) we both got our clothes bags and pulled out presents for one another. These had to be lightweight, but deliver maximum pick-me-up value. Jonesy went first and gave me my present, it was a penguin beanie. We hadn't seen any of the little blighters when we left the coast and there was zero chance of seeing one in the interior of Antarctica. It made us laugh as I whacked it on.

Then it was my turn. I first gave Jonesy a Christmas card that I'd made a few nights before. I'm a pretty terrible artist, but I'd drawn two stick figures skiing with sleds and wrote this:

Dear Jonesy,
This is our third expedition together. Thank you for being a massive part of my life. I wouldn't be whole without you. Yeah, sure we have our differences, but for the last fifteen years you've been my best mate, something I hope I can call you in fifty years' time. You have so many qualities I admire and love and after much thought over the past fifty-five days, I want you to be the best man at my wedding.
Love you bro, Cas

The previous couple of months had given me plenty of opportunity to think about our relationship and the twists and turns that it had endured. Our friendship started when we were two tubby teens with a shared love for the outdoors. Through these formative years we shared a common confusion and a lack of confidence in where we fitted into this world; and equally embarrassing stories about trying to date girls. The outdoor adventures we shared helped develop our self-belief – something drinking and partying couldn't do. We then shared the five-year Crossing the Ditch project, starting our own business and now the last three years with this Crossing the Ice project. Jonesy and I have developed an unusually powerful bond and understanding of one another. Despite my anger towards him in Punta Arenas, this trip had made clear in my mind that I valued his friendship enormously and I wanted that friendship to last for the rest of my life.

I then handed Jonesy a food bag that contained every single meat snack ration I'd been allocated with for the previous two weeks. I knew Jonesy would love the meat, it was what he'd been craving the most. On a deeper level, I hoped making a 'food sacrifice' showed my commitment to our friendship. And it was a peace offering for all the bad stuff I'd said. He was overwhelmed and started sobbing.

Before we both got too emotional we hit dessert. We poured dehydrated cheesecake over Louisa's brandy-soaked Christmas pudding. We could both taste home and the love that went into making it. We savoured each spoonful and licked our bowls clean, and by the end of the meal we were completely stuffed. It was absolutely delicious, and a Christmas we'd never forget.

Video journal – Christmas Day 2011
www.casandjonesy.com.au/extremesouth

DAY FIFTY-EIGHT

Ration Day 11

Random recipes going through my head:

Terrines and rolls

Turkey breast, prosciutto, fetta, cranberries and sage

Roast chicken stuffed with fetta, breadcrumbs, pine nuts, basil or sage, cheese

Lamb injected with garlic butter, oregano

Roast rib eye roll

Wrapping in industrial gladwrap

Chicken, ham, salsa verde, fetta

Chicken cordon bleu roll

Boil versus roasting

After all the emotional excitement of Christmas, I found it hard to get to sleep. Before I knew it the alarm went off and we had our tent down, sleds loaded, and were on the trail earlier than we had been all trip: 7.50 am. We intended to push out some enormous days, and hoped to average close to 40 kilometres a day. As I gingerly stepped out of the tent I noticed how stiff my hip flexors, knees and ankles had become. The plateau was a brutally cold –30° Celsius (without wind chill) causing the moisture clinging to the hairs in my nostrils to snap-freeze, and any warmth in my fingers to be sucked away instantly.

As soon as we started skiing, the beautiful glide that we'd experienced on Christmas Day became a distant memory and we were back to slower progress. Our bodies struggled to warm up after each break. The cold was so piercing that we got in the habit of leaving our parkas on for thirty minutes after each break in the hope that would help, but it didn't. I was chilled to the bone and it was by far the coldest I'd felt all trip. We were well and truly up on the plateau and fatigue, the higher altitude and the loss of fat stores were clearly starting to take a toll. I couldn't help thinking again about Mike Stroud, the explorer who collapsed with hypothermia during his 1992 expedition with Ranulph Fiennes and how that had almost resulted in tragedy. Fortunately, the extra fat we had piled on before we departed definitely helped provide additional insulation and reserves and I didn't feel close to collapsing in my tracks, well not yet anyway.

Frustrated: that one word summed up how I was feeling all day. I was frustrated with the intense cold and our lack of speed, but more to the point I was frustrated that we weren't at the South Pole and on our way back to the coast. Aleks had enjoyed a couple of rest days and had begun his return journey to the distant Hercules Inlet – 1100 kilometres to the north.

To help lighten our sleds in order to hopefully pump out the kilometres, we laid our final cache. We left our spare ski, ski pole, tent pole and one solar panel, we trimmed everything that was non-essential. We were taking six days' food and fuel to get us to the Pole and back, a distance of 230 kilometres. Yes, we were going light and if we were dealt some crap weather or we had a critical piece of equipment break the best case was that it would spell the end of the trip, the worst case would've been even more ugly. It was bold and risky but if we wanted to make it back to Hercules Inlet (which we did, we'd re-energised that plan) we needed to start making these decisions on an almost daily basis. The Push was on.

DAY FIFTY-NINE

CAS DIARY ENTRY – 27 DECEMBER 2011

Ulcer forming on upper lip which is making eating annoying and frost blisters [on inner thighs] scabbing and bleeding. Less than 100 kilometres left to the Pole ... Murphy's law: another tent pole broke tonight and spare back at last cache. Used pole splint we cut in half. We got a good night's sleep and full rations today, mood was much better. Sleds quite light now, approx sixty kilograms. One side of tent fading more than other. JJ's lips bleeding today and he has lost a heap of weight.

JONESY DIARY ENTRY – 27 DECEMBER 2011

Spent some time composing an email to Gravy once Cas went to bed to start working on his bucks party. Now that I'm going to be best man. I wonder what his thoughts are?

Felt flat on the trail and getting extremely hungry. Cas once in the tent was irate at how late it was. 8 pm before he got in.

Ah, the bliss of a good night's sleep. It doesn't just translate to a better mood but also results in us travelling further and faster. My inner thighs weren't giving me too much grief, but I had to pay attention to them and try to do everything I could to avoid infection. Something I desperately didn't want to deal with again.

It was a solid day's skiing under blue skies that saw us cross over the 100-kilometres-to-the-South-Pole mark. It made me think about Shackleton's Nimrod expedition, when Shackleton, Marshall, Adams and Wild reached the furthest south any man had travelled – a mere 180 kilometres from the South Pole. They made the gut-wrenching but sensible decision to turn back knowing they could've reached the South Pole, but would've died on the return.

Jonesy and I had a chat about Shackleton's decision and we both understood how conflicted he must have been. We truly believed in the integrity of the return journey and neither of us felt a personal drive just to bag the Pole, but we wouldn't risk our lives more than we already were to make it happen. It was all about managing risk. But this journey wasn't just about us. Many of our sponsors and media partners, the ones who had made our journey possible, were heavily invested in us reaching the Pole and it was this perceived pressure that almost crippled me in the first month of the expedition. To some, us reaching the Pole was more important than achieving the return journey. If we were a self-funded expedition, like Shackleton, this day – Day Fifty-nine – would've marked our 'turn-around' point, just short of the Pole, to make the point that adventure isn't about conquering peaks, oceans or other geographical markers but about the journey. However, we were an expedition that had set goals and had made commitments to our stakeholders and so we were going to reach the Pole and then push back as far north as we could. That section of the journey, the return, was the part that we were doing solely for ourselves, and it motivated us as adventurers.

Finishing skiing for the day, we unrolled the tent and for the first time all trip I said to Jonesy, 'Mate, let's be really gentle setting up the tent tonight, 'cause all our spares are at the last cache.'

'Good call,' Jonesy slurred through his swollen, bleeding lips.

But sure enough, a tent pole snapped. We repaired it with a splint and some strapping tape as best as we could and hoped that it'd hold for the next five days until we got back to the cache and could access a spare. I crossed my fingers that nothing else would break.

When we crawled into the tent I noticed that all the lovely notes that family, friends and You Can patients had scrawled had started fading on one wall. Because the wind had been consistently driving from the south-east we'd positioned the tent on the same angle relative to the sun for close to two months. Some messages we could hardly read anymore, which showed how time was passing.

With the longer day, we didn't get the stove started until 8 pm. This made us edgy and irritated, and when Bec passed on some feedback from Matty McNair's daughter, Sarah, that suggested we weren't doing enough we felt deflated, similar to how we felt after speaking to our mate Tink on Day Thirty-Two. Antarctica had already taught us some valuable lessons over the previous two months about patience. We had to work with (and not fight) our bodies and the environment. Although we were in the final phase of the expedition, there was no room yet to bolt for the gate, we needed to remain disciplined and have belief and resolve in knowing the big miles on the return would come. If we smashed ourselves (like we had leading up to Day Twenty-eight) our bodies would fail. It was hard to ignore Sarah's feedback, as it caused a niggle of doubt. But we had to trust our experience. Would we regret not pusing harder? Only time would tell.

DAY SIXTY

Ration Day 12

Want to start a cookbook. Wherever I travel I'll take lessons, also from people like Louisa and Alicia, etc. Photos are a must.

Feet get cold on the trail.

We were slogging away lost in a daze when, ahead, a black smudge appeared on the horizon. At first we thought it was a shadow cast by large sastrugi but there were none around, then I was sure it moved. Aleks? Just the thought was exciting, but the odds were ridiculously remote. We skied eagerly in its direction while our eyes played games with us. One moment we were convinced it had moved, the next we thought it was our imagination. The anticipation was killing us!

We zeroed in on the black dot with much more energy and speed than normal. After ten minutes we were convinced it was a person, and the only person that it could be skiing *away* from the South Pole was Aleks! We drew closer and closer and when we were about fifty metres away we knew. It *was* Aleks. We couldn't stop smiling and laughing. We shouted out to one another and just as we got to a distance where we could make out facial features we noticed he looked strange. The crazy Norwegian was wearing a Scream mask! We embraced emotionally, and at that moment I experienced a feeling of pure joy. This was the only man on earth who knew what we had gone through and we were forever bonded by this. We shared a mutual understanding of what we'd all suffered through. After Aleks removed the mask, I was quite shocked to see how weather-beaten and gaunt his face looked. His clothes were draping loosely off him, he told us that he'd weighed himself at the Pole and that he'd dropped 20 kilograms and was expecting to lose a further 10 kilograms on the return. I noted in my diary that evening:

> **Was quite a big morale boost to see him like that cause I have been thinking he is just a terminator. He is human and he is hurting – JJ and I both look healthier, fatter and less beaten.**

Aleks told us that he took 'support' at the South Pole in the form of using toilet paper and a toilet and going inside the South Pole station. He also had a bag dropped there with his sponsor's flags (and a life-size female blow-up doll for photos!). Hearing this gave me an even deeper respect and admiration for Aleks. He didn't care about the rules, he was undertaking his expedition on *his* terms and his terms only. He was out for an adventure – he wanted to try to survive on his own in Antarctica for the entire summer and ideally get back to Hercules Inlet. With no common set of rules for an unsupported expedition, Aleks defined a set of parameters that he felt made sense and that he believed in, and he stuck with them. And so what if us or others didn't agree with what he constituted as support? Frankly, he didn't care!

When he told us about the toilet paper, he started laughing and said, 'I'm technically supported, so it's up to you guys now.' It really highlighted the absurdity of it all, but it also made me realise that if we stuck to the commonly accepted idea of an unsupported expedition then Jonesy and I could satisfy all our sponsors and media partners by becoming the first team to achieve an unsupported return journey, even if Aleks beat us back. I can't describe how liberating this felt knowing that we could still satisfy all the people who had backed us.

We stayed with Aleks for about thirty minutes and shared war stories, and lots of laughter. We found out that Aleks was also having trouble sleeping. During the days he was taking French lessons on his iPod and listening to a whole range of podcasts and music, and each night he watched a couple of episodes of *South Park*. Aleks looked like he could keep chatting all day, but my fingers had turned into frozen sticks and we needed to get moving. We said our goodbyes and parted ways, us skiing south, Aleks north. It took a good forty-five minutes for the blood to move back into my fingers causing the worst screaming barfies I'd had on the whole trip. It was worth the pain though, because seeing Aleks was a massive boost to our morale. He was so encouraging, supportive and friendly. We drew enormous strength from his courage, passion and unfailing optimism. When I'd asked him if he was struggling he replied, 'I think I've had one bad day, where I got down for a few hours, but apart from that it's been great!'

I knew the pain and suffering, and how far Jonesy and I had pushed ourselves and I couldn't believe Aleks sounded like he was describing an evening stroll. Truly inspiring.

My good mood stayed with me all afternoon and I lost myself in the unfamiliar cirrus clouds of the plateau. They're the light wispy ones that normally sit really high but oddly they felt really close, like I could reach up and touch them. The effect was probably caused by the elevation of the plateau and the way the light was refracted at the bottom of the earth.

By this point, we were getting close enough to the South Pole for my brain to digest the thought of the return journey. It had been too overwhelming earlier, but now I was able to start visualising it. The thought of finishing at the South Pole in a few days' time didn't feel right, it was too early and not the complete journey. We had to press on.

DAY SIXTY-ONE

Jonesy had a shocking night's sleep and that set the mood for the rest of his day. He was still struggling with the cold and his fingers were as stiff as boards for most of the day and would take close to an hour to warm up after breaks. His lips were constantly bleeding or scabbing up and even though he'd just finished a course of antibiotics he was definitely doing it tougher than me.

Watching Jonesy fiddle with his iPod with fingers that just didn't work was horrible, his body was breaking down and there was nothing I could do. I was starting to regret the ill feelings I was having towards him a few weeks back when I was wanting him to hurt. If I'd been suffering from the same ailments he was dealing with, I don't know whether I'd have been able to muster the strength to continue past the South Pole. He kept on going, though.

We were getting closer and closer to the Pole. Skiing along on the high plateau had a strange eeriness to it. It's hard to pin down exactly what was so strange about it, but the general atmosphere was a little intimidating. The deep blue sky that we'd seen on good days at the beginning of the expedition had changed to a wispy light-pastel colour. There was a misty cloud constantly hanging on the horizon in all directions and the weather seemed very volatile and changed quickly.

Adding to my sense of uneasiness was a rare sun dog (scientists call it a parhelion), where the ice crystals in the sky refract the light from the sun and cause a second sun to appear on the horizon. This same light hitting these ice crystals had also formed a perfect halo around the real sun. The ice crystals acting as a prism beaming the light are called diamond dust, similar to fibreglass particles. It was a weird phenomenon and I felt lost in a science fiction movie.

As we were skiing along, looking up, the ground underneath us suddenly let out a thunderous WHOOMP. We froze. The surface immediately around us had collapsed ten centimetres. My heart was beating fast but after a few moments waiting for the ground to disappear beneath our feet nothing happened. We skied on gingerly and after only a few minutes ... WHOOMP! There it went again. It sounded a bit like a stockman cracking a whip. Our ears rang with it. Surely there were no crevasses this high on the plateau? We probed around, praying that when we stabbed our ski poles into the ground they wouldn't puncture through a thin crust and reveal a gaping chasm below. There was nothing. After establishing that we weren't skiing through another crevasse field we kept going, albeit cautiously.

Every now and then there'd be the same thunderous sound and the ground under our feet would sink. We'd tense up expecting the worst. It was tremendously unnerving. We finally worked out that a hard crust must have formed over a bed of soft snow and the weight of our bodies and sleds on the surface made it snap and collapse. The cracking of the crust was the sound that we were hearing.

I knew how much Jonesy's body was struggling and how tired he was towards the end of each day, but skiing behind him agitated me more and more. His technique has never been great but it was deteriorating further and he looked like he was waddling like a duck. Because of his method he was burning more energy and wasn't able to use the skis to glide forward. But who was I to judge? He'd been stronger than me for most of the trip. Just as it had when we were paddling, his dogged determination and strength got him through. I tried not to watch him skiing and focused on the Australian flag on the back of his sled.

We were only one sleep away from reaching the bottom of the earth, the Geographic South Pole. I'd been dreaming about this moment for so many years but now that I could almost reach out and touch it, I felt let down, like it was a non-event. In my mind the real journey began when we turned to head back north. No-one had done it before. Could we? My thoughts started racing, thinking about what we needed to do to get back to Hercules Inlet in less than one month. Considering the start that we'd had, we'd done well to be getting to the South Pole in sixty-two days, but it meant there was a massive time pressure on the return. We would only have twenty-seven days to ski just over 1100 kilometres. The last ALE plane for the season departed from Hercules Inlet on 26 January and then winter closes in. If we didn't finish by then, we'd have a choice of either wintering there until the following summer (which would mean missing my wedding) or paying US$50,000 per day to keep the base open to wait for us (again, not really an option!). And that was only if the weather stayed clear enough for a plane to land.

After ten hours and fifteen minutes' skiing, we set up our camp a mere 12 kilometres from the South Pole. We discussed our Pole strategy for the morning and got our gear ready for the push. The plan was to treat the South Pole like the summit of any mountain we've climbed in the past. After sixty-one days' toil, we were finally at high camp. The next morning we'd leave our tent, sleeping-bags, stove and all our other gear at this camp and push on double-hauling one sled with our parkas, snacks, water, cameras and flags. No other team in history had skied away from the safety of their shelter down here. It was bold, as getting lost or not being able to find the tent on the return was a death sentence. If we injured ourselves or an issue cropped up, again, our margin of safety was non-existent and the repercussions would be severe. We both felt the risk was worth taking. Not only from a physical perspective, in that it would be much lighter and faster skiing with just the one sled, but more importantly from a psychological perspective. Many of the teams that had attempted the return in the past had said to us that the pull from seeing other people and knowing that the suffering can end by simply walking inside and having a cuppa is too hard to ignore – especially if you spend some time at the South Pole Base, it breaks your rhythm and focus. By leaving our tent 12 kilometres away, it was forcing us to turn around.

The same emotions that run through me prior to a big wall climb or a summit push on any mountain were rampant that evening. Jonesy was equally as excited and nervous. We were about to stand on the bottom of the world, where all meridians of longitude converge and the only way to go is north.

DAY SIXTY-TWO

CAS DIARY ENTRY – 30 DECEMBER 2011

Wow! We stood at the South Pole today. Who would have thought when I had my groin infection that we would reach the South Pole one month later. Woke at 6.45 am to cloudy/windy conditions. Set off dragging one sled with camera, gear, food and flags – it really had the excitement/anticipation/fear of a summer's day mountaineering. It felt naked – like two turtles going for a walk without their shells. As much as we were excited about reaching the South Pole unsupported, we were both feeling anxious and kind of wanted to get it out of the way. We still have so far to go. We are now as far away from our start point as we will be –

we have 27 days to ski 1130 kilometres – basically one marathon per day. Can we do it? Not sure. My body and spirit are psyched – we are in for an epic, we are not going to give up. We plan on aiming to average greater than 37 km per day to 88 degrees (which should be around 11 or 12 hours on trail) then we will need to pick it up. This is adventure. Sure things could be better – more time/fuel/food, etc., but today I feel I would not want it any other way than we have got it. This is what makes an adventure an adventure – the element of the unknown.

We made a big effort to not go into ALE's mess tent at the South Pole cause to us that represents 'support', and it does, big time. It is a cold business taking pics at the South Pole and standing around and it would have been so nice to go inside both before and after pics. We had strategies in place to ensure we didn't get too cold – i.e. took break 20 mins prior to arriving, wore PrimaLoft pants today, wore big jackets for last bit of skiing to build heat momentum, wore apex gloves inside polar mitts, etc., – it required careful management and we strongly believe going inside constitutes support – was fun knocking on tent window. One lady – Carol from Canberra who was doing a last degree trip – was so lovely and overwhelmed at being at the South Pole and meeting us. She's been following the trip back home and gave us the biggest hug ever! So warm.

Richard Weber's clients were also very friendly, said that he'd read about us in the paper back home and thought we'd have no chance. His views have changed now – he reckons we're legends and have got it in us.

Carol also mentioned that all of Australia is behind us. Leaving SP station they gave us three Aussie, Aussie, Aussie, Oi, Oi, Ois! The whole experience pumped us up big time.

Ration Day 13

Hit the South Pole today. It is unbelievable that we are now on the way back. We definitely have looked forward to this more than a halfway point and a reason for change in conditions.

The sun on our face, wind on our back and it really feels like it's coming home or downhill! It feels like a lot of the pressure is finally off us now, now we can just push it. Leave nothing left in the tank.

It's make-it or break-it time.

Video journal – South Pole
www.casandjonesy.com.au/extremesouth

Prior to 1956, all that had stood at the Geographic South Pole were the tattered remnants of the British and Norwegian flags from Scott and Amundsen planted in a sea of snow and white. Then, between 1956 and 1958, a wooden scientific base was erected. In 2003, an enormous scientific base was built, which stands about 400 metres away from the South Pole. This is what we saw as we skied in. At this base they don't do any polar research, but use it for the most hardcore, 'Area 51-ish' science for the nerdiest of the nerds. Pretty cool. They do stuff like upper-atmosphere physics, meteorology, geophysics, glaciology, biomedicine and astrophysics. In winter a core staff of about fifty stay at the base and this number of scientists explodes out to about 200 in the summertime.

There are actually seven South Poles. Yep, that's right – seven! They are: Geographic Pole, Geomagnetic Pole, Tectonic Pole, Pole of Relative Inaccessibility, Cold Pole and the Ceremonial Pole! Today we were skiing towards the Geographic Pole, that's the dime the earth spins off, marked as 90 degrees south with a longitude of zero degrees. This point is moving at a rate of ten metres per year due to the ice shelf in Antarctica moving in the direction we came from in Hercules Inlet. As a result, each year on New Year's Day the scientists at the Pole move a small stake in the ice to the new location. We missed this ceremony by two days!

Sitting very close to the Geographic South Pole is the Ceremonial South Pole, which is an area set aside for photo opportunities at the South Pole Base. Marking this point is a shiny metallic sphere on a plinth (a one metre high red and white barbers pole), surrounded by the flags of the Antarctic Treaty signatory states. Two weeks earlier, back on 14 December, this is where the centenary celebrations were held. A beautiful ice statue of Roald Amundsen had also been sculptured for the centenary and sat two metres away from the plinth.

There were also quite a few smaller satellite buildings positioned all around the main scientific base. It was quite confusing knowing where to go. We skied towards the biggest building in what looked like a deserted ghost town, as everyone was snug and warm inside the base. Unfortunately, behind the big building there were tractors, boxes and containers strewn in an area that looked more like a rubbish dump or ghetto. It's crazy to think that for two months we had hardly seen a trace of humanity or life and now we were looking at a rubbish tip. The buildings were functional, but the structures and storage yard were horribly ugly. I felt ashamed, and reflected on how different the scene around us was to what Captain Scott would have seen – a lone Norwegian flag.

> The Pole ... Great God! This is an awful place and terrible enough for us to have laboured to it without the reward of priority. Well, it is something to have got here, and the wind may be our friend tomorrow. Now for the run home and a desperate struggle. I wonder if we can do it.

The scene around us reminded me of something American polar explorer, Richard Byrd once said: 'This is the way the world will look when the last man dies.'

To be fair, the base operates on New Zealand time (we were still on Chilean time), which was probably why there wasn't a single person walking around. We skied over to a long blue tunnel-tent that had 'ALE' written on the side and not knowing quite what to do I asked Jonesy, 'Now what?'

He looked just as blankly at me and replied, 'Why don't we knock on the windows and see if someone is up?'

We started fumbling over the mounds of snow anchoring the mess tent down. I whacked my mitt against the iced-up window not knowing if anyone could see or hear me. No answer.

Then after about a minute or so the door swung open and a gaggle of people (Yes, people! How great is this! People!) stuck their heads out and smiled warmly.

'Cas and Jonesy! Welcome to the South Pole. Come in!'

The temptation at that moment to cross the threshold and feel the warmth that was billowing from the door was immense. I couldn't stop staring at the flushed pink cheeks and warm bare hands of those peering out ... ah the joys of normality!

Just as we were about to explain that due to the unsupported nature of our journey we couldn't enter, a small lady in a big puffy jacket, with a strong accent muscled her way past the others and eagerly threw her arms around us. Carol (from Canberra) completely overwhelmed us with her unbelievably friendly and welcoming manner. It was so incredible to see another Aussie down there and one who knew all about our expedition too. Her encouragement and support was overwhelming: 'Everyone back home is rooting for you,' she said. 'You guys can do it – you're bloody legends!'

Standing quietly behind Carol was Richard Weber – the first man (along with Mikhail Malakhov) to have completed an unsupported return journey to the North Pole. His face was expressionless as he cast a critical eye. I wondered what he was thinking. The same motivations that saw us turning around from the Pole also drove him seventeen years before to leave the North Pole. It was fitting that he was there and I kind of felt like he was passing the baton onto us, but it was hard to tell.

After a few minutes chatting, the lovely Carol along with a guide stationed at the Pole escorted us to the Geographic South Pole. Carol wasn't any kind of hardcore polar explorer but her attitude and excitement at being at the South Pole was electric. Carol taught me a big lesson: you don't have to be pushing the limits of polar travel to experience adventure. It is different for each and every one of us, relative to our risk profiles, experiences and expectations. Adventure is not an objective word – it's relative. Who is someone else to define whether you've had an adventure or not? At the end of the day we are the only ones who truly know. Some hardcore adventurers may label Carol a tourist, but seeing her eyes light up at being in Antarctica, I could tell it was the biggest adventure of her life and her excitement was beautiful to see.

The pure elation on Carol's face made me ask myself why I wasn't feeling the same jubilation. It was because this wasn't the end of the expedition, it was the real start of the adventure. I was still proud though, because less than ninety people had ever skied from the coast of Antarctica to the South Pole without assistance. That's not many, considering that over five thousand have climbed Mount Everest. By far the biggest joy for me came while taking photos of us with our sponsors' flags. We were the youngest team to ever ski unsupported to the South Pole and we had delivered to our sponsors what we'd said we'd do. It felt good to acknowledge their belief and assistance. And then it was time to head back to our tent.

Carol and the others who had come out to greet us gave us both a big hug and as we skied off they chanted 'Aussie, Aussie, Aussie, Oi Oi Oi!' Richard Weber didn't join them, but just as I was turning to leave our eyes locked and he gave me a steely nod of approval, before quietly adding, 'Good luck. You can do this.' And on that note, we were off.

I constantly looked back over my shoulder as the base became a black shadow and then disappeared from view entirely. We were alone once more. Having the sun in front of us and wind on our back for only the second time this trip, we reflected positively about the dream-like events that had just occurred. Surrounding the sun was a magnificent rainbow halo which danced brightly making things even more magical. We were on the 110 kilometre homeward stretch. We found our tracks from earlier that morning and followed them all the way back to our lonely tent, sitting just the way we'd left her.

As Captain Scott wrote:

Now for the run home and a desperate struggle. I wonder if we can do it.

DAY SIXTY-THREE

Thinking about cooking cakes:
- Orange and walnut
- Madeira, sponge, carrot

Washed socks.

We woke early to a cloudy, misty morning and a stiff breeze blowing from the direction of the Pole. When we'd arrived back at the tent the night before, it was 5 pm and we'd realised that we didn't have enough time to break camp, ski for a couple of hours then re-establish another camp further north. As a result, we enjoyed what would be our last relaxed evening. To get back to Hercules Inlet we needed to average over 41 kilometres each day, every day for the next twenty-six days. I wasn't sure that was even possible. Considering our biggest day to that point had been 37 kilometres it was a big ask.

We had a few things going for us: the headwinds that we'd been battling the whole way to the South Pole would now be on our backs giving us a bit of a push along and, technically, it was all downhill now – we were sitting at an altitude of 2800 metres and Hercules Inlet was almost at sea level. In addition, with the way we planned to structure our days, the sun would now be on our faces as we travelled (initially we thought this would tire us more, like when you drive into the afternoon sun, but we would find it kept us warmer and was a morale booster); we'd established our four food caches so our sleds were lighter; our ski technique was more efficient (well, most of the time) as was our efficiency with all our tasks, from eating food at breaks to setting up and breaking camp;

and finally, from a psychological point of view (which should not be underestimated), we very much had the feeling that we were heading home and that in four weeks we'd be back in Australia.

If only we could stay focused on all the positive stuff. Unfortunately, there were a whole lot of other factors that played with our minds when we drifted into darker moods. Things like how every second day we were going to be on half-rations, so our weight, which had already fallen enormously, was going to continue to fall and meant the cold would penetrate our bodies more deeply. More than two months in an environment where humans aren't designed to live meant we were already battling fatigue and our bodies were slowly (or in the case of Jonesy's lips, rapidly) breaking down. And then there was the worst psych out of all, who were we to think we could average more kilometres per day than the single biggest day of strong, seasoned teams like Fiennes and Stroud, Kevin and Jamie, the IceTrek guys – Muir, Hillary and Philips – and Ian Brown, Peter Treseder and Keith Williams (the first Australian team to ski unsupported to the South Pole)? These guys were our heroes, they were bloody tough men whose books we'd read and re-read for years; men who had inspired us to attempt our Antarctic expedition in the first place. Why should we think we could do mileage they couldn't?

All we could do was take it a day at a time and trust in ourselves. We extended our sessions out to three hours between breaks. We started the day with three three-hour sessions and punched out two hours for the last one, making a total of eleven hours of skiing and only thirty minutes of breaks. Towards the end of each session we both felt horribly hungry, which was a real worry as we were on full rations all day – how were we going to go on half-rations? Despite the hunger, our spirits remained high from the Pole visit. However frustrating me were two massive air bubbles that had formed in my compass, which made the needle dance unreliably, and to get an accurate bearing I had to stop and let the needle settle. Hopefully, when we got off the plateau and into denser air the bubbles would disappear.

We were stoked to finish up the day having done 38.4 kilometres considering the plateau surface continued to be granular and slow, but we also knew that each day we didn't hit 41 kilometres was only going to put additional pressure on the back end of the journey. By the end of that first big push the mist cleared as we pitched our tent and the sky was full of those light fluffy clouds you see in the opening credits of *The Simpsons*. I was exhausted but hopeful.

Video journal – Not all bad!
www.casandjonesy.com.au/extremesouth

DAY SIXTY-FOUR

JONESY DIARY ENTRY – 1 JANUARY 2012

Ration Day 14

Another freaking cold night, I can't feel my toes at the moment and I'm cocooned in my sleeping-bag.

A hard day today – 37 kilometres but very hungry and flat. Hamstring aching – I hope it dissipates – can't have my body break down. We are finally at the business end.

Happy New Year's Day! Waking at 6.15 am, we looked out at conditions very similar to the previous evening, predominantly blue sky with the odd small fluffy cloud reaching to the horizon. Both of us slept well, the longer hours skiing were having more of an impact than any of the sleeping tablets ever did. The first few sessions always seemed to go the slowest and were the most difficult. Day Sixty-four was no exception – it felt that time had slowed and it really hurt to look down at my watch every few minutes and see the numbers had barely changed. The clouds built throughout our sessions and by early afternoon there was no sky visible at all. We were at the mercy of the gods. If it snowed, our progress would slow and our chances of reaching Hercules Inlet in time would go from slim to zilch. If we copped weather like we experienced at the start of the expedition we had zero chance of making it and with the limited food we had, the horrible fate of Scott and his men was staring us in the face. In Scott's message to the public, he wrote:

> On our return we did not get a single completely fine day; this with a sick companion enormously increased our anxieties ... I do not think human beings ever came through such a month as we have come through, and we should have got through in spite of the weather.

The change in weather made us both edgy and we prayed to the weather gods to show us some mercy. I remembered the pilot's words about how he was only a phone call away. In bad weather that certainly wouldn't be the case.

We slogged on in the worsening conditions, and the cold tore through our clothing and penetrated our bones. Jonesy's fingers were constantly numb and mine were not much better. And if Jonesy didn't already have enough ailments to deal with, his left

257

hamstring started to really throb. Popping a couple of painkillers was the only remedy that'd help take the edge off the pain for a while. At least there was one highlight: we'd saved our hot chocolate from the night before and we had it at the end of the second session. It made an enormous difference – getting the calories into our bodies on the trail was more important than in the tent at night time.

Even when we finally burrowed inside the tent, we didn't really warm up. The cloud cover was a barrier to the lovely warming rays of the sun. We jumped into our sleeping-bags, and even they didn't warm up for hours. We needed something to take our minds off the cold, and I had just the thing. Not knowing that Jonesy had brought the red and white Santa hats for Christmas, I'd also packed a couple of hats – party hats with tinsel on them. Once he had Christmas covered, I'd decided to save mine and surprise Jonesy for New Year's. That night we sat eating dinner with our little sparkling cone party hats on. We talked about what a crazy year 2011 had been and what we had in store when we got back in 2012. To celebrate the New Year, we each had one of Louisa's precious homemade cookies for dessert.

DAY SIXTY-FIVE

CAS DIARY ENTRY – 2 JANUARY 2012

Didn't sleep the best last night. Woke at 5 am needing to do a wee and didn't get back to sleep. Really affected me breaking camp but was all good on the trail. This morning we made great progress, picked up our 89 degree 'Push Cache' and kept a good pace all day.

Keen to be getting a little more glide today, incredibly satisfying picking up cache, awesome to think that we laid it. The trip is now a cache-hunting mission.

Tired so will keep this short.

I thought that the way back meant we'd be going down! NOT UP! The last two sessions felt very uphill.

Picked up cache – glad we filmed it. Cas has spares and fuel and I have the food.

Gamme yesterday on the phone made a really nice comment – 'I'm so impressed with you guys, I am Norwegian but you guys are Australian. I was born with skis on. I don't know how you're doing it.'

Bowels been f**ked the last three weeks. Shat myself for the second time today and had to shit on the trail in the first break. Something is not right. So hungry. Finished Cas's Christmas present today.

We were making great pace in the morning, and then during the second session a small dot appeared in front of us – 'The Push' cache. Picking up our food, fuel and spares really filled us with a sense of pride and self-sufficiency. We'd carried all that stuff for fifty-eight days and we were beginning to reap the benefits of our early toil. I guess we'd only left that cache a week earlier, but were surprised at what good condition the snow blocks were in – it looked like we'd just constructed it.

It was good to have the security of more food. Captain Scott and his men averaged approximately 4428 calories per day. It is widely claimed that this was insufficient for the demands of manhauling and that it was one of the primary factors that led to the demise of Scott, Wilson, Bowers, Oates and Evans. With the rationing we were now implementing we were consuming fewer calories than these men, and skiing longer hours each day with fewer rest days.

Was this sustainable? No, it wasn't. But the real question was could we keep up this intensity for another twenty-four days? This is what we didn't know, and this is what we were about to find out.

In the overcast conditions, as I was struggling towards the end of the third session, Steve and Carol's words rang in my ears and I repeated them over and over, 'We're setting a new benchmark by turning around from the Pole', and 'Make history'. When these words weren't strong enough and I was really struggling, I thought of the lyrics in that Eminem song, 'Lose Yourself' – about having one shot, one opportunity to capture all you want and not letting it slip away. These lyrics had held me strong for session after session pulling tyres and were now keeping my legs pumping forward like pistons.

Ever since we hit the plateau, Jonesy had also been dealing with really volatile bowels. Sometimes he was constipated, other days he had diarrhoea. There is nothing worse than busting to go to the toilet, however I was agitated that 'toilet breaks' had taken thirty minutes out of our day.

'Jonesy mate, can you try and hold it in until we finish for the day in forty minutes, that way you can do your poo while I'm setting up the tent?'

Immediately I knew he was incensed and that I'd been an insensitive bastard. It wasn't a matter of holding it in, he'd stopped because he'd actually shat himself. I'd misunderstood the urgency of his nature call and it understandably caused friction. We stopped, Jonesy cleaned himself up with some snow and we finished the day with Jonesy angry at me and the indignity of the situation, and me feeling like a real prick.

DAY SIXTY-SIX

It was a 'eureka!' moment. We discovered the absolute best way to kick-start the day ... ready for it? Instant coffee mixed with chocolate F.I.R.S.T powder! It was just like a mocha and the only issue we had with it was that because of our rationing we needed to wait another three mornings until we had our next one.

Under blue skies and with the wind blowing at less than 15 kilometres per hour we were able to ski next to each other and have a really good chat. It'd become quite apparent that in the first month of the expedition, my body took a much bigger beating than Jonesy's, culminating in my extreme breakdown. Since then, my body seemed to have adapted to the conditions and was coping at least for the moment, while Jonesy's had deteriorated. Why was this? We came up with three logical answers:

1) In the first month with a heavy sled, soft snow and shorter days on the trail, hauling was more a strength exercise, now the longer days and lighter sleds made it more about endurance. My body has always been better suited to endurance whereas Jonesy has lion-like strength over shorter distances.
2) Over the past sixty-six days, we'd lost an estimated 20 kilograms each, which meant I was sitting at about my normal weight, whereas Jonesy was below.
3) Jonesy seems to have worse circulation, so the thinner air of the plateau could have been having more of an impact on his extremities.

Interestingly, Jonesy was able to separate his mental outlook and morale from his physical discomfort and pain. It wasn't like that for me. The spiral that I suffered after twenty-nine days shows that my physical and mental health are closely linked. Having said that, on other shorter trips I'd never let physical ailments affect my outlook like they had in Antarctica, I had been more likely to embrace them as a challenge, something to overcome. Although, I suppose on those trips I wasn't ever pushing myself as hard or for as long, and was probably well inside my comfort zone.

I asked Jonesy who he'd prefer to have an injury out here – me or him? It was sobering to hear him say that prior to leaving he'd have said me, but after seeing me battle my groin infection he'd decided it would be better if it was him. He spelled it out in his diary:

> **Physically if he's down, mentally he's down. Me, I can dissociate my mental and physical states – good for an expedition, my body is hurting but I can still push ... Managing him back then was like trying to manage a ticking time bomb. He was so emo and irrational, telling me he couldn't do this and that 'You aren't listening to me, I just can't.'**

I agreed Jonesy was dealing with pain better than I was and it was less likely to bring him to breaking point. Admitting this embarrasses me a little, it doesn't sit well with the view I have of myself. Is it something that can be changed? I hope so.

During the afternoon, I started thinking about what life had in store for me after Antarctica. I'd made the promise to Mia that this was going to be my last big adventure before settling down, getting married and maybe even starting a family. Especially during the first month of this expedition, I was feeling that I never wanted to find myself in a position like we were in again. I'd suffered enough. Reaching 90 degrees south and feeling the excitement and uncertainty of the return journey had got me contemplating this promise. Could I live without adventure and big expeditions? Could I shut my mind to other dreams I have longed for, like climbing Mount Everest, and big walls in Patagonia and Pakistan? What about the North Pole?

As strong as the passion to live out these wild dreams is, the dream to have a family with Mia and live in the Blue Mountains is just as strong. To be a dad and see our kids grow up in a loving family environment is incredibly important to me. The death of Robert Scott and how devastatingly that must have impacted on Kathleen and their son Peter haunted me. I'm not sure I could put Mia through that potential pain. I just wasn't sure it was fair to try and live out both these dreams concurrently. I didn't believe a fulfilling family life could exist while pushing boundaries in adventure.

But the previous few weeks had reignited my passion and love of adventure and the feeling of contentment and inner peace I get from an expedition. I was loving being out there. I'd let go of what had happened earlier in the expedition, and was happy to be pushing myself and following a dream. Could I get this same feeling of contentment without big adventures in my life? Unfortunately, the only way I'm going to be able to answer that is by trying it. No matter what the voice in my head yells, it'll be my heart that'll drive my decisions about adventure in the future.

While I was contemplating a family, Jonesy had been doing some thinking of his own. During the second-last break for the day he paused while scoffing food to say, 'You know, Cas, everyone has the capacity to do an expedition like this. But what stops most people is the lack of mental drive.'

I thought about this for a while, and he was right. There's nothing special or gifted about Jonesy and me, we're two pretty average Aussie blokes. We're not talented athletes, we feel pain and suffering like anyone, we hurt, we cry, we have bad days, but I guess what differentiates us from others is that we push on when others give up.

At the final ten-minute break before the last session I was so glad I'd put aside two extra spoonfuls of trail mix from our full-ration day. After nine hours' skiing I knew I was going to need every gram to get me through the next two hours. We punched out this last session at a good speed and again knocked out our biggest day – 39.1 kilometres. The tent went up quickly and after a long day, we began psyching ourselves up to do it all over again in just ten hours' time.

After I went to sleep Jonesy called Gravy on the satellite phone and started planning my bucks party. Fortunately I had my earplugs in and was asleep within seconds of hitting my parka pillow. After the phone call, just before he closed his lids for the night, Jonesy made a big mistake, he allowed himself one spoonful of the next day's snacks. Yum – what's another one? Just one more mouthful . . . and another. And before he could stop himself, he'd demolished half of his snacks for the next day. As he drifted off to sleep, he had already started to regret his actions.

DAY SIXTY-SEVEN

CAS DIARY ENTRY – 4 JANUARY 2012

Eating has become a chore since we started 11-hour days – don't really enjoy dinner. Poo this morning resembled a slug. Was tiny from half-rations yesterday. Both feeling all-over stiffness and very tired. Really struggled today, no gas in the tank, feeling so flat –

how can we keep this up for another three weeks? Got ready in record time this morning – on trail by 0730. Did radio interview. Terrain changing and getting more bumpy.

Terrible sleep last night. Took a Temtab.

Woke up very drained and both Cas and I struggled on the trail the first session. Couldn't wait to eat food. Just wish I hadn't eaten so much yesterday (midnight snack). Hopefully after five more ration days (10 days total) we can go back to full rations. Until then, at least we can start splitting 2 x 6000 cal days into three days and a full maybe on the fourth day.

This morning the session just felt so long!

The third session – last 1.5 hours is harder at the moment but we're doing what we can. Last session is always brilliant.

Thinking a lot about going to the Supermarket in Punta Arenas and getting ice cream, ham, cheese, bread, hot dogs and churros (and beer and wine of course).

Over Harry Potter.

Belly button now infected. WTF. Got to get out of here soon.

We can do this but the start of the day is just getting so much harder.

Toes hurting more today.

Pus – lanced it yesterday and cut nails two days ago. Have lost feeling in finger tips. Not going to be able to climb in Thailand!

DAY SIXTY-EIGHT

It was an early wake-up at 6.15 am and we were on the trail skiing by 7.25 am, giving ourselves plenty of time to knock out a big day. Sometimes there's a decent reason why you're in a good or not so good mood (for example, your toes are all pusy and painful or you've had a bad night's sleep). Other times there is no reason why you should be in a great mood, but you are. Jonesy and I both woke up in one of those positive moods. Particularly for Jonesy, objectively things weren't looking too great: his toes were a mess, his fingers were constantly dangerously cold, his bowels were still playing up and his lips and face ... yuck. From the tip of his nose, a crusty yellow scab was crawling across his face while his bulging lips resembled the bad collagen job of an ageing Hollywood actress. Instead of red lipstick, blood oozed from open sores and ice hung from his bleached moustache. I summed it up best in my diary:

> JJ's face looks like a leper's and he's lost a shitload of weight, starting to look like a POW victim – I think a lot more than me. With the issues he's having (toes, guts, face, fingers) it's incredible he doesn't whinge or complain.

Jonesy was teaching me such a valuable lesson about life. Often things pop up that you have no control over (like Jonesy's ailments), but you are able to control how you perceive these issues and how you act. Jonesy just got on with the day and suppressed his pain and discomfort quietly. Witnessing this made me reflect on the way problems in my life back home are often worse in my head than they actually are. If Jonesy could put up with all that he was dealing with and not complain, surely I could do the same in other areas of my

266

life. Wilson, who accompanied Scott on his fateful march in 1912, once said: 'The best sledger is the man who sees what has to be done, and does it – and says nothing about it.' And that was Jonesy.

One of the downsides of this staunchness of character was that it made us more impatient and less sympathetic towards people's problems back home in Australia. *Seriously?* How bad is work really? Or the traffic? Or that person over there who's annoying you? These are manufactured problems and stresses that seem so trivial compared to the constant struggle of life in Antarctica. I had to be careful I didn't alienate others with this mindset.

We were making good miles, and passed through some stunning sastrugi fields. I could not resist setting up the camera to shoot video, I just loved these majestic shapes more and more the longer I was out there. They could look like vibrant roses or gushing waterfalls and I would never get tired of their beauty. And then finally, in the mid-afternoon after having skied around 1500 kilometres since our journey began, I spotted a sastrugi that I'd been searching for the entire trip. About 20 metres to our right there were smoothly rolling sastrugi that looked like a dolphin's back, and in the middle of one of these was carved out an 'oval window'. The sun was perfectly composed for the frame and before I unclipped from my sled I knew it was one of the shots I'd been visualising the entire expedition – and it was finally here. I threw myself on the ground and directed Jonesy to ski into the frame. Like a twitcher who'd found a Blue-billed Curassow or Gorgeted Wood-quail, I was highly excited. I snapped the shot and the result came out even better than I'd imagined. Wow! Perfecto! The sun threw beams of light across the image like the spokes of a bike wheel. I was buzzing all afternoon after that, my only regret was not also setting up the video camera, but we simply didn't have the time, we needed to ski.

In the afternoon we picked up the Christmas Cache we'd left at 88 degrees. Once again we were both filled with a sense of pride, relief and self-sufficiency. We laid that! We wrestled with the snow blocks covering the cache and picked up six days of full rations that would sustain us till our next cache at 86 degrees – 230 kilometres to our north. As we skied off from the ice rubble, Jonesy kindly offered me a red frog that he'd saved in his pocket. It was an incredibly warm and giving gesture which really symbolised to me the strength of us working together – we were in it together all the way to the end.

The weather had been perfect all day and as we descended off the plateau it was finally warming up as well. During the day we dropped another 175 metres of altitude, which made skiing so much fun. By 7.30 pm we'd skied eleven hours (and had been on the trail for twelve hours) and we finally beat our average target with 42.1 kilometres. You beauty! Now all we had to do was press the replay button another twenty-one times – 900 kilometres to go.

DAY SIXTY-NINE

CAS DIARY ENTRY – 6 JANUARY 2012

'Do a long polar expedition if you want to know what you'll look like in 30 years' time.' Aleks Gamme

We woke up at 6 am, fifteen minutes earlier than usual. Not sure if that fifteen minutes made a difference, but both of us were particularly rattled and weary, the kind of tired that makes your head and bones ache and your temper short. Fortunately when we stepped outside the tent, it was hard to be grumpy, the sun was parading its full rays against a perfectly deep blue sky. There was a gentle breeze on our backs, encouraging us forward, and it was one of the rare times on the expedition when we didn't feel that we were fighting Antarctica, but that she was giving us a bit of positive reinforcement. Not that these feelings made us complacent. It was still bitingly cold at –20° Celsius and after we'd packed up the tent Jonesy's hands had once again deadened like wooden blocks. As we started marching for the day he tried to warm them up by clenching and unclenching his fists, and spinning his hands like a Ferris wheel around his head to try and force the blood into the extremities.

After forty minutes' skiing he was still doing these motions, which meant his fingers still hadn't warmed. Jonesy was doing such a great job at moderating his emotions but he is human and it does affect him. He was quite grumpy on the trail and lost his temper a few times. It started with when his fingers wouldn't warm up, then he took a couple of falls and then he expressed the frustration his bowels were causing him. These outbursts weren't at me, more at what was going on with his body. Adding to the angst was the fact it was a half-ration day, Jonesy wasn't at his best when he was hungry.

Even though our bodies were taking a beating, ever since we'd reached the Pole an overwhelming sense of positiveness had engulfed us. For the first time I recorded in my diary the feeling that we had a chance of getting back to Hercules Inlet: 'It's going to be tough but we think we can pull it off.'

Jonesy had kept the faith much more than I had in those early, dark days. He had never given up on the return journey, but he respected the way my head worked and had tried not to put pressure on me. Back then, I had emotionally distanced myself from completing the return journey and was more focused on just reaching the Pole. The return seemed too far, too impossible, and I needed to keep the expedition broken into bite-sized chunks. Although it was a big slice still left, I now felt I could digest it.

After twelve hours of skiing we set up our tent on a plot of snow indistinguishable from the one we'd stopped at the night before or the night before that. Bec wasn't able to do a sked, so Jonesy ran it through with Mia. Our routine was so monotonous it was a surprisingly exciting change to our day.

Jonesy had been so considerate all trip with the sound levels of his eating, but he just couldn't prevent the ravenous slurping of dehydrated spaghetti bolognaise. Although his bleeding, swollen, minced lips prevented him from shovelling the meagre rations in too quickly, they were so sore and sensitive, he couldn't help himself and tried to swallow a large spoonful. It caused the skin on his lips to rip; blood became the dominant flavour of the rest of the meal. As he was cleaning out the central cooking bowl, I glimpsed him sipping the left-over remnants in the pot with his bleeding lips. Until that point I'd felt sorry for Jonesy, but all I could think was that we'd done a great job in isolating the infection to Jonesy's face by not sharing spoons and cups. He wasn't thinking and was just starving but I was incensed by his lapse in concentration. Let's face it, if I also developed the infection, it could really make life horribly unpleasant, for both of us.

DAY SEVENTY

JONESY DIARY ENTRY – 7 JANUARY 2012

Ration Day 17

Had a chat to Cas this morning where he got some things off his chest. He thinks that I've been filming just myself (and pics) – especially at the back-up of the Go Pro [camera] his gloves are covering his face. I do have a tendency to say 'I' and 'me' rather than 'we' but this is especially evident when we are discussing food rations which 'I' have taken responsibility for! He used the example of the broken ski pole but I KNOW I also explained how it broke not just how 'we' broke it and how 'I' had to fix it.

F**king sensitive – all that conversation did was make me feel terrible about myself all morning – does he think about all the little things that I do, like giving him frogs out of my rations when I'm starving? Or getting up earlier to make him tea. Giving him my iPod at night. The pre Xmas rest day – he did nothing all day. Or that I deliberately take more weight. The last 2–3 days all the food we've eaten has come from his sled!

I woke up in a foul mood. Adding to the discomfort was the fact that for the first time all trip I was constipated – my body was needing every gram of nutrients I gave it and then some. Fairly or not, I directed much of this frustration towards Jonesy. We'd both become ridiculously sensitive and emotional. If you spend enough time with anyone, there'll be personality traits that cause you to clash. I noted in my diary that 'JJ always has the attitude that he's doing more which is really starting to piss me off.' His air of superiority is a trait that he's always carried and is something I've come to understand and accept. That's Jonesy, and back home I ignore it. But out here it was creeping under my skin, and each additional day that passed was irking me more and more.

We had hopes of knocking out our biggest mileage of the expedition with what was our biggest drop in altitude all trip. Unfortunately, along with the drop came heavy sastrugi fields, which slowed our progress north. These fields played havoc with the sleds – at times it felt like the sastrugi had claws ripping at our sleds that prevented forward momentum:

I felt like a dog being walked by an owner that kept pulling the leash – sent a violent shock through the body each time. The constant jerking and start/stop slowed progress.

It was a long, tiring day. Thrown into the mix was the occasional uphill sections which highlighted just how weak we'd both become. The strain of pulling our comparatively light 70-kilogram sleds up these inclines had us panting and heaving like it was the first week of the expedition. Although the previous ten weeks had forced our bodies to become extremely efficient at skiing, the flat ground on the plateau had masked how weak our bodies had become.

Interestingly, most of our stabilising muscles had deteriorated and when we found ourselves off balance our core didn't have the strength to steady our shakiness. As a result, we were beginning to fall over more frequently. With the downhill sections on this day, Jonesy had five falls. It was a bit of a worry because it was through falls that we were going to break equipment and damage ourselves. It required us to concentrate more, which then sapped more energy, which led to us being more tired towards the end of the day, we'd then fall over more and so the cycle continued its downward spiral.

I'd finished listening to the Harry Potter audio books a few days before and dove straight into listening to an iPod that a climbing friend, Jules, had kindly given me just before we left. On it were a whole heap of his favourite audio books, a number of which I'd been meaning to read for years but just hadn't got round to. I've always loved non-fiction, and Peter FitzSimons' *Kokoda* was keeping me well engaged. It got me thinking. Most people of my generation in Australia have grown up in relatively calm political stability. Not that Iraq and Afghanistan aren't horrific wars, it is just that most of us haven't been affected by them. We've been lucky. Not like our parents living through the Vietnam War, or our grandparents fighting in World War II and their parents in World War I and both coping with the Great Depression. There are some aspects of hardship and war that played a role in developing and shaping the character of men in prior generations. As young men we crave adventure and to experience danger and the excitement of truly living on the edge. In our current cotton-wool lives this isn't available in domesticated, middle-class living and as a result many of us search for these experiences through avenues like drugs, alcohol and driving like an idiot. Young men are programmed to push their boundaries. Being out here on a trip like this had given Jonesy and me that excitement and danger and more importantly forced us to grow up.

All day the weather was jumpy and volatile. We had woken to beautiful conditions, then by midday there was complete cloud cover blanketing the sky. As a result, the temperature plummeted making our breaks hideously unpleasant. Within a few hours, the cloud cover blew off and revealed a stunning sun dog which we used to navigate off. Making it more spectacular were the colourful outer-rings that formed around the main rainbow to the horizon. Having had the longest day on the trail yet – a full thirteen hours – it was really exciting to see the sun travel a full 200 degrees around us. I felt like we were at the centre of its orbit. We'd made a solid day of 40 kilometres, but solid just wasn't enough at this stage of the expedition, as Jonesy so eloquently summed up in his diary: 'Both exhausted and made dick-all miles.'

Earlier in the expedition we could only have dreamed of this kind of mileage; but now, 40 kilometres was still not enough to get us back to Hercules Inlet in time. We needed to go further.

This pressure made Jonesy, for the first time, start questioning in his diary whether we were going to make it:

Doubt creeps in slightly. This next 19 days are going to be very tough – I hope that we/I can handle it. My body is not happy.

DAY SEVENTY-ONE

At 2.15 am I stirred, feeling that I was on a ship rocking violently, and feeling incredibly nauseous. Ripping my eye shades off my face, I realised that it wasn't a dream and that I was actually physically ill. I hurriedly unzipped the rear vestibule, stuck my head out and began dry retching. I was sure I was about to vomit. My hands had gone all clammy and my forehead gleaned a light film of sweat. I coughed and heaved but all that came out was blood from my chesty cough. When a spot splattered on the pristine white snow it made me really worried. What could be causing this? My dry retching woke Jonesy and he looked on with sympathetic concern. When I didn't feel like I was about to get anything else up, Jonesy kindly handed me a couple of Panadol. Although my head was still spinning, as soon as I hit the pillow I fell asleep and by the time we woke at 6.45 am I felt completely normal. This place was doing weird things to me.

When we woke, an angry ground storm was in full force outside. The wind was belting above 50 kilometres an hour and the snow particles scouring the outside of the tent made us both want to hide in our sleeping-bags. Once we finally got ready, we could not believe how much assistance the strong wind was giving us while skiing – it was incredible! We were finding that the push along from the wind was helping us more than any downhill slope ever had.

After reaching the end of the *Kokoda* audio book, I thought to myself, 'Who the hell are we to whinge?' Even on half-rations we were consuming 3000 calories, those poor diggers went days with absolutely NO food or water but kept on fighting. I similarly reflected on Tom and Jess, the two You Can teenagers I'd met at the expedition media launch, who'd been thrown into the pit to fight cancer. None of them had chosen their challenging battles. We had. It's just what I needed. 'Toughen up, mate,' I said to myself.

The strong wind on our backs helped push us to our biggest mileage yet – a whopping 43.4 kilometres! As Jonesy said in his diary:

I woke dreading the howl of the wind outside BUT it really makes a difference! Wind – wind is the key. We did our best mileage and in the shortest amount of time.

For Jonesy, the couple of hours after dinner had become the worst for hunger pangs. He struggled to sleep on an empty stomach and got in the habit of eating a decent chunk of his next day's snacks just before he slept. It helped him fall asleep, but if he woke during the night he dug into the snack bag for a few more scoops. He dealt with hunger on the trail better than I did and preferred to be full when he fell asleep.

DAY SEVENTY-TWO

What a grind of a day. The blustery conditions had calmed and outside our tent we were greeted by pleasant, balmy weather – a roasting -10 to -15° Celsius with only a gentle wind on our back. You little ripper! We were so excited to ski in just our thermal tops, it was the Antarctic equivalent of swimming nude at the beach. The freedom of not wearing five layers was liberating, and the warmer temperatures meant Jonesy's fingers stayed thawed all day. The big downside of this warmth was that as we skied our energy drained quickly as sweat gushed off our bodies like free-flowing taps. The increased heat and no wind meant that by the end of the day we were massively dehydrated and more knackered than we'd been in days.

I was completely spent. The stuffiness seemed to also slow time – all I could think of was that Salvador Dali painting of the melting clock. Minutes felt like hours, and the terrain didn't change once all day, not once! We didn't see a single sastrugi and the ground was one big flat, monotonous snow field in every direction. My feet overheated causing my big toe to swell with an angry red rash. Apart from the blisters on my heels in the first week, my feet had held up remarkably well until now. Looking at (and smelling) Jonesy's feet had made me extra vigilant with washing, drying and airing my own feet each night. Now that I had developed some random rash, I became hyper-paranoid. If the weather stayed like this I was going to remove my Vapour Barrier Liner (VBL) layer and try and keep the gaiters unzipped because my feet were getting far too warm.

Although the heat was taxing, we still managed our required daily marathon in just over eleven hours. We were on track. After we pitched our tent it was warm enough to take off our thermals outside and see what state our torsos were in after seventy-two days. I was no longer fat! It looked like I was back to my normal weight of about 80 kilograms (remembering that I started the expedition at 102 kilograms) and Jonesy – wowsers! Jenny Craig, eat your heart out. We ran around the tent like two excited schoolkids at lunchtime!

After dinner was served (and quickly scoffed) Jonesy handed out the snack bag for the next day. Holding a tiny bag that wasn't bigger than a couple of big mouthfuls, I asked, 'I thought we were doing ration days every second day? Isn't tomorrow a full-ration day?'

He replied straightaway that he didn't think I'd mind if we did three half-ration days in a row. Well, I did! On the half-ration days one of the big motivations that helped me to get through the deprivation, was knowing that the following day we were treated to full rations. To have this routine altered and a tiny food bag handed to me without any discussion really bent me out of shape. All our decisions – from navigation, to hours that we planned on skiing, how much to push, how much to rest – were always talked through together. If we had a disagreement we'd often try to find the middle ground and compromise. I couldn't understand why Jonesy had suddenly taken it upon himself to make a call on when we would or wouldn't be rationing food without talking to me. Adding to my frustration was the way he tried to justify himself. When I asked him how he'd feel if at the end of a long day's skiing I suddenly announced, 'I've decided we're going to ski another three hours', he told me he'd been spewing. Exactly! I think he got it then, but he didn't apologise.

Even after all that I was feeling surprisingly good about where we were at. There was no way that forty-odd days previously I would've written this in my diary:

Mentally I'm doing alright and can keep going so long as I get a reasonable amount of SLEEP, for me that is the key. When I have a few bad nights' sleep in a row – that's what kills me more than anything. The distance and speed we are making and the knowledge we've got less than twenty days is so motivating – both feeling psyched that we can do this.

DAY SEVENTY-THREE

We woke to the horror of a dully lit tent and the sound of gentle fluttering snow softly falling on the tent. Jonesy had a shocking night's sleep and as soon as I poked my hands out of my sleeping-bag, I knew we were in for a cold day. Setting off, Jonesy's hands were already frozen solid, and he let out an almost primal yell in frustration. With a thin dusting of snow hampering our progress and Jonesy in a bad mood we skied next to each other in a moody silence.

Mid-morning, we spotted our 86-degree Centenary Cache. It stood out like a lighthouse on the desolate, dreary plain. It took us forty minutes to finally pull up next to it and we quickly got to work knocking, kicking and tumbling the snow blocks off the pyramid and digging out the provisions we'd left behind. We were relieved to be there, but nervous about the 460 kilometres we had to cover to the next stash of food, the Gateway Cache. If we could reach it, without suffering the same fate as Scott and his men, then we were determined we could go all the way to the coast. The next fourteen days would decide the success of our expedition. One hundred years before, Captain Scott had scrawled with his frostbitten fingers, a message to the public blaming 'misfortune' and the weather for their untimely demise:

> ... our wreck is certainly due to this sudden advent of severe weather, which does not seem to have satisfactory cause [and] the storm that has fallen on us within 11 miles of the depot at which we hoped to secure our final supplies.

Jonesy and I had read this harrowing transcript that many times, we knew it by heart. We were similarly throwing caution to the

278

wind, and our fate to the weather. With the meagre food rations we had in our sleds, our margin for safety was tight. At full rations, we had nine days' food to ski 460 kilometres – we'd be required to ski over 51 kilometres per day. It was a mammoth task even on full rations. If we copped a similar weather system to what we experienced in the first month of the expedition, we'd be in a horribly dire situation and the truth was there would be no rescue.

These thoughts were playing on my mind, as I'm sure they were on Jonesy's. I wrote in my diary that evening:

The little food we've got puts us in a very similar position to Capt Scott – he needed to reach One Ton depot, us the Gateway. Let's hope we don't get pinned in by storms like him.

Once we farewelled the cache, the day turned from bad to worse. Under gloomy skies our progress slowed further with the weight of the food, fuel, spares and rubbish that we'd taken on. The extra provisions were proving both a blessing and a curse.

With Jonesy's fingers numb and clumsy from the cold, our breaks crept out from our previously rigid ten minutes to twelve … to thirteen minutes. Everything was more difficult for him and his frustration was obvious as his mind was telling his hands one thing, but they just wouldn't respond.

And then suddenly we spied a small, moving black dot on the horizon in front of us. Unsure what it was, we picked up our pace and before long realised it was a lone figure running next to a Transformer-like vehicle. It was a fellow Aussie – Pat Farmer – who was nearing the end of his marathon 21,000 kilometre run from the North Pole to the South Pole. His face was gaunt and his clothes hung loosely from his jagged, skeletal frame. We shared a few quick words and mentioned that we needed to catch up for a meat pie and a beer when we returned from Antarctica. All of us were chilled to the bone so we set off quickly, us to the north, Pat to the south. For the remainder of the afternoon it was inspiring following Pat's small footsteps and thinking about his remarkable journey.

By the time we called it quits for the day we'd been out on the trail for 12.5 hours but had only skied for eleven. We had 37.2 kilometres to show for our efforts, which wasn't enough, and that made me antsy. Time had slipped through our hands like sand through filming, picking up the cache, seeing Pat and skiing less energetically than we could have. It just wasn't good enough and I was disappointed in us both. Put simply, if we kept at this inadequate pace our food would run out and we would not make it to the Gateway Cache. If providence was on our side, the weather might permit a rescue or food drop, but if not we would starve to death, that's if we didn't freeze first.

DAY SEVENTY-FOUR

After the previous day's dismal performance we woke determined to get things back on track. It was our nineteenth half-ration day and neither of us could escape the hunger, it was all-encompassing. We were only pooing every few days, and when we did it was no bigger than a wombat's poop. The hunger pains came in waves. The first contractions in the morning were distantly spaced, but as we expended more effort skiing we grew hungrier throughout the day and they'd strike more frequently and for longer. By the end of the day stomach cramps forced us to stop skiing at times, we'd have to cradle our torsos until the waves passed. Fortunately, in the evening when we crawled into the tent it was easier to manage; scrunching into the foetal position was the most effective way to deal with the contractions. Jonesy made a note in his diary: 'My body is bloody starving. This is the skinniest I've ever been and my body knows it.'

Despite the hunger, we hit the day with more vigour, and were out skiing under light cloud cover at 7.20 am. Our catchphrase for the day was 'to keep it tight'. Breaks were kept to a maximum of ten minutes and we skied north knowing that everything depended on each and every step. As the clouds cleared during the day, the Thiel Mountains revealed themselves 20 kilometres off to our left-hand side. Though our route didn't take us right alongside them, we still fed off their energy. Apart from a number on our GPS screen, it was the first geographic sign since leaving the Pole that we were making progress. It might sound strange but their presence gave us company, a feeling we weren't alone. Adding to this excitement was that we were now at an altitude of 1500 metres and the air had a certain thickness to it that had been absent on the plateau. We were definitely warmer and the sleds were gliding more smoothly.

As Jonesy led strongly in session three, my eyes flickered from the mountains out to our left, to the weather-beaten Australian flag sewn onto the back of his sled. I had used it as a focal point during tough times and though it was looking tired and worn, seeing the blue, white and red of our national flag made me quite emotional. But I also thought that if seventy-four days out here makes a flag look like that, I wonder what these hostile conditions have done to our faces?

The overheating of my feet earlier in the week had made me super paranoid that they'd suffer the same fate as poor Jonesy's feet. To address this issue I'd removed my outer sock but, in typical T.I.A. style, this led to a blister forming on my heel again. Great. At least having dealt with my blisters in the first month had given me the confidence that they could be managed and treated effectively.

At the end of our final session we'd skied for eleven hours and forty-five minutes and only taken thirty minutes in breaks all day. It was by far our biggest day and our discipline was rewarded – we'd skied 43.6 kilometres! We were back on track. Through his bleeding lips, Jonesy inhaled his spaghetti bolognaise in the time it took me to take two mouthfuls. His ravenous eyes followed my spoon's every movement as I finished my dinner. I felt sorry for him and handed him my last couple of mouthfuls.

DAY SEVENTY-FIVE

After seven hours' sleep, we woke at 6 am and the weather had cleared – beautiful bluebird skies and conditions warm enough for us to ski without our shell jackets. Unfortunately, within a couple of hours the wind picked up, cloud rolled in and temperatures plummeted big time. Our moods plummeted with the barometric pressure. Regardless of what the weather was doing we still kept the discipline and focus and stuck rigidly to our timings. The blister that had formed was causing a fair bit of grief and discomfort for the first ten minutes or so after breaks, but then it warmed up and I hardly felt it.

Skiing behind Jonesy, I could see how his clothes hung off him – there was no meat on his bones. Antarctica was sapping more from our bodies than I ever thought possible.

With the Thiel Mountains behind us and familiar nothingness all around, it was quite déjà vu-ish. We skied for a total of 43.86 kilometres, and as I lay in the tent that night my mind went off on a weird tangent.

I've always been fascinated by how the men of the Heroic Age of Antarctic Exploration were able to control their sexual fantasies and desires. Back then, people didn't talk about sexual matters, it was taboo and information was hard to come by. The men didn't write about it in their diaries, that's for sure. How did those early polar explorers cope with being in the company of only men for up to three years? How did they control their sexual longings? Finding answers to questions such as this is one of the many reasons that has driven me to pursue a life of adventure. I wanted to feel, touch, smell exactly what those explorers of yesteryear had endured. And now I think I had the answer. Interestingly, for the past month we'd been so tired the sexual fantasies and erotic dreams that we'd both had at the beginning of the expedition had vanished, there'd been no more wet dreams, pounding the bald moose or shaking hands with the general, we didn't have the energy now, every bit of physical exertion was being used to keep us warm and move us forward. Jonesy summed it up in his diary: 'Sexual desires were rampant in the first month but non-existent now.' We were just too exhausted.

DAY SEVENTY-SIX

We woke to horrendous weather – it was an all-too-familiar reminder of the conditions we'd experienced in the first few weeks of the expedition. A complete white-out engulfed us, with snow falling and terrible contrast. It was oppressive and claustrophobic. This weather meant we were once again alone, no-one could reach us if something went wrong. The worst-case end-game frightened us both. Having spent days over the previous couple of months listening to the Harry Potter audio books, we coined the term 'Dementor weather'. Just as J.K. Rowling's dementors drained any hope or happiness, so too did this weather.

Adding to my negative mood was that, for the first time all trip, my feet were starting to give me a fair amount of grief. I wrote about it:

Feet are now starting to fall apart – the skin on soles (especially on heels) of feet are sanding/falling off.

Mawson had suffered an extreme case of this, primarily caused by a vitamin A overdose from eating dog's liver. Fortunately, I wasn't suffering from anything that extreme, but it was a clear sign that until we returned to civilisation our bodies would continue to break down. My feet had spent too much time stuffed in sweaty boots and the effects of having walked 1700 kilometres were showing.

All trip, whenever I'd been in a really dark mood, Jonesy had more often than not been there to pick me up and vice versa. Not on this day. He was struggling more than I was and I ended up leading all afternoon as Jonesy's diary noted:

Hardest day on the trail in a long while. Feel empty. Cas put in an awesome effort in the last two sessions.

We were both popping painkillers quite regularly to help dull the pain, but it never fully dissipated. At least we made ourselves laugh coming up with a tagline for a Nurofen advertising campaign: 'Why hurt when you don't have to?' Maybe not the best shoutline in history, but we liked it.

There was only two weeks until the final plane flew out for the season and we had just under two weeks' food and fuel (assuming we made it back to the Gateway Cache). Fortunately, we'd used less Nurofen than we'd budgeted for, which now meant we started gulping them down every few hours.

Jonesy continued to struggle with the lack of food. Although funny, the desperation of this statement in Jonesy's diary highlights how ravenous we'd become: 'You know you're hungry when you find it hard to spit out your toothpaste.'

DAY SEVENTY-SEVEN

When we woke, the complete white-out had partially cleared to reveal an overcast day. In these constantly volatile weather conditions I sympathised with what Scott recorded in his diary on 21 January 1912:

> Is the weather breaking up? If so, God help us with the tremendous summit journey and scant food.

We now had visibility, but the cloud cover ensured that none of the sun's rays warmed us. The snow from the previous day made conditions underfoot slow, and our 60-kilogram sleds felt more like they weighed around a hundred.

After three days' constipation, I made a right mess of myself. I forced out a small Vegemite-textured nugget which smeared all over my bum cheek and hand. Even though temperatures were mildly warmer now, having bare hands exposed to the cold meant they froze quickly and made the clean-up job infinitely harder. It was disgusting and messy. By the time I was clean enough to jump back in the tent, my fingers took some time to warm up. This constipation was a sure sign of deteriorating health. Our bodies were using every bit of nutrient from our diet. The lack of food and our sluggish bowels were playing games with our stomachs and making us both feel ill. As a result, we decided to try a laxative after breakfast, hoping it would ease the discomfort the following morning. This was treading a fine line, knowing if it worked too well, having to stop constantly on the trail would by far outweigh what we were currently experiencing.

As is always the case, people interpret events differently. While writing this book, I've used Jonesy's diaries and my own to try to retell our story based on the facts. But sometimes, though we were together every step of the way, our views on the facts differ. On this day Jonesy wrote: 'I was pushing it harder and better than him today!' I didn't exactly agree with that and wrote in my diary: 'I took some weight off JJ (3 kg) after first session cause he was going slower.'

Who to believe? Well, me of course!

We both agreed that our progress was steady all day, but Jonesy's technique once again agitated me. The energy he'd save if his skis moved parallel to one another would have been enormous but when I tried to tell him he clammed up, got defensive and that was that.

DAY SEVENTY-EIGHT

The situation was turning dire. We were heading into our fourth day in a row of overcast, low-light conditions. I was worried:

> On trail started to get very concerned re: Captain Scott's ending. These conditions are slowing us down – we've only got 7 days' food to get to 82 degrees. In these conditions rescue/ food drop is near impossible – we're alone and need to be self sufficient.

Although the weather was crap, the laxatives had done wonders. My mood kicked off to a great start but deteriorated when I went to don my clean undies (I'd washed them the night before). They hadn't dried because of the overcast conditions, so I was forced to revert back to a normal pair of briefs (without the G-string insert).

Jonesy was struggling right from the moment we took our first step. He was on lead but with the low light and poor contrast he was moving slowly and falling often, which on one occasion resulted in him hurting his ankle. After forty-five minutes of slow progress, I took the working compass off him and navigated out front for the next nine hours. We're all different and it's been interesting to observe how, where and when we've both struggled. With the enormous weight loss and the various ailments plaguing our bodies, we really were in a race, not because of Aleks, but because of our own bodies and our dwindling food supplies.

At our third break, we had a heated altercation. Just as I had struggled being the weaker one in the months of training and at the start of the expedition, Jonesy was starting to feel a similar frustration. Handing over the compass was symbolic of the changing dynamics between us, something Jonesy was having trouble accepting. At this break he checked our position on the compass and to our horror we realised we were 2.7 kilometres to the right of our correct heading. What? How could this happen? I thought I'd been attentive in keeping on our bearing and steering us to the Gateway Cache and had been proud of my stint out front. We were both agitated, and handled the argument immaturely. I blamed the problem on the fact that Jonesy had set our bearing to a waypoint 150 kilometres away and he blamed it on me for not paying close enough attention to the compass. I was less worried about being off our bearing than him, but more intimidated by his explosive anger. His ill-temper was getting more volatile and he raged like a wounded bear. It was frightening to be near but I felt the way he reacted was not just about the bearing but also about the way his body was failing him:

Today almost broke me. Cas was strong . . . I hate having to rely on him in some sessions but it goes both ways I guess.

But he wasn't the only one having issues with his body. Unfortunately, my scrotum was still sensitive from the infection on Day Twenty-six and not wearing the G-string had caused chafing. It highlighted the great job the homemade lingerie was doing and fortunately I only had to suffer until my undies dried. After four days of horrible weather, the clouds started to break up and by late afternoon we finally had blue sky above. The improvement to our morale was enormous and psyched us up. We both prayed once more for the weather to hold.

By evening I noticed my lips had developed four big ugly cold sores. I couldn't help remembering Jonesy drinking out of the central cooking bowl. I did everything I could to try to treat them and hoped that prevented them deteriorating any further.

DAY SEVENTY-NINE

We woke at 5.30 am with the hope of pushing out our biggest day ever. As the alarm buzzed, I felt like the walking dead. Famished, tired and grumpy. By 6.55 am we were skiing and managed to increase our session times to three hours fifteen minutes – about the time it takes to run a marathon – and we planned to do four of those a day from now on. Towards the end of these long sessions we weakened, and progress slowed. We had little choice with our limited provisions required to get us back to the Gateway Cache. It was going to be touch and go. The stress we were putting our bodies through was enormous and the outcome of the expedition could fall either way. Doubt continued to plague my thoughts:

'Can we keep this intensity up for the next ten days? If so we'll make it, if not we won't.'

Each day had become the hardest day we'd ever experienced, either in the outdoors or in life to date. We were pushing past any boundaries we thought we had, physically, emotionally and mentally. At times we did want to rest but we refused to give up and kept clawing forward. I drew on everything I could. The fear of letting people back home down, which drove me at the start of the expedition, was now the furthest thing from my mind. Sometimes my motivation was to make Mia and my family proud, at other times it was to discover what I was truly capable of. We were now in an unfamiliar place, where our expectations and self-boundaries had been left far behind. On other occasions it was the inspiration I received from the unspoilt beauty of Antarctica that drove me forward:

> **Passing through a beautiful sea of sastrugi – wind has made waves (all kinds: breaking waves, heavy waves, dumpers, even ugly white wash waves), dolphins, sharks ... Such beautiful sastrugi today just love looking at them – don't think I will ever get over the shapes.**

As we continued to reach massive milestones, these provided an enormous boost to our morale. Just after lunch we crossed the line that marked the previous longest, unsupported manhaul in history – 1800 kilometres. This was achieved in 2009 by Cecilie Skog (Norway) and Ryan Waters (USA). I reflected on their journey and some of the other significant journeys of recent explorers who have set benchmarks in polar travel. All their stories played a role in inspiring me and Jonesy to undertake our own journey and I almost couldn't believe what we had now achieved. We had travelled so far and survived out here for so long, yet we still had *another* 400 kilometres to go. Although we'd been out on this icy continent for eighty odd days, it didn't lessen the intimidation of the ten days we still had to go. I was menaced by our lack of provisions, the distance we needed to ski each day and my worsening sleep deprivation.

Having crossed this elusive 1800 kilometre milestone taught me how we can achieve more than we give ourselves credit for. Often we dream too small and as a result only achieve small things. I'd heard all this rah-rah motivational stuff before, but never truly believed it until that moment. Believing is very different to hearing and I hope I never forget this valuable life lesson.

The wind crescendoed all afternoon and by the time we set up the tent it was peaking close to 40 kilometres per hour. We'd skied for twelve hours and twenty minutes and had clocked up an impressive 45.1 kilometres. The mileage was brilliant, but the demands of these hours were starting to affect my body as severely as they were Jonesy's. To my horror, my lips exploded into a mine of blisters – cold sores mixed with a bacterial infection. It was creeping over my face making it considerably more susceptible to cold damage. Eating our fish pie for dinner, chunks of flesh fell off my lips. They looked like I'd tried to kiss a blender and made every mouthful of my meagre rations difficult to eat. I had watched exactly the same thing happen to Jonesy but still I got too greedy, tried to swallow a large spoonful and the skin ripped. Blood dribbled down my chin and dripped into my bowl.

DAY EIGHTY

CAS DIARY ENTRY – 17 JANUARY 2012

Long, long, long day. My mood was better than yesterday (I definitely am most affected by lack of

sleep) but it just seemed to go on and on. JJ had a real tough day ... I don't know how he keeps going, his body is completely ruined.

Ration Day 22

Blood in my shit in the morning. Was constipated and had blood. On trail needed to shit all of a sudden, ok – manageable. Session 4 break shat myself (blood too), F**K, then had to go again at the end of the day. Was able to push hard for sesh 3 and 4 and we managed our best day yet. All I could think about was the 10 mins we lost because of me shitting ... felt guilty.

In the evening Cas had a go at me because of the set-up shot. I stumbled and ruined the shot. It is still usable, we just need to work on it in the edit but he's right. He was f**king furious at me saying he was going to give up filming. I apologised after a while, but he told me to tell someone who cares and passed me the camera. I think he meant this as a joke but I'm dealing with so much baggage currently with my body that I broke down.

It's the first time on this trip that I truly felt alone ... I cried. I'm so sick of having to just put up with the pain, etc. This was just the last straw. My toes, my bowels, my fingers, my ankle – I think I have a stress fracture and I was sick of or just incapable of ignoring it anymore.

To make matters worse, Cas was really impotent during this time, he watched his iPod (well, mine) patted me on the shoulder, asked if I was okay and then just went to bed. I still had to split food after sked and talk to Greg Quail, wash undies, get brekkie ready, etc., and then I woke him up accidentally and he got angry at me and said he couldn't get up at 5.30 am and it'd have to be 6.

When he was like this (like me crying) at day 30, I provided him with all the support I could NOT this token bullshit and then pull this selfish anger that he did.

I know we can do this trip, I always have but I really got overwhelmed today.

I hope it's not cancer.

The days out on the trail were now so long and we both experienced a vast array of different emotions all in the one day. I continued to marvel at how Jonesy kept going while dealing with chronic pain and constant discomfort. Growing up, he'd had a pretty cushy life at home, but from somewhere he'd developed a ridiculous inner strength and a deep reserve of will power to call on when he needed to. Anyone else would just give up but Jonesy kept plodding. It helped pull me along too. My lips had deteriorated more, which meant shovelling snacks into my gob in the allocated 10 minutes break time was painful. I was so hungry that I felt all that was giving us the strength to keep marching was the brilliant rays of sunshine shining down. The surface was firm and fast but every now and then we passed over a field of coarse gravelly crystals that refracted the sun's light. It was like skiing over glittering diamonds, and helped take my mind off the pain.

Those moments of beauty out there helped but the truth is often there's nothing sexy or attractive about realising a dream. Most of the time it's boring and bloody hard work, and unfortunately that doesn't just apply to a South Pole return journey. This journey taught me that back home – with all the distractions and worthy excuses for not sticking with a goal – it's often easy to jump from one thing to the next. It's easy to be flippant with excuses when challenges arise. But in Antarctica we didn't have that luxury. Our goal was finite and the only real choices we had were whether to give up or to keep fighting, there was no middle ground. Once I understood this, I started to demolish previously established boundaries and kick down walls that were limiting what I thought possible for my life. In a weird way, through this monotonous plodding I'd inspired myself to achieve bigger, bolder dreams in the future. How can anything back home be as hard as this? Establishing a successful business? Getting fit? This trip gave me the belief in myself that I can achieve.

After twelve hours and ten minutes of skiing, we'd covered a massive 46.5 kilometres. During dinner we brought the camera inside to play the video from the set-up shot that morning. I was really excited – I knew it was going to be a stunner! I nervously pressed play and the shot appeared on the camera's LCD even better than I imagined. I fast-forwarded until my ski tip entered the right corner of the frame and before long my body and sled were right in the middle of the picture – it was a ripper! And then Jonesy entered the shot. The following frustration was described in my diary:

> **Really pissed off with JJ. This morning I set up an epic/ awesome video shot – just looked at footage in tent and saw that JJ tripped and fell in background of shot and tried to pretend it didn't happen and he didn't say anything – ruined the shot. Disappointed cause I visualised the shot the night before, rushed in morning to set up shot properly, was really excited about the framing of it and for JJ not to care really upsets me –**

293

we've got such limited time for shooting video and when we do it, we need to nail it. Why am I driving the shooting/doco? I'm the one setting up most of the shots, coming up with shot list, etc.

I felt hurt. Jonesy was the one who was meant to be making the documentary but he'd been doing little filming over the past month, so I'd accepted it as one of my responsibilities, had written a shot list in the back of my diary and tried at every opportunity to film. I was really enjoying it. I should have been more sympathetic in understanding that Jonesy's body was in such a bad state that he was well and truly in survival mode now. He was channelling all his willpower into moving his body north and just didn't have the energy to be thinking about filming. It was a distraction and took effort away from the mission.

I let Jonesy know how annoyed I was about the whole situation, and combined with his physical disintegration, it all became too much and it caused him to break. Everything completely overwhelmed him and he started bawling. I'd never seen Jonesy like that. He was a mess, and his body a broken shell. It was an eerie reminder of what I must've looked like on Day Twenty-nine. I never want to have to see anyone cry and cry, let alone my best mate. Snot dripped from his nose as tears ran down his face. It was getting late and we had to be up at 5.30 to ski the next morning. I tried to comfort him as best I could, before putting in my earplugs and trying to get to sleep. This devastated Jonesy – he felt abandoned. I knowingly acted selfish and cold. We were both so far beyond exhaustion, we were treading a tightrope between collapse and the ability to stagger on for a few more steps. I needed to sleep or else I'd be the next one to break. My selfishness was purely driven by a survival instinct. Yes, I should've comforted him. Do

I regret my decision? No. We were at the stage in the game where we needed to put our own survival and self-preservation first before we could look after each other. It was a scary place to be.

Video journal – On the edge
www.casandjonesy.com.au/extremesouth

DAY EIGHTY-ONE

I woke at 6 am after a fitful night of tossing and turning with vivid nightmares of Jonesy's breakdown. I expected to be in a foul mood and the lack of sleep to destroy any strength I had left. Surprisingly, I wasn't and didn't even feel too tired. Jonesy was still troubled after his breakdown and his ankle was giving him grief so I took the lead for most of the day. He noted it in his diary:

> **Cas did an awesome job leading most of today in these low-contrast conditions. I have to go slower because of my ankle. I feel weak having to rely on him but I guess it's fair considering the crutch I've been for him and that I've been taking more than my share of the weight – I'm so proud of him.**

Strange things were happening. On so many occasions time had slowed ridiculously, but on this day it was the complete opposite. It was racing forward, out of control. The first time I looked at my watch, four hours had passed without a break.

We crossed our 83-degree campsite in the afternoon and we both clung to a small glimmer of hope that we might be able to recover the food we'd dumped on Day Thirty-two. We hadn't laid a cache, because we didn't think we'd make it back. Our GPS navigated us right on top of where our campsite had been, it looked just as void and desolate as everywhere else and there was no sign of where we'd been fifty days earlier. Back then I had given up hope of the return journey and had been lost in a feeling of despondancy and failure. On Day Eighty-one I was back at the same location and believed we had a chance of achieving our goal. What a tumultuous journey the previous fifty days had been. Like searching for an avalanche victim, we probed our spare tent pole into the snow. There was nothing. It was like looking for the proverbial needle in a haystack – the chances of finding the food were remote. We kicked ourselves for not having left a tiny cache just in case. Jonesy was like a man possessed. He refused to give up. It had to be there, surely? After fifteen minutes of digging he accepted it was lost. We had been rationing our food on the basis that if we'd found the dumped food it would be a bonus, but if we didn't recover it we would still have three days' food to get us back to the Gateway Cache 115 kilometres away. We then had to decide whether we should cut our rations even further to give ourselves a buffer. If we'd decided to cut down, there was no way we could've continued to push out the thirteen or so hours we'd been doing. We talked it through and made the call to consume all the food we had to reach the Gateway, hopefully in three days' time, but that gave us no room for errors, injuries or delays. We were committed.

It was do or die. We refused to accept a similar fate to Scott, and in that moment we both felt we'd prefer to be found strapped to our sleds with snow under our fingernails than lying in our tent waiting for the end.

DAY EIGHTY-TWO

Ration Day 23? – Augmented

We're dying at the moment.

After an insufficiently short six-hour sleep, I felt the most tired I had all trip – bags drooped under my eyes, my head pounded and I felt nauseous. The poor night's sleep two night's before had caught up with me – I should have known, you couldn't hide from reality out there. My movements in the tent were heavy and clumsy. When I stuck my head out the tent door, the Dementor weather had returned and, if such a thing was possible, my heart sunk even further. The only thought that motivated me to get out of my sleeping-bag was the realisation that we only had one more week to go. If it was any longer, I would've rolled over and refused to budge:

> **Had to use all my willpower to keep going today – just wanted it all to be over. The constant discomfort and doubt about distance still to go is very tiring. Can we keep pushing for seven more days? I don't know, but we have to.**

When we got skiing at 6.55 am the ground conditions were all furry, which made our progress slow – neither of us was firing on all six cylinders and we plodded along in our own worlds of discomfort. Each step was laboured and our morale was bleak.

My lips had gone from bad to worse and the infection was spreading into my gums and cheeks. I was struggling to eat my snacks at breaks and cruelly the salt from the food stuck to my

297

bleeding lips causing them to sting for a good chunk of each session. We had two more days' food left to reach the Gateway. It was going to be a close call. We were both craving food and sleep. It was so tempting to just lie down for a few minutes or set up camp and rest for a bit. We were so low on energy, it felt like we were sucking only the thin air high up on Everest.

If this were a mountain we are now well and truly in the death zone. Each day now we can feel our bodies dying.

This was no exaggeration. Our bodies were burning energy they didn't have. Somehow we managed a gruelling 43 kilometres in tough conditions. The tent went up quickly and we collapsed on our sleeping-bags. It took us a few minutes to muster the energy to put on the dinner. Jonesy summed up how we were feeling best in his short, ever succinct diary entry: 'So f**king tired – Bones aching.'

DAY EIGHTY-THREE

CAS DIARY ENTRY – 20 JANUARY 2012

Being this fatigued is almost worse than physical pain for me – I feel nauseous. I can't keep going with this lack of sleep – need a sleep-in tomorrow. Six days is still six days and there needs to be some level of sustainability. Zero fun today – fatigue headache and short temper. Ground conditions improved and sky is clear – please hold out. Hercules Inlet still feels so, so far away. Now skied 2019 kilometres – I honestly can't believe that we've skied that far! Skied strong on trail today. Cried a few times under my goggles thinking about Mia, Lil, Mum, Dad and Clary.

Shoulder getting worse – had two falls. Ankle worse, RHS [right-hand side] little toe bleeds through the day and looks to have a tumour.

Cas – vile in the AM. 'I'm tired and my lips are flaming and it's all your f**king fault.' I fired up.

Slippery – hazardous. Cas session 4 – low, I don't think he likes seeing me ahead. Feeling better than yesterday because at least we got mileage.

Fingers perpetually tingling.

Big dinner but could eat three of them.

DAY EIGHTY-FOUR

The lack of sleep was killing me. We treated ourselves to a lie-in and woke at 6.30 am feeling half-normal. I was greeted with a F.I.R.S.T mocha – it'd been three mornings since our last one. Yum! We got off to a solid start and found ourselves skiing with a little more zip in our stride. The morning stint went without incident and then, on the horizon off to our left, we thought we saw something. After fifteen minutes with eyes fixed on the object dead ahead we hoped, no we prayed, that it was the Gateway Cache. There were a few 'yes it is … no it isn't' moments, until we got to within one hundred metres and recognised the weather-beaten flag standing tall on top of a mound of snow. Relief washed over us.

The reason it hadn't stood out like a beaming lighthouse as the previous depots had, was because Antarctica had battered the lonely cache for ten weeks. Without the flag, the mound would've looked like any of the countless sastrugi that dotted the landscape. It now had a long, firm tail caused by snowdrift and the fifty centimetre thick snow blocks that covered our precious reserves had been wind scoured, leaving our provisions open to the elements on the windward side. The homemade flag on top of the bamboo stake told its own story. Of all the caches we'd left behind, this originally bright orange flag was now bleached almost white. Only half of its original now-tattered fibres still fluttered – the rest had been torn off and cast into the wind.

We had arrived at this critical food cache with less than half a day's provisions between us. As we pulled up alongside the cache, I removed my skies and collapsed on my knees holding the pile of snow. My head touched the mound and I began to sob. Hidden in the snow was all the food we needed to make our dash back to the coast. No more rationing, we now had three full days of food to ski 115 kilometres. What luxury!

We dug the provisions out and loaded them into our almost empty sleds. We now had ample food to reach our final depot – the Hidden Cache, a mere 130 kilometres from Hercules Inlet. As we left the mound of broken snow we bumped our mitts together like we were raising our glasses at the pub, but instead of saying 'cheers!', we looked into each other's eyes and said 'Kia Kaha', which means 'stay strong' in Maori. These powerful words had kept us going on the Tasman Sea and out on the ice had again become a common expression. After every break and each time we started shuffling forward this was our war cry. Each time we said it to one another, I felt my shoulders raise a tad and my chest swell.

300

Leaving the Gateway Cache behind, a tsunami of relief washed over us. For so long we'd been fighting to reach this small pile of provisions – an oasis that would surely keep us alive and moving forward for another week. Jonesy skied strong all afternoon and when we stopped for the day, I said in a thick Aussie accent, 'Jonesy, you're as strong as a bloody Mallee bull.'

He seemed chuffed by the compliment. We had again knocked out our required distance of 45 kilometres and set up our home on another virgin patch of snow. Routine was the glue holding us together now, but the surprise we had waiting for us was about to give us the strength to get back to Hercules Inlet. We ran through our skeds as usual and then as we were tucking into our *full* rations of dinner, the phone rang. Jonesy answered and I heard through the crackle of the satellite phone:

'Yo Jonesy! It's Aleks here. How are you?'

'Great, Aleks. Just picked up our second-last cache today. You must be getting close now?'

Reaching the Gateway had filled us both with pride and given us confidence that we were in with a real shot of getting all the way back to the coast. The completion of the journey however was going to be slightly bittersweet. Aleks, who'd been absolutely inspiring and encouraging, was going to beat us back. I'm ashamed to admit this, as I keep saying I'm a firm believer that adventure is not about being the first, the fastest, the longest or any -est, but I still couldn't help feeling disappointed that we weren't going to be the first. Of course we'd be proud of succeeding, and the way we'd overcome so much, but, if I am honest, deep down the jubilation of completing the journey was going to be dulled. I was thinking about this while Jonesy chatted on. My ears pricked up when I heard him congratulating Aleks for being a day away from finishing.

I yelled out, 'Have a beer for us'. We were both genuinely happy for Aleks even if I was wrestling with the impact his success would have on us.

I was only half listening to Jonesy as he chatted on but I felt his whole body suddenly change and looked over.

I could see a tear run down his face as he raised his eyebrows to me and he smiled the biggest grin I'd seen on his face for months. I wasn't sure what was going on and I listened to him say, 'Aleks that is incredible. You are a bloody legend.'

Aleks had decided to wait for us so we could ski into Hercules Inlet together. He wanted to celebrate with us.

Only a moment before I had been struggling with the notion that I wasn't going to fulfil what I had set out to do. Despite everything we'd done it cut deep and for all my noble ideas of what adventure should be I'd still felt hollow. And then Aleks made this astonishing gesture and the biggest example of sportsmanship that I could ever imagine. What he was offering us underpinned exactly what adventure is all about and I felt incredibly humbled and ashamed for the way I'd been thinking minutes before. I felt almost an electric shock of excitement course through me as the reality hit. We were on track to complete what had thwarted many other explorers before us. We were no longer skiing to Hercules Inlet just for us, we were also doing it for Aleks. We were about to live out the dream we had spent years thinking about and planning for. And we were going to do it with one of the most impressive men I'd ever met.

DAY EIGHTY-FIVE

The incredible gesture from Aleks and his remarkable show of friendship would have made sleep hard to find but on top of that had come the disappointing news that Channel Seven (the network we signed our exclusive relationship with prior to the expedition) had decided not to send a crew down to film our arrival at Hercules Inlet. Stupidly, I let this bother me and I woke at 3 am with my head racing with it all and then had trouble falling back to sleep.

Our alarm rang early and once again I felt like death on a stick. I'd only got three or four hours' sleep and the fatigue was making me ill. My head spun and before sipping on my cold tea I thought I was going to vomit. Fortunately, rationing was a distant nightmare and now we could enjoy the luxury of having three days' rations for every two days of skiing. Cruelly, my lips were worse than ever and so eating became a real challenge. Although we were both severely fatigued, the result of these increased provisions was evident immediately – we had more energy skiing and travelled faster.

Mid-way through the day, thick clouds started brewing on the horizon to our right. As the afternoon progressed, thin clouds clawed across the sky like long fingers. To our left, the spectacular jagged peaks and nunataks of the Patriot Hills revealed themselves. Although still a long way away, they were the chequered flag marking our finish line, Aleks was down there waiting for us and we couldn't keep him from a hot shower for too long. After twelve hours and twenty minutes' skiing, we'd clocked up another record day – 50.59 kilometres! Jonesy summed up how we felt about breaking the fifty-kilometre barrier for the first time:

The miles we did today will remain a mystery. I don't know how we did it considering how we were feeling, but biggest day yet.

Looking at our waypoints on the GPS, the ground we covered in that one day had taken six painful days on the outward journey.

No wonder we'd felt despondent and constantly questioned our futile efforts in that first month. As I sat writing in my diary that night I looked up at the ragged clothes hanging on the rack above my head and couldn't believe the number of holes in my socks, undies and tips of my gloves. My underpants were shredded between the legs and, not surprisingly, had started to cause chafing again. We'd had two pairs of undies each for the entire expedition, and it was lucky that we were almost finished because like our bodies, our clothes were falling apart.

DAY EIGHTY-SIX

CAS DIARY ENTRY – 23 JANUARY 2012

Feels like we're getting close now! Less than one degree to go. Biggest concern are my lips – both top and bottom blistered and swollen and painful – its made eating a chore and an unpleasant one at that. Started antibiotics tonight for them cause they're steadily getting worse.

JONESY DIARY ENTRY – 23 JANUARY 2012

I can't believe the level of animosity Cas bears me for his lips. He blew up at me again for it whilst I was on sked to Bec (I was getting caught up in detail again). But it is not as if I was deliberately trying to pass them on, although unlikely, it's possible he just got them. I had it for a month and he thinks that he alone can own the monopoly of suffering. Such victim mentality is below him.

The routine each morning was well and truly drummed into us by now, which was a good thing because we were so tired we were running on autopilot. Alarm rings. Good morning. Stove's lit. Snow melting started. Sleeping-bags into vestibule. Clothing on. Boots on. Breakfast. Load sleds. Pack tent. Ski. We'd become robots.

The fatigue was painfully straining our relationship. We were both annoyed and frustrated towards one another at the slightest provocation. Jonesy was becoming slower each day on the trail, his damaged fingers caused break times to blow out, he was being short and rude during sked time, his temper was flaring more than ever and his pedantry was at an all-time high. The whole lip situation had me harbouring more resentment towards him than was justified. We were caught up in our own; mostly dark, thoughts and so were distant and detached. In the dull afternoon light we picked up our final depot – The Hidden Cache. We now had all the food we needed to get us back to Hercules Inlet.

We both cracked a rare smile when Jonesy stopped to go to the toilet and his one sheet of toilet paper was ripped out of his hand by the cheeky wind. With pants down round his ankles, he launched himself after it with more determination than a beggar chasing a one hundred dollar note. At least we could still share a laugh.

DAY EIGHTY-SEVEN

CAS DIARY ENTRY – 24 JANUARY 2012

We're like two walking dead men. I don't think I've ever pushed myself as hard as this. We're both dying out here now – absolutely exhausted physically, mentally and emotionally – there is nothing left. Constant nausea from

fatigue and my lips are making one of the most enjoyable aspects out here (eating) something I dread – all basic human needs are stripped away from you out here.

About forty-five minutes after waking, Jonesy was outside removing the snow from the snow flaps and I was packing up the kitchen box inside, and I just started crying. I reached over to Jonesy's side of the tent, grabbed the camera and started babbling to myself:

Pain in my lips is making life unbearable. As you can see they're absolutely shredded like biltong. The end is so close, we can almost reach out and touch it, I'm so desperate to be there. We've just pushed so hard I would never have thought it possible to do what we've done to ourselves and cover the distance we have. If we can do this we can do anything! Anything! Alright. Let's go skiing.

Talking to the camera lifted a huge weight that had been crushing the air from my chest and gave me what I needed to step outside and face another day. To think during the first month of the expedition I was whingeing that Crossing the Ice was too similar an experience to Crossing the Ditch. 'What's the point?' I had asked myself, 'What am I learning?' But it was only by living the past three months that I'd grasped the true meaning of something a Greek philosopher called Heraclitus wrote 2500 years ago: 'You can not step twice into the same river; for other waters are ever flowing on to you.'

I'd heard the saying 'you can do anything if you put your mind to it' so many times and some days I'd believed it more than others. At this point, in our tent in Antarctica, I believed every word more so than any other time in my life. Only by pushing way past my boundaries and sticking with the expedition had I discovered what I am truly capable of – which was more than I'd often given myself credit for.

We'd travelled 2190 kilometres but I still questioned whether we could keep it up for another 80 kilometres. Another 48 hours, could we do it? Doubt continued to linger even though I knew Aleks was waiting and we wouldn't let him down.

I spent most of the day lost in thought reflecting on the journey. Then out of nowhere a small bird – a delicate black skua – appeared. For three months, apart from the occasional human, we hadn't seen a single piece of flora or fauna. It was so beautiful and utterly surprising. Jonesy and I stood like two confused 'roos startled by the headlights of an oncoming vehicle. We didn't quite know how to react. What was this crazy bird up to? It was dancing into the wind, heading towards the South Pole. Seeing this skua was a sure sign we were approaching the coast. It reminded me of when we were out on the Tasman – four days away from pulling into New Zealand, a dandelion had floated by the bow of the kayak. This felt strangely similar. It was like the world was coming back into our consciousness. The blustery wind in the morning had brought thick cloud cover and it looked like it was snowing on the horizon so it wasn't the pitch-perfect weather we'd have liked, but we were nearing our final march.

Throughout the previous week I'd reflected constantly on Scott and his men. The question that had plagued me ever since I read about his tragic end had circled in my head for weeks. Why did Scott not die on the trail, fighting to reach his final depot? Our journey gave me the ability to perhaps understand and I recorded how I was feeling:

Our mood is so dark and oppressive, can understand completely how Scott and his men died – it [Antarctica]

wears you down slowly and the end pounces up quickly – JJ and I are just holding on but if we had much longer out here we wouldn't make it – last couple of weeks I've felt our bodies dive and not recover.

We were at the brink of collapse. If Aleks wasn't waiting and a blizzard had whipped up, like it had done for Scott, I don't know if we could have mustered the energy to continue. Even though we were so close to the end, it still seemed so far. For Scott and co., One Ton Depot was not the end, it was their equivalent of our Gateway Cache. They still had a further 220 kilometres *after* the depot to get back to the hut at Cape Evans. Exhausted, starving, cold beyond imagination, and believed to be suffering from scurvy, resting in the tent would have been an overwhelmingly alluring option.

After an enormous 48.4-kilometre march, we were ready to crawl into our own tent, but were forced to erect it on our knees as our legs could no longer bear our weight. The weather had closed in and in the final half-hour of the day it began snowing. I spent that night praying for clear weather because we still had to negotiate the same crevasse fields that had almost swallowed me up on Day Two. If conditions remained overcast, negotiating the crevasse fields would become even more dangerous.

DAY EIGHTY-EIGHT

All going well, this would've been our last full day alone in Antarctica. Jonesy's body had reached the point of near collapse and he stumbled and fell constantly on the trail. It made us slower, but after twelve hours we'd covered 43.7 kilometres. We were almost there and I felt a darkness lifting, but the physical aches and mental fatigue meant there was no feeling of jubilation yet. ALE warned us of a weather system moving in so we had to make it to Hercules Inlet to fly out the next day. Two jagged nunataks, which I felt I could reach out and touch, marked our final descent. One day to go.

DAY EIGHTY-NINE

This was it. We woke early and hit the trail by 7 am. The visibility was fair, but complete cloud cover blanketed the sky. We skied a couple of kilometres on flat terrain, and then just past the two nunataks the ground steepened. Ten kilometres in front of us was Hercules Inlet.

I was nervous as we made our way across the crevassed ground. It was much harder and icier than it had been when we were last there and the memory of that yawning crevasse flashed through my mind's eye and frightened me. Fissures started to emerge, and the further we skied, the bigger they got. Before too long we were gingerly inching forward over crevasse bridges. Our balance was unstable and the icy surface made it hard to stop. Jonesy was finding it especially difficult staying on his feet and kept falling. There were myriad crevasses delaying our progress to the inlet. The safest way to cross them was perpendicular and fast. Slot after slot we skied over, but suddenly Jonesy found himself gathering speed and was out of control. He was nearing the widest crevasse we'd yet encountered, it would have easily swallowed an entire train carriage, and he tried to slow himself, but to no avail. He leaned back and centimetres short of the crevasse wall he hit the ground hard. I winced as he screeched in pain, but I was grateful that he hadn't broken through the ice. With no meat left on his rump, Jonesy thought he might have cracked his coccyx. I made my way over to help him to his feet and we both stopped and stared in horror at the bridge in front of our ski tips. I smacked my pole into it and its surface crumbled to reveal an enormous chasm reaching down into the darkness. The hairs on the back of my neck prickled. If Jonesy's fall had been one metre further on ... I couldn't believe he'd been that close to certain death.

It shook us both terribly. We had to continue on with our precarious descent, trying our best to stay in control on the icy surface and cross the bridges at their narrowest. We had to keep mentally focused during every inch. And then finally, just when I thought I'd reached my limit, the worst was over. As we got closer to the inlet a small dot appeared on the icy slopes. Initially we thought it might have been a random rock, but as we skied nearer I realised it was a tent. After another fifteen minutes the dot started edging towards us. It was Aleks. He lifted his arms in the air and let out a massive cheer: 'Congrats guys, we've made it!' he yelled.

I couldn't believe we had actually done it! The three of us embraced and I started to cry. It was completely overwhelming to know we had achieved history. Jonesy and I both knew that despite some emotionally raw moments we were more bonded than ever before. When we'd arrived in New Zealand after our 3318 kilometre paddle we had 25,000 people waiting to greet us on Ngamotu Beach and the noise had been deafening. On this final day, we were whooping and crying and embracing and all around us the ancient continent of Antarctica watched silently. As unmoved by our triumph as she'd been by Scott's death.

Video journal – The three amigos
www.casandjonesy.com.au/extremesouth

Skiing in a line, with Aleks in the middle, we made our way down to Hercules Inlet. I couldn't imagine a better way to be celebrating Australia Day. We chatted casually, all childishly excited, and although I had an enormous sense of pride and fulfilment, I mostly felt an overwhelming sense of gratitude and respect for Aleks. His actions, his encouragement and his patience in waiting for us was the ultimate gesture of sportsmanship and kindness. I will be indebted to him for the rest of my life. The way that he had cast ego aside was tremendously humbling and I felt honoured to share this moment with him. He was a remarkable human being. So Zen-like, so calm, and he didn't seem to have suffered the massive emotional troughs that Jonesy and I had experienced.

While I was contemplating his emotional maturity it was perfectly exhibited. Aleks carried a blow-up beach ball that looked like a pumpkin, on which he'd drawn a face. During the past three months this had been his only company. He'd named it Wilson, like the ball in the movie *Cast Away*. As we skied towards the inlet, Aleks attached Wilson to the top of his sled, so he could enjoy the moment. He talked fondly of the time the two of them had shared together and when he turned around to ask Wilson a question, he was gone!

We scanned the snowy wilderness behind us but our eyes revealed nothing. For a moment I could see a look of horror on Aleks's face and tried to comfort him.

'Aleks, do you want us to ski back and have a look for Wilson?' I asked.

After a brief pause, Aleks replied with a smile on his face, 'No. No, it's alright. It was meant to be – Wilson wanted to stay in Antarctica.'

And that was that. Such an event would've devastated Jonesy and me. But Aleks just adapted to the situation and moved on.

As we skied along babbling to one another my skis crossed and I fell over. I felt like an obsessed Formula One fan who'd just stalled at the lights next to Michael Schumacher. I was so embarrassed! Unlike Aleks's calm demeanour over the loss of Wilson, this incident stewed in my head making me feel slightly inadequate until literally a few minutes later when Aleks did exactly the same thing. But he just got up and dusted himself off, not at all fazed. It made me wonder why I'd been so worried. It also made me realise that Norwegians are human too.

Finally we skied into the inlet and that stranger's shadow which had been cast onto the icy slopes of Hercules Inlet back on Day Two had now lost its unfamiliarity. As the journey unfolded the shadow had become my friend. And now that shadow was me – I was that Polar Dude. Our pick-up plane buzzed over our heads in a circle. We cheered and yelled and waved. We were going home and our happiness at the thought bordered on delirium. The plane circled, and continued to circle. We stopped and watched, wondering when they'd land. After twenty minutes, they banked away from us and Aleks astutely said, 'That's a bit odd, why are they preparing to land downwind?'

'Maybe they're not,' I replied, suddenly not so joyous.

'They're not leaving us here are they?' Jonesy asked. Dreams of unlimited plates of food had dulled the pain of his throbbing coccyx over the previous few hours.

They were and they did. The plane got smaller and smaller and the sound of the engines roaring in the cold air became ever more distant. The plane disappeared. We jumped on the satellite phone and called the comm's operator at Union Glacier.

A thick South African accent delivered the bad news. 'Sorry guys, the pilot says the contrast and flat light make it impossible to land the plane. We'll have to wait for conditions to improve.'

We stood there in deflated silence looking at one another for a moment or two, and then we got to work. We set up Aleks's tent, then staked out a runway with all our spare bags, sleds, poles, anything we could fashion into markers so that when the plane did come back there'd be no problems.

We bunkered down for the night and had our fingers crossed that conditions would improve by morning. By 8 pm, the fatigue from the past couple of weeks made me feel ill and I fell asleep quickly with the knowledge that in the morning there was no more skiing. We'd done it!

DAY NINETY

I slept like a baby. When I woke I could hear Aleks speaking to the pilot about the weather. Conditions had improved marginally but still weren't really any better than the day before. I hadn't let myself think about this scenario, but if the plane didn't get down to us soon, our food supplies would reach critically low levels. All three of us had rationed our supplies to get us to Hercules Inlet and no further.

The pilot understood the seriousness of the situation and made the call to come and have another look. If he wasn't able to land, he'd at least drop some food down to us that would last a few more days. An hour later the plane circled around our heads, before lobbing a small package to us. He wasn't going to land – but, food! Fresh food at last! There was a lovely note from the base staff and we immersed ourselves in frying the bacon on our stove and slicing up the fresh bread. Our senses exploded at the delicious smell.

While we were occupied stuffing our faces, the pilot had not given up. He landed 20 kilometres to our east under a patch of blue sky, hoping that if a clear window opened he could dart across and pick us up. After only a few hours, he flew back and, third time lucky, he landed the plane lightly and before we knew it he taxied up next to us. We jumped around like crazed loonies yelling, 'We're going home, we're going home!'

The muscles in our legs had become so used to shuffling forward that stepping into the Twin Otter was a real challenge. Our quads had wasted completely and we needed to help one another on board. With us and our sleds in, the plane roared to life and skipped across to Union Glacier camp where a whole heap of the staff had gathered to cheer as we disembarked the plane. Steve was there smiling and the comms guys who we'd been speaking to every night were also there. Everyone was so excited. It was such a relief to be among other humans again. From that moment on the three of us couldn't stop eating, drinking and sleeping, in no particular order. Jonesy had three months worth of cravings and recipes in his head that he needed to satisfy and he got to work quickly. Mid-way through his third plate of dinner his face turned an ashen white and all at the table asked if he was alright.

'I think I ate too much,' he replied. 'Might just go outside and get some fresh air.'

He returned to his plate fifteen minutes later and finished off what was left, then went and helped himself to a pile of brownies. I was relieved. When Jonesy can't eat there is definitely something wrong.

The doctor at the base examined us and the good news was that there were no permanent injuries. The nerve damage in Jonesy's fingers would take a few months to repair, and a strong course of antibiotics and some ointment would sort out my face and Jonesy's toes. The main thing we needed was rest, and we were told we'd need to allow our bodies the time for our wounds to heal. We were well acquainted with this, as after the Tasman it had taken us a good nine months to recover from our fatigue levels and short-term memory loss.

Video journal – Back at base camp
www.casandjonesy.com.au/extremesouth

So what about our weight? We jumped on the scales and we both weighed 76 kilograms! Considering Jonesy started the trip at 106 kilograms and me at 102 kilograms, the total weight loss between us was a phenomenal 56 kilograms. Jonesy was the lightest he'd been as an adult and found it hard to take his eyes off the mirror when he wasn't wearing a shirt. For the first time in his life he could see his abs (and between you and me, he loved it!).

The realisation that Aleks, Jonesy and I had managed a feat that would become a page in Antarctic history – that we'd conquered one of the last great polar adventures – was still sinking in. I felt immensely proud and grateful. And I was ready to go home.

'The unknown journey of life is the
ultimate destination.'

David 'Gravy' Johnston, 2007

POSTSCRIPT

Within a few days, we'd touched down on the tarmac at Sydney International Airport. The anxiety of being around people again intimidated me and I was nervous about the cameras, the media and the excited group of supporters who had gathered early on a Sunday morning to welcome us home. As we passed through the customs gates I immediately locked eyes on Mia, who was crying, and as soon as she saw me she started running in my direction. She was more beautiful than I remembered. With her face snuggled into my ratty neck-beard, she held me like she never wanted to let go. I was home.

Over the next few weeks, we had numerous media and sponsor commitments as well as an extremely fun welcome-back party down at Bondi. We were stoked to find out that while we were on the expedition we raised $60,000 for You Can.

Never being one to remain idle for too long, I had a wedding to get ready for! Mia had done such a fabulous job while we were down south, organising pretty much everything, however a little walk in Antarctica wasn't going to get me out of all my groom's duties. After we arrived home from the airport she sat me down at our dining table and handed me my 'wedding to-do list'. What a contrast from being on the ice! On the list was sorting out my wedding attire, wedding rings and, most importantly, learning our wedding dance. Dancing has never been one of my strong points and the anticipation of those couple of minutes scared me more than any crevasse in Antarctica ever did.

Just as Mawson was wedded to Paquita weeks after arriving home from Antarctica, my marriage to Mia took place within a month of leaving Antarctica. Seventy of our closest friends and family travelled to an idyllic spot in the south of Thailand with the most spectacular beaches on this planet (oh, and how can I forget – the best climbing too!). For months I'd dreamt of my wedding day. As Mia walked down the aisle, I stood next to my best man, Jonesy, and we all cried. We'd scrubbed up okay, though the odd scar from cold injuries on our cheeks and noses were still evident. Luckily, after copious amounts of conditioner and oil Mia had managed to unmatt my hair so I didn't have to cut it. That day was everything I had hoped it would be and more.

Now that we're back in Sydney and normal (married) life has resumed, I constantly reminisce on our ninety days in Antarctica. Of course that resentment I thought I could sense from Mia on the other end of the satellite phone had been completely manufactured in my head and things between us had never been better. I've been busy writing this book and Jonesy has been working on our documentary. Sometimes when I go for a run or head into the city, I stick earplugs in my ears to experience that same deafening quietness that became our friend in Antarctica. I miss it.

We've started sharing our keynote talks to corporations around the country, which audiences are responding to extremely well. The expedition was only a couple of months ago and the raw scars are still visible. It's both difficult and emotionally draining explaining to audiences where the journey took our minds. Answering the question 'How hard was it?' is still challenging – because we pushed so far past anything we thought possible, we have no other frame of reference to compare it against. All I can say is that it was a truckload harder than crossing the Tasman. I hope this book goes some way in showing what we experienced.

Over that last month, Jonesy and I trod the tightrope between collapse and just scraping through, and although we pushed hard, we cannot dismiss the fact that luck played a vital role in getting us back to the coast. We were lucky that temperatures did not plummet towards the end of summer, we were lucky that the weather held. Captain Scott and his Pole party did not have this same good fortune. He said himself in the diaries found next to his body:

> The causes of the disaster are not due to faulty organisation, but to misfortune in all risks that had to be undertaken.

Since 17 January 1912, when Scott's party reached the Pole, Aleks, Jonesy and I are the only people who have turned our backs on the South Pole after establishing caches on the outward journey. The complexities of cache plans, calculations and figuring how much to leave behind and how much to keep carrying was one of the most challenging and rewarding aspects of our journey in Antarctica.

Critics argue that many factors led to Scott's death. It is hard not to declare that Scott's biggest mistake was that he simply didn't have a sufficient buffer to accommodate for poor weather and unfavourable conditions. Like Scott, we knowingly had a tight buffer, aware of the consequences that poor weather could bring. Both his expedition and ours were at the limit of human survival at our time in history. When pushing these boundaries of human endeavours there is only limited room on an expedition for spares of equipment and food. The heavier the sled, the slower the progress and the less chance of success. There are only so many kilograms that one can pull in a sled. If the weight of our sleds was much more than the 160 kilograms we started with, we would've been required to shuttle loads forward, which aside from being extraordinarily slow, would've been suicidally dangerous in poor weather.

I can now understand why Scott lay in his ice-encrusted sleeping-bag and waited for death. Mentally, when Antarctica has destroyed you (like it did me on Days Twenty-nine and Thirty) it is very difficult to keep fighting. At the end of the first month, I had given up on the expedition. No amount of coercion from Jonesy, no thoughts of family and friends or anything for that matter, could buoy my spirits. I was broken. The pain, the suffering, the intimidation and the weather had all become too much. Scott's body was even more ruined than mine. He had not received the mental boost that would've come with claiming sovereignty of the Pole and he had been out there for five months. He didn't have his best mate there with him either, something I know made a huge difference for me.

In Antarctica, Jonesy and I went through incredible highs and devastating lows. At times we came close to hating each other and we said some heavy things when we were at our worst. But we were also able to encourage and help each other to get to the end. No matter what, there is no-one else I could've done that with, and if I had to do it all again, I'd need him by my side to do it.

Though there is one person who I want to share every adventure with from now on – my wife, Mia. We have moved out of the expedition headquarters and are enjoying married life. I'm still struggling with the notion that our expedition in Antarctica may have been my last one. Adventure is ingrained in my DNA. I've always said that when I have a family I'd put them first, but at the same time I cannot deny who I am. I think the size, scope and scale of my expeditions will have to wind back. Will I be satisfied downsizing these adventures? This is perhaps the biggest challenge I face, as two parts of my heart are ripping me in different directions. Yes, at times I dream of the bitter North Pole but I also dream of raising a beautiful family with Mia in the Blue Mountains. And just days before this book was finished I was able to tell friends that I am going to share one of the biggest adventures of all with Mia – we are expecting our first child. This news gave me the same excitement that adventure has always done – it's that feeling I experienced paddling out onto the water with the Tasman stretching before me, or watching the Twin Otter fade into the distance from Hercules Inlet – it's knee-trembling anticipation and exhilaration.

But even if I never do another big outdoor adventure again in my life, the lessons that Crossing the Ditch and Crossing the Ice have taught me will still be with me. These two four-year projects have seared a framework into my head on how to take on the impossible. The first step was allowing myself to dream big enough – failure is never quite so frightening as regret. By undertaking this journey and achieving what we did, it has allowed me to dream even bigger.

Dreams can come true, but only through bloody hard work. The success of any big expedition comes from detailed risk-management work, planning and scrupulous preparation. Believe it or not, both Jonesy and I are pretty risk-averse guys. Fortunately, we enjoy piecing the puzzle of possibility together. Our mate Gravy is always telling us life is about the journey, not the destination – and he's right. Our journey began years before we touched down on the ice and it was all part of the experience.

Both of us were terrible skiers and had never experienced the brutal cold. So how did we succeed where others had failed? The lessons we learnt from these prior attempts were invaluable. Perhaps the biggest lesson these teams passed on was advice on equipment and training, and on the head game – the mental side of things. Viewing the South Pole as the summit of a mountain was a critical factor in preparing to turn around. Further, the strength of our friendship and the attitude that we were one unit trying to move across the ice as fast as we could as a team – not individuals – led to our success. Finally, we refused to give up. Regardless of whether we were going to make it back to the coast, we were in for all fifteen rounds. It wasn't going to matter how many times we got knocked down, for us the challenge lay in getting back up again.

I don't think Antarctica has radically changed who we are or what we stand for, but it has definitely put into perspective many of life's everyday challenges. Late to work? Not as bad as being stuck in a white-out for two weeks! Feeling a bit tired? Nothing will compare to Day Eighty-nine of the expedition! Car broke down? Prefer that to our ski pole breaking in Antarctica!

Our ninety days in Antarctica forced us to accept responsibility for our actions. This is one of the things I love about adventure – you are ultimately responsible for your own safety and survival. We live in a society where we are becoming more and more risk averse and want to outsource responsibility when things go wrong. Risk cannot be eliminated but it can be managed. Accepting responsibility allows you to address risk. Without risk there is no adventure, as the outcome would be assured. Without this excitement of the unknown, I strongly believe there is very limited room for growth as an individual. In my life, it has been the times that I've really extended myself that I've learnt the most valuable lessons about who I am and what I'm capable of. Australia is now one of the most litigious countries in the world and our experience in Antarctica taught me there is something incredibly liberating about accepting responsibility for the good and the bad. Antarctica taught Scott the same lesson:

We took risks, we knew we took them, things have come out against us, and therefore we have no cause for complaint.

Sure, we had a great team from all over the world who were instrumental in putting our bid together. But as soon as we hit the ice in Antarctica, if something went wrong it was not their fault but ours. The responsibility either came down to a fault in our leadership or a lack of proper understanding regarding a particular facet of the journey. Taking ownership of a problem expedited the path to finding a solution.

Antarctica also reinforced Newton's physics law: 'for every action there is an equal and opposite reaction' – T.I.A., we dubbed it. In our lives back home there are also ripples from our actions, but often these are minimised or muted due to the structure and developed nature of our society. Antarctica has taught us to be more aware of the repercussions of our choices and actions.

It's a massive honour that the Powerhouse Museum has agreed to acquire our gear from the expedition. Our clothing and equipment now sit next to Douglas Mawson's gear – a hundred years separates our expeditions yet surprisingly there are few differences. As I look at the two sleds my mind wanders back to the POW – will this be the future? What will gear look like in one hundred years' time?

Jonesy has had a rougher time integrating back into normal life. His family is scattered all over the place and without the all-consuming focus of the trip, at times he feels isolated and alone. I know that feeling from years past and it isn't good, but I also know Jonesy is a very good man and he will find his way.

Finishing the journey with Jonesy and Aleks Gamme has forged a bond between us that I don't think will ever be broken. Aleks is the only other person on the planet who truly understands what we went through out there. I find it difficult to express the respect and admiration we have for him. Aleks showed us that a much higher level of self-fulfilment (and respect) can be achieved when the prize is not winning or beating one another. When I reflect back on the 2000 Sydney Olympic Games I struggle to remember who won gold medals but deeply etched in my thoughts are timeless scenes like when a small man from Equatorial Guinea nicknamed 'Eric the Eel' swam the 100-metre freestyle in 1 minute 52 seconds (twice as slow as the rest of the field) and yet he stole the hearts of so many Australians. Similarly to Eric, Aleks's act of sportsmanship showed how competition can be transcended. Everything we do in life is competitive – our careers, the partners we desire, where we live, how we live – it is often dictated by the inbuilt human mechanism to 'one-up' each other. Skiing into Hercules Inlet alongside Aleks and Jonesy was an infinitely richer finale to our adventure than if we'd 'beaten' him, and in hindsight I would like to think we also would have waited for Aleks. Through his kindness, Aleks not only taught me what adventure is all about but, more importantly, what life is all about. It has little to do with self-gratification and accolades, and more to do with the power of sharing life's little victories and experiences with others. Recently I asked him about why he waited and this is what he had to say:

> It seemed like everybody expected a new race, this time for the last milestone in Antarctica. We both wanted to succeed and we both wanted to be first. But I couldn't bear the thought of 'racing' for three months, that would have totally ruined the whole experience for me. Every day I was just pushing as hard as I could, but I have to admit that I was relieved that I got a lead on you after the first weeks. Being in front made it easier for me to be less competitive and more supportive. Then, as the weeks went by I felt we developed a bond and I definitely wanted us both to succeed.

This idea of a perfectly scripted dream-finish was encouraging and very motivating for both of us. Aleks continues:

> Someone messaged me a note telling me I could risk my trip and not be considered solo if I finished the last stage with you. Honestly, I thought 'f**k off'. Why am I here? I would rather have the experience of life and be a supportive team player, instead of making winners and losers out of all of us. After the tremendous effort the three of us had been through I just couldn't do it. Those last days I was waiting in my tent like a child waiting for Christmas Day. I can't describe the feelings of happiness when I saw you, up there on the slope ... it was one of the best days of my life. I can still cry just thinking about it. I didn't envy you your last two weeks, really, it was tough but you didn't look as bad as I thought you'd look. I also remember you offering to go look for Wilson when he disappeared. That was impressive given your condition and the efforts it had taken to get back to Hercules Inlet.

Aleks is now back in Norway and is hoping to do a trip through the jungles of Borneo. He's obviously had enough of the cold.

It took this scruffy Norwegian to teach me something that crossing an ocean and a continent didn't: that it is the simple things about being human that bring the greatest joy, and on 26 January 2012, we celebrated just that. Three blokes skiing over an arbitrary finish line, with a stadium of silence roaring all around. Along with the blood, sweat and tears – a fragment of my soul will always remain in the extreme south.

GLOSSARY

ALE (Antarctic Logistics and Expeditions) – The company that flies expeditions to Antarctica and provides logistical support. They operate the Union Glacier Base and would be the organisation to effect a rescue if needed.

Amundsen, Roald – Led the first successful expedition to the South Pole, arriving 14 December 1911. His success was primarily due to his meticulous planning and preparation.

assistance – Any external power aids used for significant speed and load advantage. Typical aids used in polar expeditions include wind power (kites), animal power (dogs) or engine power (motorised vehicles). Only human-powered expeditions are considered unassisted. The use of human-powered equipment such as skis, snowshoes and sleds are not considered as assistance. Usage of a navigation aid such as a compass and GPS are not considered as assistance. Usage of safety aids such as radios, satellite phones and location beacons are not considered as assistance.

Baffin Island – An island in Northern Canada, Arctic Circle, where we trained for the Antarctica expedition with the world's best polar guides.

cache – Stores of food that are left on the way out to the South Pole to be picked up on the return journey. We gave our caches individual names:

81 degrees cache – The Hidden Cache

82 degrees cache – The Gateway Cache

86 degrees cache – The Centenary Cache

88 degrees cache – The Christmas Cache

89 degrees cache – The Summit Push Cache

crevasse – A deep fissure in a glacier or other body of ice. Crevasses are usually caused by differential movement of parts of the ice over an uneven ground underneath or the pressure of one ice body pushing against another. They can have a partial crust form over the mouth (a snowbridge) hiding them from sight.

EPIRB (Emergency Position Indicating Radio Beacon) – A distress radio beacon.

fartlek – a form of running training where the speed is varied throughout a run, not unlike interval training.

Gamme, Aleksander – Norwegian polar guide and adventurer who set out to achieve an unsupported solo return journey to the South Pole at the same time as us.

Hercules Inlet – A landmark on the continental coast of Antarctica. The start and end point of our journey.

Ilyushin 76 – A Russian cargo plane that flies in and out of Antarctica from South America. Chartered by ALE.

Iqaluit – The base town for our polar adventure course on Baffin Island.

katabatic wind – Wind that generally pushes downhill due to gravitational pressure and air temperature. Especially prevalent in Antarctica and the reason we were pushing into headwinds for the first half of our expedition.

Mawson, Sir Douglas – Australia's pre-eminent polar explorer of the early 1900s.

McNair family – The family of polar guides who trained us up on Baffin Island in the Arctic: Matty (mother), Eric (son) and Sarah (daughter). Eric completed a big kite-skiing expedition in Antarctica at the same time as our expedition and came to Sydney during preparations to help check our equipment.

nunatak – An isolated rocky peak surrounded by ice or snow.

Philips, Eric – Australian polar guide. Provided logistical support and advice on expedition strategy, gear and training. Also supported Pat Farmer (Pole to Pole runner) when he was in Antarctica.

pulk – A sled. We used these to carry all our equipment, supplies and food. Generally dragged behind the expedition on (hopefully) slick runners.

return trip – A return trip has the same start and end point.

sastrugi – ridges of snow found in polar regions formed and shaped by the wind.

Scott, Captain Robert Falcon – Led the second party to reach the South Pole. Unfortunately, Captain Scott and his fellow adventurers did not survive the return journey.

sked – A slang term for a scheduled radio talk.

skins – Nylon material much like carpet, attached to the bottom of skis. Provides grip in one direction, glide in the other.

solo – A travel style that refers to the expeditioner being alone with no support.

support – Outside help received by an expedition. The most common form of support is to pick up supplies from an external party including food, fuel, equipment, etc. Support can also be extended to entering a tent to receive the benefit of warmth and shelter from the conditions.

Thiel Mountains – The mountain range that we skied past on our way to and from the South Pole, approximately halfway between Hercules Inlet and the South Pole.

T.I.A. (This Is Antarctica) – A phrase we used on our expedition whenever something unfavourable occurred in accordance with Murphy's Law, or when a solution to one problem would result in another problem.

trace-lines – The line that attached us to our sleds. Also called traces.

Twin Otter – A small twin-propeller plane that ferried us from Union Glacier to Hercules Inlet and back again.

Union Glacier – The base where we entered and left Antarctica. This base is run by ALE and is in the Chilean-managed portion of Antarctica.

SOUTH POLE RETURN TRIPS – COMPLETED

Surname	First name	Nationality	Starting point	Starting date	Arrival at South Pole	Days	Kilometres	Support	Assistance
AMUNDSEN	Roald	Norway	Bay of Whales	20 October 1911	14 December 1911	54/25	2700	–	dogs
BJAALAND	Olav	Norway	Bay of Whales	20 October 1911	14 December 1911	54/25	2700	–	dogs
WISTING	Oscar	Norway	Bay of Whales	20 October 1911	14 December 1911	54/25	2700	–	dogs
HASSEL	Sverre	Norway	Bay of Whales	20 October 1911	14 December 1911	54/25	2700	–	dogs
HANSSEN	Helmer	Norway	Bay of Whales	20 October 1911	14 December 1911	54/25	2700	–	dogs
McNAIR	Matty	USA	Hercules Inlet	2 November 2004	23 December 2004	51/70	2260	resupply	parasail
McNAIR – LANDRY	Sarah	USA	Hercules Inlet	2 November 2004	23 December 2004	51/70	2260	resupply	parasail
McNAIR – LANDRY	Eric	USA	Hercules Inlet	2 November 2004	23 December 2004	51/70	2260	resupply	parasail
DICKINSON	Conrad	UK	Hercules Inlet	2 November 2004	23 December 2004	51/70	2260	resupply	parasail
DICKINSON	Hillary	UK	Hercules Inlet	2 November 2004	23 December 2004	51/70	2260	resupply	parasail
GAMME	Aleksander	Norway	Hercules Inlet	29 October 2011	24 December 2011	57/30	2260	–	–
CASTRISSION	James	Australia	Hercules Inlet	30 October 2011	30 December 2011	62/27	2260	–	–
JONES	Justin	Australia	Hercules Inlet	30 October 2011	30 December 2011	62/27	2260	–	–

EXPEDITION NOTES

DAY ON TRAIL	CHILEAN TIME 2100	POSITION	DAY SUMMARY					WEATHER			
			DISTANCE TRAVELLED (km)	CUMULATIVE DISTANCE (km)	AVERAGE DAILY DISTANCE (km)	TOTAL ELEVATION (metres)	HOURS ON THE TRAIL (inc breaks)	AVERAGE TEMP (Degrees Celsius)	WIND SPEED (km/hr)	VISIBILITY	NOTES
1	30–Oct–11	79057.002"S 79055.916"W	9.12	9.12	9.12	130	3hr	-25	40-50	Relatively good	
2	31–Oct–11	80002.423"S 80015.127"W	12.10	21.22	10.61	200	7hr	-25	40-50	Good	
3	1–Nov–11	80006.225"S 80042.179"W	11.10	32.32	10.77	500	7hr	-23	25 (am) 10-15 (pm)	Very good	
4	2–Nov–11	80012.753"S 80037.733"W	12.80	45.12	11.28	700	8hr 15min	-23	50	Good during day, reduced to 20m once tent was set up	
5	3–Nov–11	80018.767"S 80025.356"W	12.20	57.32	11.46		8hr	-20	30-40	Poor, 20m white-out all day	
6	4–Nov–11	80025.398"S 80016.393"W	13.00	70.32	11.72	750–770	8hr 20min	-20	20-30	Start 20m throughout day increased to 40m white-out again	
7	5–Nov–11	80031.770"S 80005.229"W	12.60	82.92	11.85	750–770	8hr 20min	-15-20	10-20	Varies 20-60m	
8	6–Nov–11	80036.795"S 079059.039"W	9.76	92.68	11.59	750–770	8hr	-15-20	10-30	Majority day 20-40m, cleared to 100m for a bit, then snowed again, snowing all day	
9	7–Nov–11	80040.695"S 079058.005"W	7.40	100.08	11.12	750–770	8hr 20min	-15-20	20	100m give or take	
10	8–Nov–11	80044.260"S 080001.592"W	6.70	106.78	10.68	820	7hr	-20	up to 50 died off in evening	Clear	
11	9–Nov–11	80050.233"S 080003.836"W	11.40	118.18	10.74	800	8hr 20min	-15-20	10-25	White-out 50-100m	
12	10–Nov–11	80056.344"S 080004.754"W	11.30	129.48	10.79	750–770	8hr 20min	-15-20	up to 25	White-out 200m	
13	11–Nov–11	80056.344"S 080004.754"W	0.00	129.48	9.96	750–770	0hr	-15-20	up to 50	Clear	Rest day, 3 days' provisions dropped @ Hidden Cache for return journey
14	12–Nov–11	81001.008"S 080002.028"W	8.70	138.18	9.87	830	8hr	-15	up to 80	White-out 20-30m	
15	13–Nov–11	81006.400"S 079054.940"W	10.20	148.38	9.89	800	8hr 50min	-15	20	White-out 30-100m	
16	14–Nov–11	81008.269"S 079054.169"W	3.50	151.88	9.49	730	4hr 25min	-15	10 to 50	100-200m	
17	15–Nov–11	81016.349"S 079053.547"W	9.40	161.28	9.49	820	8hr 50min	-20	10-15	Clear	
18	16–Nov–11	81017.368"S 079053.324"W	7.50	168.78	9.38	720	8hr 50min	-20	10-15	Clear	
19	17–Nov–11	81023.292"S 079055.929"W	11.00	179.78	9.46	730	8hr 55min	-15-20	5-10	Clear	
20	18–Nov–11	81029.100"S 079059.279"W	11.00	190.78	9.54	700	8hr 55min	-15-20	10-25	Clear, partial cloud cover	
21	19–Nov–11	81039.316"S 079057.725"W	19.80	210.58	10.03	790	9hr 55min	-15	5-15	Clear	

DAY ON TRAIL	CHILEAN TIME 2100	POSITION	DAY SUMMARY					WEATHER			
			DISTANCE TRAVELLED (km)	CUMULATIVE DISTANCE (km)	AVERAGE DAILY DISTANCE (km)	TOTAL ELEVATION (metres)	HOURS ON THE TRAIL (inc breaks)	AVERAGE TEMP (Degrees Celsius)	WIND SPEED (km/hr)	VISIBILITY	NOTES
22	20-Nov-11	81045.637"S 080001.046"W	11.70	222.28	10.10	790	8hr 50min	-15-20	20-40	Clear, partial cloud	
23	21-Nov-11	81053.581"S 079059.143"W	14.70	236.98	10.30	810	9hr 55min	-15-20	30-50	Clear, slightly cloudy	
24	22-Nov-11	82000.320"S 079059.475"W	12.50	249.48	10.40	880	8hr 10min	-15	5-20	Clear	3 days' provisions dropped @ Gateway Cache for return journey
25	23-Nov-11	82010.051"S 079048.040"W	18.20	267.68	10.71	860	8hr 25min	-15	20-40	Clear	
26	24-Nov-11	82021.452"S 079054.401"W	21.25	288.93	11.11	890	9hr 50mins	-15	5-20	Clear	
27	25-Nov-11	82030.726"S 079059.537"W	17.22	306.15	11.34	1000	10hr 50min	-20	20-50	Clear	
28	26-Nov-11	82040.734"S 079059.477"W	18.60	324.75	11.60	1030	9hr 30min	-15-20	5-25	Clear	
29	27-Nov-11	82040.734"S 079059.477"W	0.00	324.75	11.20	1030	0hr	-15-20	5-20	Clear	Rest day
30	28-Nov-11	82040.734"S 079059.477"W	0.00	324.75	10.83	1030	0hr	-15	0-10	Clear	Rest day
31	29-Nov-11	82051.866"S 080001.280"W	21.00	345.75	11.15	1060	8hr 50min	-15	5-15	Clear	
32	30-Nov-11	83002.326"S 079058.928"W	19.50	365.25	11.41	1100	9hr	-20	10-30	Clear	
33	1-Dec-11	83015.461"S 080002.389"W	24.40	389.65	11.81	1119	9hr 30min	-15-20	5-20	Clear	
34	2-Dec-11	83026.078"S 080003.197"W	19.70	409.35	12.04	1178	9hr 15min	-15	0-15	Pretty much clear, low contrast, lots of cloud cover – couldn't see what you were stepping on	
35	3-Dec-11	83039.268"S 080005.113"W	24.50	433.85	12.40	1235	9hr 20min	-15-20	0-25	Clear, partial cloud	
36	4-Dec-11	83053.245"S 080008.164"W	26.00	459.85	12.77	1280	9hr 25min	-15-20	5-20	Clear, partial cloud	
37	5-Dec-11	84006.227"S 080011.201"W	24.10	483.95	13.08	1303	9hr 25min	-15-20	15	Clear, cloudy day	
38	6-Dec-11	84019.459"S 080017.603"W	24.60	508.55	13.38	1259	9hr	-15	0-10	Cloudy, extremely low contrast	
39	7-Dec-11	84032.577"S 080025.166"W	24.40	532.95	13.67	1273	9hr 20min	-15-20	0-20	Clear, sunny	
40	8-Dec-11	84046.577"S 080025.166"W	25.10	558.05	13.95	1270	9hr 25min	-15-20	0-15	Clear, partial cloud	
41	9-Dec-11	85000.044"S 080043.820"W	26.00	584.05	14.25	1350	9hr 45min	-20	0-20	Clear, some cloud	
42	10-Dec-11	85011.370"S 080053.072"W	21.10	605.15	14.41	1356	8hr 40min	-15-20	0-20	Clear, light cloud	
43	11-Dec-11	85023.279"S 08106.497"W	22.20	627.35	14.59	1360	9hr 25min	-15	0-15	Clear, cloudy, low contrast in afternoon	
44	12-Dec-11	85036.921"S 081019.275"W	25.40	652.75	14.84	1465	9hr 50min	-15	0-15	Clear, low contrast in morn, cleared as day went on, slight touch of snow this morning	
45	13-Dec-11	85051.218"S 081033.585"W	24.90	677.65	15.06	1597	9hr 20min	mind 15	0-10	Clear	Best day we've had

DAY ON TRAIL	CHILEAN TIME 2100	POSITION	DAY SUMMARY					WEATHER			
			DISTANCE TRAVELLED (km)	CUMULATIVE DISTANCE (km)	AVERAGE DAILY DISTANCE (km)	TOTAL ELEVATION (metres)	HOURS ON THE TRAIL (inc breaks)	AVERAGE TEMP (Degrees Celsius)	WIND SPEED (km/hr)	VISIBILITY	NOTES
46	14-Dec-11	86007.521°S 081036.296°W	30.20	707.85	15.39	1742	9hr 55min	-10-15	0-10.	Clear, now cloudy and overcast	Skied in thermal top for a while. 6 days provisions dropped @ Centenary Cache for return journey
47	15-Dec-11	86021.492°S 081038.400°W	26.00	733.85	15.61	1791	9hr 30min	-15	5-15	Overcast, low contrast, couldn't see much around them	
48	16-Dec-11	86036.113°S 081041.453°W	27.20	761.05	15.86	1892	9hr 50min	-15-20	5-20	Overcast now, clear, good day	
49	17-Dec-11	86051.083°S 081044.045°W	27.85	788.90	16.10	2010	10hr	-15	10-25	Clear	
50	18-Dec-11	87007.114°S 081046.007°W	29.82	818.72	16.37	2183	9hr 55min	-20	5-15	Clear, overcast to clear	Going up getting colder
51	19-Dec-11	87023.080°S 081050.462°W	29.70	848.42	16.64	2336	10hr 05min n	-20	5-10	Clear	
52	20-Dec-11	87037.148°S 082028.168°W	26.40	874.82	16.82	2476	9hr 45min	-20-25	5-25 North	White-out, low vis	
53	21-Dec-11	87052.186°S 082000.708°W	28.05	902.87	17.04	2532	10hr 55min	-20	5-15	Clear when woke up, now cloudy	Last night freezing in the tent. No sun. Windy. Both had cold feet for a while.
54	22-Dec-11	88006.139°S 082006.715°W	26.00	928.87	17.20	2606	9hr 45min	-20-25	5-35	Clear, light cloud	6 days' provisions dropped @ Christmas Cache for return journey
55	23-Dec-11	88006.139°S 082006.715°W	0.00	928.87	16.89	2650	0hr	-20	10-20	Clear, overcast, low contrast, batteries at 80-90%	Rest day
56	24-Dec-11	88025.173°S 082013.651°W	35.40	964.27	17.22	2710	10hr 45min	-10-15	0-10	Clear, some cloud cover which meant low contrast	
57	25-Dec-11	88045.124°S 082032.742°W	37.10	1001.37	17.57	2740	10hr 40min	-15	5-20	Clear, cloudy then clear	
58	26-Dec-11	89002.076°S 082053.130°W	31.50	1032.87	17.81	2740	11hr 5min	-23	5-25	Clear, light cloud	Colder this morn. More wind wind this morn. 6 days' provisions dropped @ Gateway Cache for return journey
59	27-Dec-11	89020.084°S 083037.886°W	33.50	1066.37	18.07	2764	10hr 45min	-25	5-15, 20 (am)	Clear, light cloud patches	
60	28-Dec-11	89037.540°S 085037.495°W	32.50	1098.87	18.31	2808	11hr 20min	-15 to 20	0-15	Clear, light cloud	
61	29-Dec-11	89054.369°S 058051.745°W	32.70	1131.57	18.55	2817	11hr	-20-25	5-20	Clear, cloudy, clear patch, then cloudy, misty, light snow, changing a lot, confused weather	

			DAY SUMMARY					WEATHER			
DAY ON TRAIL	CHILEAN TIME 2100	POSITION	DISTANCE TRAVELLED (km)	CUMULATIVE DISTANCE (km)	AVERAGE DAILY DISTANCE (km)	TOTAL ELEVATION (metres)	HOURS ON THE TRAIL (inc breaks)	AVERAGE TEMP (Degrees Celsius)	WIND SPEED (km/hr)	VISIBILITY	NOTES
62	30-Dec-11	89054.369"S 058051.745"W	23.80	1155.37	18.64	2817	8hr 25min	-15 to -25.	5-20 (am), 20	Clear, strange weather, mist on the horizon	Overnight overcast and freezing, cold in the morn
63	31-Dec-11	89034.409"S 084044.443"W	38.40	1193.77	18.95	2804	11hr 30min	-15 (day), -25 this morn.	5-20	Clear, cloudy, misty in the morning, clear in the avo, patchy cloud	Most winds this morn
64	1-Jan-12	89014.431"S 083020.261"W	37.20	1230.97	19.23	2770	11hr 55min	-20-25	5-20	Clear during day, clear now but overcast and cold	
65	2-Jan-12	88054.268"S 082042.334"W	37.50	1268.47	19.51	2725	11hr 45min	-20	5-15	Clear, overcast this morn, freezing last night, clear now	Windier in the am died off in pm. Picked up the Push Cache.
66	3-Jan-12	88033.245"S 082022.106"W	39.10	1307.57	19.81	2735		-20	5-15	Clear	Perfect day
67	4-Jan-12	88012.208"S 082010.020"W	39.10	1346.67	20.10	2664	11hr 55min	-20-25	5-15	Clear, perfect day	
68	5-Jan-12	87050.011"S 082001.528"W	41.30	1387.97	20.41	2514	12hr 5min	-20	5-25	Clear, bluebird day	Picked up Christmas Cache
69	6-Jan-12	87028.887"S 083012.765"W	39.60	1427.57	20.69	2350	12hr 5min	-15-20	5-10	Clear	
70	7-Jan-12	87007.784"S 081046.333"W	40.00	1467.57	20.97	2140	12hr 25min	-20	5-15	Clear, alternated between cloudy and fine	
71	8-Jan-12	86044.503"S 081042.606"W	43.30	1510.87	21.28	1924	11hr 25min	-15 to -20	5-30	Clear	
72	9-Jan-12	86022.393"S 081038.372"W	41.10	1551.97	21.56	1791	11hr 35min	-10	0-10	Clear, nicest days of trip	
73	10-Jan-12	86002.377"S 081035.639"W	37.20	1589.17	21.77	1650	12hr 15min	-20 (am) then to -15	5-20	Low, overcast, light snow in am	Wind was in face this morning. Picked up Centenary Cache.
74	11-Jan-12	85038.943"S 081021.053"W	43.60	1632.77	22.06	1467	12hr 15min	-10-15	0-15	Clear, started out cloudy, then really nice	
75	12-Jan-12	85015.439"S 080056.741"W	43.86	1676.63	22.36	1371	12hr 15min	-15	5-20	Clear, started out sunny then overcast and patchy cloud, snowed this afternoon, just a dusting of snow – enough to take away glide, wind drift meant we had to ski over bumps, wind from East – across us.	
76	13-Jan-12	84054.881"S 080040.124"W	38.30	1714.93	22.56	1359	12hr 15min	-15-20	5-30	Low. 200. Low contrast.	Wind from the East

			DAY SUMMARY					WEATHER			
DAY ON TRAIL	CHILEAN TIME 2100	POSITION	DISTANCE TRAVELLED (km)	CUMULATIVE DISTANCE (km)	AVERAGE DAILY DISTANCE (km)	TOTAL ELEVATION (metres)	HOURS ON THE TRAIL (inc breaks)	AVERAGE TEMP (Degrees Celsius)	WIND SPEED (km/hr)	VISIBILITY	NOTES
77	14-Jan-12	84033.685"S 080040.124"W	39.50	1754.43	22.78	1279	12hr 15min	-10-15	5-15	Clear but overcast, bit of light this arvo	
78	15-Jan-12	84011.982"S 080010.828"W	40.44	1794.87	23.01	1303	12hr 20mn	-10-15	5-25	Overcast am, low vis, couldn't stick to track, only last session cleared up, good vis now	
79	16-Jan-12	83047.746"S 8006.405"W	45.11	1839.98	23.29	1277	13hr 05min	-10-15	10-35 (started to get close to 40 when we were talking)	Clear bluebird day	Feels colder
79	16-Jan-12	83047.746"S 8006.405"W	45.11	1839.98	23.29	1277	13hr 05min	-10-15	10-35 (started to get close to 40 when we were talking)	Clear bluebird day	Feels colder
80	17-Jan-12	83022.742"S 080003.792"W	46.54	1886.52	23.58	1145	13hr 15min	-10-15	5-20	Clear, blue bird day	
81	18-Jan-12	82059.845"S 079056.651"W	42.65	1929.17	23.82	1085	12hr 15min	-10	5-15	Overcast, low contrast, cloudy	
82	19-Jan-12	82036.693"S 079054.524"W	43.10	1972.27	24.05	1032	13hr 15min	-5-10	5-15	Clear, but overcast, cleared up in afternoon	
83	20-Jan-12	82011.268"S 079047.720"W	47.36	2019.63	24.33	842	13hr 15min	-10	5-20, dropped during day	Clear, light cloud	
84	21-Jan-12	81048.174"S 079057.215"W	43.06	2062.69	24.56	800	12hr	-10	5-20	Clear, started as overcast, turned to sunny	Picked up Gateway Cache
85	22-Jan-12	81020.999"S 079053.289"W	50.60	2113.29	24.86	723	13hr 15min	-10	5-30	Clear, light cloud	
86	23-Jan-12	80055.613"S 080005.804"W	47.37	2160.66	25.12	755	13hr 15min	-10	15-50	Clear, windy, light cloud, wind from south-west rear LHS	Picked up Hidden Cache
87	24-Jan-12	80029.804"S 080025.951"W	48.41	2209.07	25.39	806	13hr 3Cmin	-10	15-40	Clear, cloudy, overcast now	
88	25-Jan-12	8006.319"S 080025.951"W	43.76	2252.83	25.60	712	12hr 15min	-10	10-30	Clear, ranging between cloudy and blue	
89	26-Jan-12	79057.002"S 79055.916"W	20.93	2273.76	25.55	130	6hr	-10	10-30	Overcast, low contrast, cloudy	

EXPEDITION PLANNING

1. RISK-MANAGEMENT APPROACH

After deciding that we were going to attempt a big expedition in Antarctica, we set about educating ourselves about all the aspects of this hostile continent. We had a huge gap in our knowledge and went about filling this as fast as possible. For twelve months we answered all our questions about the risks of the expedition on paper before then getting outside and putting our plans into action. Information from previous attempts, other polar aficionados and world-class guides (such as the McNair family, Eric Philips, Hannah McKeand and Christian Eide), as well as our own research led to the formation of our 71-page risk-management document. This became our 'how-to' (and 'what not to do') document. It would become the blueprint of our expedition.

The goal of attempting the first unsupported return journey was something that we came to after doing our research into previous Antarctic expeditions.

As with our Tasman expedition, our risk-management document became a valuable tool in convincing other stakeholders and sponsors about our detailed preparation. With it we were able to show that we had the knowledge, skill and desire to take on this bold expedition.

2. EQUIPMENT

The major consideration for our equipment was to keep the weight down. All items needed to have high durability and we had to make sure we had the means to repair any broken items.

Almost none of the clothing and equipment that we needed to use on the trail was ready to use off the shelf. The kit from The North Face, although brilliant, had to be heavily modified to become 'polar friendly' (meaning everything that had to be handled while in the elements needed to be able to be manipulated with our thick polar mittens on). We basically had to customise everything.

Here is our equipment list:

	Category	Type	Qty
I	**SKIING EQUIPMENT**		
	Skis	Fischer E99 Crown	2.5
	Skins	Montana Nylonfeller 40 mm Full-length	2.5
		Montana Nylonfeller 40 mm Kicker-skins	2
	Poles	Swix Mountain Poles	2.5
	Bindings	Rottefella NNN BC Manual	6
	Back-country ski boots	Alfa North Pole GTX	2
	Insulated over gaiter	Northwinds	2
	Boot inner	Wool kertunk and cover	4
	Sled	Acapulka Exped	2
	Harness	Acapulka	2
	Traces	Rope and Bungee	2
	Compass	Dual hemisphere small compass and carrying system	2
II	**LOGISTICAL SUPPLIES**		
	Food	82 days	189 kg
	Fuel	Shellite	45 litres
	Cache markers and flags	Bamboo	4
III	**CLOTHING & PERSONAL EFFECTS**		
	Footwear		
	Socks	Icebreaker Ski Plus Socks	4
		Sealskin socks	4
	Down booties	The North Face Tent Booties	2
	Handwear		
	Vapour barrier liner	Nitrile surgical gloves	11
	Liner gloves	Polypro	6
	Windstopper gloves	The North Face Apex Glove	3
	Mittens	The North Face Himalayan Mitt	2
	Over mitt	Steger design mitt	2
	Headwear		
	Goggles	SMITH Phenom Turbo	4
	Sunglasses	Rudy Project Hi-altitude Zyon	2

	Category	Type	Qty
	Balaclava	The North Face Ninja Balaclava	2
	Buff		2
	Beanie	The North Face High Point Hat	2
	Big neck warmer	Icebreaker Wool Chute	2
	Face shield	Cold Avenger	2
	Innerwear		
	Thermals	Icebreaker GT260 Thermals and Boxers	4
	Mid-layers	The North Face Momentum Fleece and TKA100 Pants	2
		The North Face Redpoint Optimus Jacket	2
		PrimaLoft Pants	2
	Outerwear		
	Shell	The North Face Lockoff Jacket	2
		The North Face Eurus Pants	2
	Down	The North Face Himalayan Parka	2
	Personal Effects		
	Personal toiletries bag	Toothbrush, creams, lip balms etc.	2
	Piss Bottle	Juice bottle	1
IV	**SLEEPING**		
	Bag	The North Face Inferno	2
	Mats	Therm-a-Rest Prolite Plus (Large)	2
		Therm-a-Rest Ridgerest SoLite (Large)	2
	Sleeping liner	Sea to Summit Reactor Heavy Weight	2
	Sleeping mat protector		2
V	**SHELTER**		
	Tent	The North Face VE 25	1
	Pegs	30 cm snow pegs	14
	Snow tools	Black Diamond Lynx shovel	1
	Snow saw	Black Diamond Flick Lock saw	1
	Navigation		
	GPS	Garmin GPSMAP 78c	2
VI	**ELECTRONICS**		
	Camera Equipment		
	Video Cameras	Canon XF 100	1

	Category	Type	Qty
		GoPro HD Wide Angle	1
		Sony Dual Screen Bloggie	1
	Still photography	Sony DSC-TX-10	2
	Timepieces		
	Suunto AMBIT		2
	Alarm clock		2
	Music Equipment	iPod Nano 4th Generation	3
		iPod 160GB	2
	Solar Recharge System	Brunton HET Feather2 20W	2
		HET Power 50 Battery	2
	Communications	Iridium 9555 Satellite Phone	1
		McMurdo Fastfind 211 PLB (with GPS)	1
		Solara tracking unit	1
		MacBook Air	1
	Misc.	Tripod – Lightweight Gorilla Grip	1
		Universal chargers for electronics	2
		Silva ADC Pro Weather Station	1
VII	**KITCHEN**		
	Cooking		
	Kitchen box	Containing cooking utensils, funnels, mugs	1
	Stoves	MSR Whisperlite Internationale and fuel bottles	3
		Stoveboard and heat shield	1
	Cookware	MSR Flex Pot – 3.2 litre	1
		Kettle	1
	Drinking		
	Bottles	Stanley Classic Vacuum Thermos	2
		1 litre Nalgene Bottles and Bottle Parkas	6
VIII	**REPAIRS**		
	Tool kit	Includes repair kit and sewing kit	1
	Spares	Various	
IX	**MEDICAL**		
	First aid kit	Painkillers, antibiotics, dressings and implements	1

3. TRAINING

An extended South Pole ski expedition requires a high level of fitness, particularly in the areas of stamina, core strength (abdominal, back and neck muscles), flexibility, mental preparedness and skill. In order to give ourselves the best chance of completing our objective we needed to make our bodies and minds as indestructible as possible.

Our training was broken down into several categories:

1. Mental
2. Physical
3. Fattening up
4. Polar and snow travel skills

Mental Fitness: It can be argued that mental tenacity and perseverance are more important on an expedition than physical strength and endurance. For this expedition both were critical. Our previous expeditions and our intensive physical training regime helped us develop the mental tenacity we were going to need. However, we would later realise that nothing completely prepares you for the endless grind in such a desolate place.

Physical Fitness: Tom Smitheringale from One Man Epic (www.onemanepic.com) designed the training program that we used to turn our bodies into the machines that we'd need in Antarctica. His fifteen-week program had us training up to thirty-five hours in some weeks.

The specific training activities that we utilised included:

- Tyre training: Pulling two truck tyres on frictioned surfaces (gravel and sand) for extended periods was the best substitute for sled hauling that we could do in the temperate climate of Sydney.
- Strength training: Focusing on muscular strength and endurance across the legs, lower back and core, this was aimed

at injury prevention and developing the muscles needed to pull the loads we would be faced with in Antarctica.

- Swimming, rowing and cycling: Low-impact cardio training helped us develop the physical capacity needed for Antarctica while giving our bodies active recovery from the high-impact training caused by tyre sessions and compounded by our fattening up.
- Flexibility training: To aid in injury prevention and recovery we had to stick to a strict yoga and stretching regime.

Polar and snow travel skills: Obtaining the following skills was a must prior to heading to Antarctica:

- Sled-hauling technique
- Back country skiing
- Extreme cold and general snow camping (e.g. tent-pitching, lighting a stove, cooking, sleeping in sub-zero environments, etc.)
- Crevasse rescue/mountaineering/rope skills

In order to gain these necessary skills time was spent in the Australian Alps, New Zealand Alps and the Arctic Circle.

4. NUTRITION

We were expecting to burn approximately 7000 to 9000 calories each per day but taking this much food for ninety days would have made for a ridiculously heavy load that would have limited our chance of success. Our diet needed to be calorie dense while weighing a maximum of 1.1 kilograms per person per day. This is more than four times what the average person uses in one day. This meant we needed to carry the equivalent of a normal person's food requirements for 360 days worth of food ... EACH!

The calorie requirements were so high because of the nine to twelve hours of heavy sled hauling and the severe cold and the altitude. These factors all affect metabolism and increase energy requirements. The goal of our approach to nutrition was to prevent fatigue and minimise weight loss so the return journey could be completed.

The diet was more than nutritionally complete and therefore no vitamin supplements were required. The only supplementary tablet we took was zinc for the first two weeks to try to prevent stomach upsets due to the sudden increase in fat we were eating.

The diet consisted of 50 per cent carbohydrates consumed mainly in the morning and in our day snacks. This was so high to prevent the body using muscle as a fuel source. This would also help with energy levels throughout the day.

The next highest contributor was fat at 30 per cent. Fat has the highest calorie per gram ratio making it helpful in ensuring sufficient calories are consumed and the weight carried is kept to a minimum. Fat = 9 calories per gram, Protein = 4.2 calories per gram, carbohydrates = 4 calories per gram.

The last nutrient to consider is protein. This is of least importance. Ideally two grams per kilogram of body weight should be consumed per day, which would equate to approximately 200 grams per day for Jonesy and me. The average protein that we consumed ranged between 120 and 150 grams per day.

Breakfast: This made up 13 per cent of our daily energy consumption.

It was either freeze–dried yoghurt and muesli, porridge; a cooked breakfast with dehydrated butter/clarified butter. In addition we had coffee and tea on alternate days, sugar (for coffee or cereal), whole milk powder (for coffee), one serve of chocolate or wild berry F.I.R.S.T powder (which we normally actually consumed on the trail).

On the trail: This had to be lots of small quick and easy snacks. These snacks made up 45 per cent of our daily energy consumption. They were made up of: mixed dry-roasted nuts, chips, F.I.R.S.T powder, chocolate, bacon/salami/cheese (Jonesy insisted), jelly lollies, Mainstay bars/Duo bars, cookies/biscuits.

Evening meal: This was higher in fat and made up 42 per cent of our daily energy. It consisted of a double-serve freeze-dried meal and meal supplement (beef mince, cheese), an occasional freeze-dried dessert (apple pie, ice cream), chocolate ice magic, added oil, Sustagen or Scandishake hospital-grade meal supplements.

All freeze-dried meals were supplied by Back Country Cuisine: www.back countrycuisine.co.nz/bcc/
F.I.R.S.T powder, supplied by Feed It:
www.feedit-global.com

Our food worked in a six-day cycle. Days one to three had 6000 calories per day at 1.2 kilograms per day; days four and five had 5500 calories per day and weighed 1.1 kilograms per day; and the last day was 5000 calories per day and weighed 1 kilogram. This made the average calories 5600 calories per day and weight 1.1 kilograms per day, without packaging. The first week we actually alternated between 7000 calories per day and our normal rations as this was the hardest part of the journey and the last week we planned on only consuming 4500 calories per day bringing the weight right down. We did however have to ration our food. This decision was made on Day Thirty-seven and continued until Day Eighty-three, every second day.

It was expected that we would lose between 20 and 30 kilograms and still be able to make the return journey.

The results astounded us. As you can see from the chart following, Jonesy, while losing a total mass of 12.2 kilograms lost only 600 grams of lean muscle mass, and I, while losing 10.8 kilograms, *gained* 1.4 kilograms of muscle. Despite having to be on half-rations the diet appeared to have worked wonders in terms of sparing our muscle tissue and using up our fat stores. We can only guess that if we had been on full rations we may have come back fatter! A massive thank you to Mia for designing one of the most effective polar diets in history. The amount of weeks that went into engineering our polar diet was one of the crucial factors that enabled us to complete the journey.

Jonesy:

Date of Scan	Bodyfat Percentage	Total Body Weight (kg)	Fat Mass (kg)	Lean Body Mass (kg)	Fat Free Mass (kg)	Change (+ / -) in Lean Body Mass	Change (+ / -) in Fat Mass	Total Weight Change to Date	Total Body Fat Change To Date
5/09/2011	22.3%	101.0	22.5	75.0	78.5	4.9	0.0	10.6	5.1
9/02/2012	12.4%	88.8	10.9	74.4	77.8	-0.6	-11.6	-1.6	-6.5

Cas:

Date of Scan	Bodyfat Percentage	Total Body Weight (kg)	Fat Mass (kg)	Lean Body Mass (kg)	Fat Free Mass (kg)	Change (+ / -) in Lean Body Mass	Change (+ / -) in Fat Mass	Total Weight Change to Date	Total Body Fat Change To Date
5/09/2011	26.3%	93.2	24.5	65.6	68.6	3.7	13.9	10.0	9.9
9/02/2012	15.2%	82.4	12.5	67.0	69.9	1.4	-12.0	-0.8	-2.1

An example of the Dexa Scans

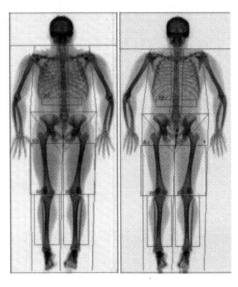

Justin before (102 kg)   Justin after (88.8 kg)

BODY COMPOSITION ANALYSIS
BY DR JARROD MEERKIN

The DEXA (dual-energy X-ray absorptiometry) results provided a real insight into the body response to stress – the stress in question was physical stress under extreme duress brought upon by the cold environment. The nutritional preparation in my opinion worked beautifully. Both James and Justin increased body fat stores successfully. For example, previous DEXA studies show James carried 12 kilograms of fat mass while Justin would normally have 16 kilograms of fat mass. Prior to the expedition this increased to 24.5 kilograms in James and 22.5 kilograms in Justin. Muscle mass remained at levels seen in previous DEXA studies – muscle hypertrophy was likely not as important as improvements in both muscle strength and endurance in preparation for the expedition hence muscle mass remained stable while their bodies' fat stores were increased.

On repeat DEXA measures once back in Sydney, James lost a total of 12 kilograms of fat tissue and Justin lost a total of 11.6 kilograms of fat tissue. Fat loss was greatest from the axial site (trunk) and less from the appendicular sites (legs and arms). One great achievement was that they both maintained their muscle mass. This may indicate that the strategy of increasing fat stores was sufficient to prevent the use of muscle tissue as fuel. If a DEXA scan was completed 'on ice' we may have seen some lean tissue loss due to glycogen depletion as food was deprived over the last week of the expedition. Lean mass may have been quickly restored upon resumption of a normal diet prior to their return to Sydney for the second scan.

These results are in stark contast to the Tasman expedition. On their voyage across the Tasman both Justin and James lost significant amounts of muscle tissue. DEXA scans prior to their departure showed that fat mass was within the bounds of what I normally measured (described above) for both of them. They did not 'fatten up' for the voyage and this may have contributed to the use of muscle tissue as a fuel. This was particularly evident in James where 90 per cent of weight lost was muscle tissue. Their lessons learnt from the Tasman expedition proved essential in developing the correct nutritional support prior to and during their polar adventure. They got it right.

A NOTE ON SOURCES
AND SUGGESTED READING

As a child, the only books I was interested in reading were the stories of polar exploration and adventure. Over the past century an abundance of literature involving the explorers of the Heroic Age of Adventure has been published – some factual, others less so. Throughout *Extreme South* I have always tried to revert back to original sources, but as I found when analysing the diaries Jonesy and I kept on the ice, there can be many inconsistencies and variances in recollecting the same event. In my research, when this has arisen I sought other original sources and used my experience in Antarctica to draw conclusions.

I've listed below many of the books that I used in researching *Extreme South*. My sincere apologies for anyone I may have overlooked or omitted:

Amundsen, Roald, *My Life as an Explorer*, Doubleday, Page & Company, New York, 1927

Amundsen, Roald, *The South Pole: An Account of the Norwegian Antarctic Expedition in the Fram, 1910–1912*, Vol. I, II, John Murray, London, 1912

Biggar, Kevin, *Escape to the Pole: Two Kiwi Guys Dodge Crevasses, Starvation and Marriage*, Random House New Zealand, Auckland, 2010

Brown, Ian, *Extreme South: Struggles and Triumph of the First Australian Team to the Pole*, Australian Geographic Pty Ltd, Terrey Hills, Australia, 1999

Cherry-Garrard, Aplsey, *The Worst Journey in the World*, Vol. I, II , Doran, Constable & Company Ltd, New York, 1922

Evans, Edward, *South with Scott*, Collins Sons and Co. Ltd, London, 1921

Fiennes, Ranulph, *Captain Scott*, Hodder & Stoughton, London, 2004

Fiennes, Ranulph, *Mind Over Matter: The Epic Crossing of the Antarctic Continent*, Delacorte Press, U.S.A., 1994

FitzSimons, Peter, *Mawson and the Ice Men of the Heroic Age: Scott, Shackleton and Amundsen*, Random House Australia, Sydney, 2011

Huntford, Roland, *Scott and Amundsen: Their Race to the South Pole*, Abacus, London, 2005

Huntford, Roland, *Shackleton*, Abacus, London, 2009

Jarvis, Tim, *The Unforgiving Minute*, Bantam Books Australia, Sydney, 2004

Laseron, Charles, *South with Mawson*, Angus & Robertson, 1957

Malakhov, Mikhail & Weber, Richard, *Polar Attack: From Canada to the North Pole, and Back*, McClelland & Stewart, Toronto, 1996

Markham, Clements R., *The Lands of Silence: The History of Arctic and Antarctic Exploration*, Cambridge University Press, Cambridge, 1921

Mawson, Douglas, *The Home of the Blizzard*, Vol. I, 11, William Heinemann, London, 1918

Mawson, Douglas, *The Home of the Blizzard*, Wakefield Press, Kent Town, South Australia, 1996

McNair, Matty L., *On Thin Ice: A Woman's Journey to the North Pole*, NorthWinds, Iqaluit, 1999.

Mear, Roger, & Swan, Robert, *In the Footsteps of Scott*, Jonathon Cape, London, 1987

Nichols, Peter, *A Voyage for Madmen*, HarperPerennial, London, 2002

Philips, Eric, *Icetrek: The Bitter Journey to the South Pole by Peter Hillary, Jon Muir & Eric Philips*, Harper Collins, 2000

Scott, Robert Falcon, *Scott's Last Expedition*, Vol. I, II, Leonard Huxley (ed.), Dodd, Mead & Co., New York, 1913

Shackleton, Ernest Henry, *South: The Endurance Expedition*, Signet, New York, 1999

Stroud, Mike, *Shadows on the Wasteland*, Jonathan Cape, London, 1993

Wilson, Edward, *Diary of the Terra Nova Expedition*, Blandford Press Ltd, London, 1972

A sincere and heartfelt thank you to all the authors who have given me a deeper understanding of those who journeyed before me.

ACKNOWLEDGEMENTS

A massive thanks has got to go out to every single person who helped make this icy dream a reality. Jonesy and I are the first people to admit we weren't the most competent polar explorers out there ... and if it wasn't for a vast support team spanning the globe, the project would never have got off the ground.

First and foremost, I want to thank Jonesy for an incredible adventure. You're my best mate and always will be. You kept me alive down south and I'm looking forward to sharing more great adventures with you in the future. Closely behind, I must thank my wonderful wife, Mia. Throughout the entire three-year journey you were a pillar of strength and support (and designed a truly incredible polar diet).

Without Bec Reil running the support of the expedition and the website, the expedition would not have been anywhere near the success that it was. Gravy, you lived this dream right from the beginning and played an instrumental role in ensuring our gear and equipment was in A1 shape when we hit the ice. Thanks, mate. Aleksander Gamme, thank you for the support and encouragement you offered us in Antarctica, but moreso, thank you for your act of sportsmanship and kindness in waiting for us to finish together. It is something that Jonesy and I will never forget.

Thanks to my family – Mum, Dad, Lil and Clary – for putting up with me through some pretty difficult times and letting us take over the garage for two expeditions now! Sorry in advance for the upcoming expeditions ... Same said for Justin's family – Rod, Chintra, Louisa and Andrew – thanks for your support and understanding. Louisa, thanks also for the Christmas cake!

Hausmann Communications, the way you handled everything was incredible. To our major sponsors – Sony, Travelscene American Express, King & Wood Mallesons and The North Face – for believing in us and providing a major chunk of the funding to make it happen.

To our other sponsors, thank you so much for your support, we look forward to building long-term relationships with each of you: Find My Super, FGI, Resi Home Loans, Dual Australia, Pretorius, Paddy Pallin, TracPlus, *Australian Geographic*, Icebreaker, Rudy Project, Suunto, Back

Country Cuisine, Climb Fit Boroughs Australia, Dick Smith Foods, Mailchimp, Chess Engineering, University of New South Wales, F.I.R.S.T, Wilderness Sports, Telstra, Sunrice.

To the whole team at You Can – thanks for doing the selfless job that you do in improving the lives of youths with cancer across Australia. Also a huge thanks to the patients of You Can, especially Jess and Fi – you helped us more than know. When we were down, we thought of you and skied on.

A special thanks to Vanessa Radnidge and Kate Stevens at Hachette, who made this book possible. Also to Malcolm Edwards, Fiona Hazard, Anne Macpherson, Jessica Luca, Pam Dunne, Roberta Ivers, Karen Ward, Olivia Porter, Graeme Jones, Christa Moffitt, Luke Causby, Andrew Hawkins, Matt Hoy, Jaki Arthur, Kate Flood and the whole team at Hachette.

Sorry if I missed anyone out, but to the following people, Jonesy and I are indebted to your countless hours spent working on the Crossing the Ice expedition: Eric Philips, Matty McNair, Sarah McNair, Eric McNair, Bruce Easton, Kevin Biggar, Jamie Fitzgerald, Tom Smitheringale, James Cracknell, Ben Fogle, Hannah McKeand, Christian Eide, Craig Thomsen, Ben Barin, Johnny Davidson, Wade Tink, Lorraine Murphy, Jen Hamilton, Hugh Anderson, Phil Harmer, Greg Quail, Uncle Colin Raftos, Nick Fordham, Andrew Fraser, Alan Cooper, Dr Glenn Singleman, Dr Jarrod Meerkin, Nick Edwards, Peter FitzSimons, Uncle H, Andy Worth, John Leece, Chelsea Kromer, Zander Pain, Steph Crowley, Iain Barnsfield, Sara Barnsfield, Melissa von Bergner, Aidan Kerr, Stacy Bien, Hugh Ward, Tara Diversi, Andrew Fraser, Maura Desmond, Sophie Gazzoli, Andy Donald, Doug Howard, Ming d'Arcy, Alexis Girardet, Wayne Dakin, Dr Con Moshegov and the team from Perfect Vision, Skye Adler and finally all the wonderful staff at ALE.

And all the other countless mates and Facebook friends who donated their time sewing, stitching and modifying gear in the garage!

For further information, please visit
www.casandjonesy.com.au
www.facebook.com/casandjonesy